How to Restore Yo[ur]
CHEVY TRUCK
1973–1987

Kevin Whipps

CarTech®

CarTech®

CarTech®, Inc.
838 Lake Street South
Forest Lake, MN 55025
Phone: 651-277-1200 or 800-551-4754
Fax: 651-277-1203
www.cartechbooks.com

Edit by Paul Johnson
Layout by Monica Seiberlich

ISBN 978-1-61325-199-7
Item No. SA331

Library of Congress Cataloging-in-Publication Data
Names: Whipps, Kevin, author.
Title: How to Restore Your Chevy Truck 1973-1987 / Kevin Whipps.
Description: Forest Lake, MN : CarTech Books, [2018]
Identifiers: LCCN 2017051160 | ISBN 9781613251997
Subjects: LCSH: Chevrolet trucks–Conservation and restoration–Handbooks, manuals, etc. | Chevrolet trucks–Maintenance and repair–Handbooks, manuals, etc. | GMC trucks–Conservation and restoration–Handbooks, manuals, etc. | GMC trucks–Maintenance and repair–Handbooks, manuals, etc.
Classification: LCC TL230.5.C45 W45 2018 | DDC 629.28/732–dc23
LC record available at https://lccn.loc.gov/2017051160

Written, edited, and designed in the U.S.A.
Printed in China
10 9 8 7 6 5 4 3 2 1

Title Page: *In order to determine if you have enough base color coverage, you can take a handheld daylight lamp such as this one and shine it over the panel. The light puts out a color temperature similar to the sun, so you will see any light spots in the finish. You can add any needed color so you have complete coverage.*

Back Cover Photos

Top: *Interior restoration is an important part of the entire restoration process. To remove the bench seat, remove the four bolts that hold the seat to the floor of the cab. Two are located just below the front of the seat toward the outside edges but parallel to the dash; the remaining two are behind the backrest.*

Middle Left: *The problem with the gauge cluster starts with the bottom left corner, just above the air vent. There's a good inch or so of cluster that's completely obscured by metal, and it won't budge. And you'd think you could roll the cluster out from the top, but you can't. Not yet, anyway.*

Middle Right: *You need to replace any piece or sheet metal part that's corroded. The guide coat allowed us to identify the damaged area. A rotary grinding tool with a sanding disc was used to knock all of the black guide coat areas down to bare metal in preparation for metal repair. For most other bodywork, you need to need to use 80-grit sandpaper on a long block to sand down the guide coat to identify the low areas, and often you can finish up guide coat sanding with 200 grit.*

Bottom: *Three coats of black base paint were applied to this truck before he put down the clear coat. Each time he'd wait until the paint "flashed" off, then tack rag again, and spray.*

DISTRIBUTION BY:

Europe
PGUK
63 Hatton Garden
London EC1N 8LE, England
Phone: 020 7061 1980 • Fax: 020 7242 3725
www.pguk.co.uk

Australia
Renniks Publications Ltd.
3/37-39 Green Street
Banksmeadow, NSW 2109, Australia
Phone: 2 9695 7055 • Fax: 2 9695 7355
www.renniks.com

Canada
Login Canada
300 Saulteaux Crescent
Winnipeg, MB, R3J-3T2 Canada
Phone: 800 665 1148 • Fax: 800 665 0103
www.lb.ca

CONTENTS

DEDICATION

To my son, Kevin Jr. (KJ), the little boy who sits by my side whenever I'm turning a wrench.

To my daughter, Kaylee, the little girl who sits by my side whenever I'm turning a wrench.

And to my wife, Kirsten, who loves wrenches.

I love you all.

ACKNOWLEDGMENTS

A lot of books have an acknowledgments section where the author claims that the book "couldn't have been done without the help of XX people," and the reader's skepticism sets in. But when I say that I couldn't have done this book without these people, I mean it. There's no way it would've happened because they were invaluable.

Thanks to Dino and Dino (Little D) at Dino's Chevy Only. Although their specialty is 1960–1966 Chevy trucks, they certainly know the 1973–1987 market, and they hooked me up with numerous contacts that helped me get the job done.

Thank you to Joe Yezzi, Rob Yezzi, and all of the Squarebody Syndicate crew. Not only did they reorganize their schedules around mine to help out with the book, but they also worked on their trucks specifically for me. That was invaluable.

A big hug and thank you to Troy and Jimbo at Borne Customs. Troy didn't know who I was when I cold-called him, but he was cool with me taking a camera into his shop and practically living there. His assistance helped me a ton.

A big thanks to Jefferson Bryant for his assistance with photos. He came through in the final moments of the project with a big score, and, for that, I thank him greatly.

I owe Cliff Ruggles a mammoth thank you for all of his help. Without his assistance with the chapter on transmissions, I wouldn't have been able to get it done. Thank you.

The same goes for Todd Ryden, without whose assistance the engine chapter would've been extremely difficult to complete.

A hearty thanks to Lonnie Thompson of Carolina Kustoms. I made a phone call to him out of the blue, then visited his shop, and he opened up everything to me. Then, after I left, he kept sending me pictures that he thought I might need. He's a great guy.

Finally, a few other people who have helped me on my path: Ronnie at C10 Talk/C10 Nation for tearing apart his crew cab for me, twice; Kevin Aguilar at *Street Trucks* and *C10 Builder's Guide* for his assistance; Seth and the crew at Switch Suspension for generally being awesome; Todd at Lowboy Suspension for being amazing; my editor, Paul Johnson, for his incredible patience; Marie Look for her moral support; and everyone else who has helped me along the way. Thank you.

INTRODUCTION

I can honestly say that writing a book is one of the hardest things to do. Holy cow was this challenging, but it's also been one of the most rewarding experiences I've ever had.

In the mid-1980s, when I was growing up in Framingham, Massachusetts, my mother owned a Chevrolet Suburban. It was a white, four-wheel-drive truck, and she named it Martha because it seemed to have a personality. The windshield wipers randomly turned on and off in that truck, and no matter how many times we took it in to have it fixed, Martha still pulled those wipers across the windshield. And she continued that process until we sold the truck in 1988.

Twenty-some years later, I picked up a 1984 Chevrolet Silverado. It was blue, the tailgate was some art piece that looked horrific, and it had a keyhole in the driver-side fender. I loved that truck. However, I eventually came to the conclusion that I could not complete the restoration myself in a reasonable time frame, so I sold it and moved on. But the bug stuck, and eventually I bought a 1987 Silverado. It was also blue. It sat and languished while I focused on other projects, such as the 1987 crew cab dually I bought without a bed. Or maybe it was the 1986 two-wheel-drive Blazer without a frame that a friend gave me. I'm not sure; I had a lot of those things.

Eventually, the whole lot was sold to a buddy of mine, and now the dually is painted and restored, and it looks amazing. My second blue truck went to another good home, I donated the Blazer to another friend, and because we moved to a new house without a mammoth side lot, my life with multiple random projects seemed to be over.

In the process of making this book, I decided that my itch for a new project had to be scratched, so I went looking for a 1973–1987 of my very own. I found one in Stockton, California, approximately 12 hours away, and picked it up for a ridiculously small amount of money. We loaded the family into our crew cab truck, hitched a flatbed trailer to the back (borrowed from Dino at Dino's Chevy Only), and headed toward Stockton. After a minor detour to Santa Cruz, we went back home with a 1981 Chevrolet Silverado (and a few black widow stowaways, too).

I did some digging on the VIN when I returned, and learned that the truck was built in Fremont, California, approximately 60 miles west of where I picked it up. The guy I bought it from found it in Tracy, California, which is even closer. And, in a weird twist, we drove right by that same GM factory on our way to Santa Cruz. Basically, I found a truck that spent the bulk of its life within a 75-mile radius of where it was built and took it home to Arizona.

That's either incredibly depressing or super awesome, depending on your perspective.

I love those 1973–1987 Chevy trucks. My friends and I always referred to them as "Squarebodies," which is ironic considering that General Motors called them the "Rounded Line." I actually have a custom license plate with the Squarebody moniker on it, even though it never was screwed to that dually (although I hope it will find its way onto my 1981).

The Chevy truck line can be separated into eras: 1947–1955 first series, 1955–1959 second series, 1960–1966, 1967–1972, 1973–1987, 1988–1998, 1999–2007, etc. The one that stands out is 1973–1987, which includes the longest run of Chevy trucks in the company's history.

For 14 years (more if you count the 1-ton trucks that carried on into the early 1990s) General Motors produced essentially the same truck in various forms. It was the first to have a factory crew cab. The company had the first dually designed for the regular buyer and not just for fleets. It had Suburbans, Blazers, long beds, short beds, Stepsides, and everything between. The Squarebody Chevy is the one that pushed the line to where it is today. That has to be worth something, right?

Historically, previous generations of trucks received all the attention. The 1967–1972 has been an extremely popular truck to restore, particularly in the early 2000s. That popularity, plus the relative rarity of the design, has raised the prices substantially in recent years, making them unattainable for most builders. The 1960–1966 has picked up steam as of late, but it's still not as popular as the 1967–1972. Previous generations of Chevy trucks are becoming more difficult to find, and if you want a 1947–1955, good luck; Old Navy bought and sold a ton of them years ago, and now people want upward of five grand for something without floors.

That leaves the 1973–1987s. Tons of these trucks are out there in every incarnation possible. Yes, the earlier years are harder to find (and therefore more desirable to some), but they're still affordable. You can find these trucks for a song, and if you're willing to put in the work, they're worth something in the end.

More important, these trucks are fun. You can find them with low mileage, believe it or not, as well as big engines. There's nothing wrong with a 454-powered standard-cab short-bed Silverado in my book, and because most are pre-fuel injection, carburetor junkies can have their fun tuning them to death. If you want a truck from the 1970s, this one almost book-ends the era, and it does the same for the 1980s.

Before I bought my 1981, I started looking for one of these trucks, and I came across a 1980s-era Suburban. It was white, with four-wheel drive and a few other accessories, and it looked familiar. Could it possibly be the same truck that my family drove West in 1987? Maybe. But alas, the owner sold it before I could find out.

Someday I'll own a Martha as my mom did, and maybe it will have the same issue with the windshield wipers. If not, maybe I'll "fix" it until it does.

FINDING A PROJECT SQUAREBODY

The best restoration project begins with a solid foundation, and that means a solid body. These trucks have very little rust and need very little mechanical work. Trucks in this condition are more difficult to find and highly sought after. On the other hand, if you start with a truck that needs substantial restoration and bodywork, you are going to spend much more for the restoration. In other words, you get what you pay for.

Before you embark on a restoration project, carefully evaluate the condition of the truck and assess the time, expense, and parts required to bring it to original condition. Some trucks are far too rusty and in such poor condition that a restoration is just too costly. In that case, a better option is to sell the truck and find one in better condition for restoration. Chapter 2 discusses how you come up with the total cost for a restoration.

Many trucks with various powertrains, trim levels, and cab and box sizes are available on the market, so you have lots of options. However, be conscientious and careful when shopping for one. You should be able to prescreen some trucks and ask the owners specific questions to reveal the condition, equipment package, trim level, and other information. Be prepared that the owner does not understand or know everything about the truck he or she owns. Some owners say they're short beds, but they are actually long beds, customized with no hope of restoration. Some owners feel that their trucks are worth six figures because that's what the TV tells them. This whole process is going to be a fun experience.

This chapter is all about figuring out the truck that best fits your needs and what you want in your next project. I start with the basics about a truck, including some analysis of the vehicle identification number (VIN), and I break down the body styles and years so that you know what you're looking for and can narrow it down. This also helps you identify the fakes from the real deals.

Whatever truck you find, it is going to be a big commitment to

For some, this truck is complete with a great patina and reliable engine. But if the ultimate goal is to return the truck to showroom condition, this truck needs bodywork and a new paint job.

The Gas Tank/NBC Issue

The first model year of the generation, 1973, introduced a ton of changes compared to the previous 1967–1972 trucks. The first change, and one that became the most controversial, came to the gas tank. In previous years, the gas tank was located behind the bench seat. As time wore on, rubber seals leaked and the interior eventually developed a noxious smell, which became hazardous.

To solve that problem, Chevrolet beefed up the frame rails and mounted the gas tank(s) on the outside of the frame. Now the gas filler door(s) sat on the outside of the bed. In addition, General Motors wanted to increase the fuel capacity to 40 gallons for marketing purposes, which required mounting a second tank on the opposite side of the truck.

This was fine until November 17, 1992. *Dateline*, an NBC program, premiered its "Waiting to Explode" episode, which was an hour-long investigation into the 1973–1991 Chevrolet trucks, including how the gas tank exploded when hit in a low-speed side-impact collision. According to the *Dateline* video (which you can easily find online), the tanks ruptured at speeds as low as 33 mph, causing them to burst into a fiery explosion, potentially killing everyone inside.

Obviously, this was not good news for General Motors. The 1973–1987/1991 trucks were, at this point, a done deal, and they had moved on to the new C/K product line. Millions of these trucks were on the road, and if the company had to compensate owners, it could cost millions and possibly bankrupt the company.

However, after the taping, one of the firefighters on the scene of the NBC demonstration contacted General Motors to report what happened. General Motors started its own investigation as a result, hiring Failure Analysis Associates (FaAA). What it found was that smoke was visible from the gas tank six frames before the actual impact of the second car. Acting on a tip received from someone involved in the *Dateline* program and after combing through 22 yards in an Indiana wrecking yard, they found the trucks used in the episode.

The results were damning. General Motors discovered that the producers of the program had placed remote-controlled model rocket engines inside the trucks' gas tanks. Just before the impact occurred, the producers triggered the rockets, causing the tanks to ignite and explode. Furthermore, the speed that *Dateline* quoted, 30 mph, was not what they actually showed on the screen. In fact, the car was traveling at 40 mph at the time of impact. When General Motors techs found the trucks used in the test, they X-rayed the tanks and determined that there were no holes at all.

As a result, General Motors sued NBC for defamation and libel on February 8, 1993, and put on a two-hour demonstration for the press explaining why the *Dateline* presentation was not possible, and that the public was not in danger. NBC settled the lawsuit by the end of the week, and Jane Pauley, co-anchor of *Dateline*, apologized publicly on the program for the error.

This is not to say that these trucks never exploded from a side impact, just that the way NBC performed the investigation was faulty. There have been several lawsuits over the years about the issue, and, as of a report in 1993 (decided just days prior to General Motors suing NBC), more than 200 people had died in full-size Chevrolet and GMC trucks of that era. At that point, six lawsuits had gone to trial: General Motors won half of them.

Today, controversy about the gas tanks continues, and entire websites are dedicated to the problem. Should you have any concern about the issue with your own project, you have a few options.

First, you can purchase a fuel cell. Aftermarket fuel cells come in all shapes and sizes, and have increased safety standards, depending on where you purchase them.

You can purchase a plastic foam-filled tank made to meet NHRA specifications and mount it between the frame rails just behind the axle.

You can purchase a gas tank from a Chevrolet Blazer or GMC Jimmy of the era, which also mounts behind the axle between the frame rails. You have to change some plumbing and wiring, but it at least has a factory appearance, even if it's not in the stock location.

Finally, you can always leave it the way it is. If you're not planning on driving the truck very often, your risk of injury is less. Plus, even if you do drive the truck every day, the chances of you being hit in the same manner that would cause the tank to puncture is minimal, so keep that in mind.

Whatever you chose to do, just be aware of the problem so that you can address it if necessary. ■

restore it, both to your pocketbook and your time. Make sure that you take those extra few days, months, or even years to find what you want in a condition that you're prepared to work with. Otherwise, you waste your time on a project that eats up your cash.

Overview of the 1973–1987 Chevrolet Pickup

Although the 1973–1987 Chevrolet pickup had the longest run of any line of Chevy trucks to date, some purists divide the generation into two distinct groups: 1973–1980 and 1981–1987. If you want to get technical, the Suburbans, duallys, Blazers, and crew cabs were available until 1991, creating, essentially, a third generation, depending on how you look at things.

Chevrolet first referred to them as the "Rounded Line" of trucks, but today enthusiasts often call them a "Squarebody." To most people, it's the most square of the current and past body styles.

Body Style Changes

The 1973 model received the "Rounded Line" moniker because almost every corner or angle on the truck had a rounded edge. For example, the windshields had rounded corners, as did the windows and front fenders. The taillights also wrapped around the bed sides, which was the first time that was done on any Chevy truck.

The purpose of the Rounded Line was to increase fuel efficiency by using aerodynamics. The bed sides also featured a double-wall construction, which, in some earlier years, also produced some rust complaints because water pooled between the two walls of the bed, causing rust. Keep an eye out for truck beds with poorly patched panels.

Three bed models were available at first. The Wideside (also called the Fleetside model) came in a short or long bed; the Stepside (called Fenderside by GMC) also came in a short or long bed; and the "Big Dooley" (now referred to as a "dually"), which was a long Fleetside bed with fend-

ers on the outsides to accommodate the dual rear wheels on the 1-ton trucks. The Stepside/Fenderside also came standard with wood floors, which were replaced by metal floors in 1980.

The cabs came in two choices: standard and crew cab. The latter had two versions: a "bonus cab" that had no rear seat and included a lockable storage compartment instead, and a "3+3" that had bench seats front and rear.

Because of these new cab and bed sizes, three wheelbases were offered for the trucks: 117½ inches for the standard-cab/short-bed pickups, 131½ for the standard-cab/long-bed trucks, and 164½ inches for the crew-cab/long-bed (or Big Dooley).

Other variants of the truck also use the same chassis, including the Custom Deluxe with camper, Blazer/Jimmy, and Suburban.

Year-by-Year Changes

The Squarebody evolved substantially over its 14-year model run, and I've highlighted most of the major changes below. This will help you find the truck that best fits your needs.

1973

Compared to the previous 1967–1972 trucks, this first year of the body style had 21 percent more glass area, an optional radio antenna embedded in the glass, and a bigger cab. Front disc brakes became standard, and the entire suspension was beefed up to go along with Chevrolet's motto, "Built to Stay Tough." The crew cab was also introduced this year. As for the engine, this was the last year that you could buy the 307 V-8; the 402 big-block available in previous years was now replaced with the 454. There was also

The body style went through a major change in 1973 and again in 1981, as was the case with this later-model example.

an inline 250- and 292-ci 6-cylinder as well as the 350-ci V-8. If you want a two-tone paint job, your second color option is white, and only white.

1974

The exterior of the truck was mostly the same, except that rain gutters became available for the areas around the side windows. Both 1973 and 1974 shared a grille commonly referred to as the recessed "egg crate" grille, named for its appearance.

1975

Higher trim levels (discussed below) came with aluminum panels on the tailgate, filling in the typically recessed area. Rain gutters were now standard on all trucks, as was a modified tailgate latch mechanism on Fleetside beds. The Scottsdale trim level was introduced. On the inside of the truck, the windshield wiper switch was modified slightly, which changed the bezels found in the 1973s and 1974s. HEI ignitions were now standard, as were catalytic converters. The front grille now featured three horizontal bars, which also eliminated the recessed feature of the previous years. This was the last year that you could find out the displacement of the engine based on the badge on the grille.

1976

Because of rust issues, General Motors added more zinc to its primer. Buyers could purchase chrome bumpers with rubber impact strips, plus they could select Rally wheels and/or a Sport model. You could now order a two-tone vehicle with a color other than white, and the Bonanza trim option was introduced. This was also the last year that the engine block was orange.

1977

Power options were available for the first time, including intermittent wipers, power windows, and power door locks. The door panels and door internal components were also different from previous years. Bucket seats came in two variations: early models had low backs and later models had high backs; it depended on when in the model year the truck was built. An inside hood release became an option and the grille changed one of the horizontal bars and four of the vertical bars were removed. A yellow/gold stripe was an option for the center of the moldings, and, other than the 1975 GMC Gentleman Jim Special Edition, this was the only year it was an option. General Motors introduced the 305 V-8, and a rear defroster also became optional.

1978

A 350 diesel engine became optional in 1/2-ton trucks. The frame was tweaked slightly to fit catalytic converters, which were now required on California trucks. This also meant that California trucks did not have a dual exhaust option available. Brushed-aluminum trim became standard on the top trim levels, replacing the wood grain. The bed received a gas door, rather than the flush gas cap found on previous years. Sometime during this model year, spade fuses were used, so glass fuses can still be found in early production units.

1979

The headlight bezels and turn signals were now combined into one unit, and General Motors added an apron underneath the grille. It also added a "decorative ridge" to the front of the hood. Trucks with a gross vehicle weight (GVW) up to 8,500

pounds now had catalytic converters as standard.

1980

The Silverado trim levels now featured rectangular headlights; other trim levels still had the round lights found in 1979. The grille gained the "egg crate" styling again (although it's different from the 1973 version), the mirrors sat lower on the cab, and cast aluminum wheels became standard. The 292 V-6 model now had a dual exhaust option.

1981

The front end of the truck was completely changed in 1981, and it stayed essentially the same until 1987. It now had a new grille with four headlights (with two as an option) and horizontal side-marker lights. There were also new bumpers and the tailgate was also changed. The dashboard changed shape slightly, as did the seats, gauge cluster, and sill plates. The 305 V-8 now came in a California-only edition and one for the remaining 49 states. The gas tank also was relocated to the driver's side of the truck. These changes reduced the truck's weight by 300 pounds.

1982

The chrome grille and front bumper were now standard features. The 6.2 diesel was introduced and came with the 700R4 automatic overdrive. The 305 V-8 with the 2-barrel was discontinued. The Cheyenne trim level was discontinued.

1983

The front turn signals were relocated from the bumper to behind the grille by the headlights, and now the 700R4 automatic overdrive transmission became optional for all trucks.

1984

The quadruple headlights introduced in 1981 were now optional equipment. The wiper controls, cruise control, and high-beam lights relocated to the turn-signal stalk.

1985

This year introduced the VorTex V-6 with a 4-barrel carburetor. Two-tone paint became optional again, and the grille changed slightly.

1986

This was the first year that didn't have any major changes to the lineup. The trucks were effectively the same as in 1985.

1987

An engine equipped with throttle body injection (TBI) was introduced, and came with computerized ignition controls. This was the last year that a Stepside bed was available; the next-generation GM trucks had a "Sportside." This was the last year of this body style, however. The 1-ton trucks, 3/4-ton trucks, Suburbans, and Blazer/Jimmys remained with few changes until 1991.

Trim Levels

In 1973 and 1974, Chevrolet and GMC offered four trim levels for their trucks. The Custom line for both brands was considered the standard model. It was the base truck and had no option code.

The next tier was the Custom Deluxe (Chevrolet) and Super Custom (GMC), considered the mid-range truck. These had an option code of Z62.

The luxury trim was named the Cheyenne (Chevrolet) and Sierra (GMC), and had an option code of Z84.

The highest-tier luxury trucks were the Cheyenne Super (Chevrolet) and Sierra Grande (GMC). They used a YE9 option code.

All of the option codes remained the same until 1987.

In 1975, the names changed again. The base model was now the Custom Deluxe (Chevrolet) and Sierra (GMC). The mid-range tier was the Scottsdale (Chevrolet) and Sierra Grande

The Cheyenne Super was the top-of-the-line trim level in 1973 and 1974, and it showed. The badging on the fenders was the first sign of something special, and the two-tone paint job and interior trim stood out as well.

This truck hasn't been restored, but it does have all of the Custom Deluxe original trim and materials, plus low mileage (less than 90,000). If you can get past the rust on the hood, trucks like this are perfect project vehicles.

(GMC). The luxury trim was named the Cheyenne (Chevrolet) and High Sierra (GMC). The top-of-the-line luxury trucks became known as the Silverado (Chevrolet) and Sierra Classic (GMC). These were in place until 1981.

In 1982, the lineup looked like this: Base model trucks were still the Custom Deluxe (Chevrolet) and Sierra (GMC). The mid-range tier was the Scottsdale (Chevrolet) and High Sierra (GMC), which was a name shift for the GMC line. There was no more luxury line (option code Z84), but the top-of-the-line luxury trim remained the Silverado (Chevrolet) and Sierra Classic (GMC). This was how the lineup looked until 1987, when the 1/2-ton trucks ended their run.

Base-model trucks had very little chrome on the exterior. There was no carpet; instead, it came with a rubber mat on the inside. The seats usually came in vinyl, although in 1982, custom or deluxe cloth became an option that you could buy at the dealer. There was also very little interior insulation, the door panels were wrapped in vinyl, there was no headliner, and the dashboard was a simple, black-trimmed model.

The mid-range model (Z62 option) was a base-model truck with a few added amenities. The exterior featured slightly more chrome, for example.

On the inside, the floor mat was now the same color as the rest of the interior, but was still not carpeted, except in certain rare cases. For upholstery, buyers could choose between "custom cloth" and "custom vinyl," which you could also buy in the Z84 and YE9 models, but the Z62 models had some unique patterns and colors that you could only buy in those trim levels. There was also no headliner, just as in the base model; the insulation still was minimal; and the door panels featured slightly more trim, including chrome and wood grain.

The next two levels, Z84 and YE9, were both considered to be luxury models, and were close to each other in options. The Z84 had a deluxe molding package, plus a tailgate insert on the Fleetside bed models. An insulated headliner appeared on the interior for the first time, as did cut-pile carpeting. The door panels were now longer in appearance, with the addition of a map pocket at the base, and they also had either brushed-aluminum or wood-grain panel inserts. Finally, General Motors added insulators located at the hood and cab to the fender, which reduced noise. The Z84 option was available from 1973–1981 only, and was likely discontinued because of its similarity to the YE9.

The top-of-the-line trim level, YE9, took the truck to even higher luxury levels. In addition to the Z84 exterior trim, additional items were added to the truck.

In 1980, the V22 chrome grille/Deluxe front appearance package became standard, although other trim level models could have the package for a price. The interior of the YE9 trucks included the BC2 Deluxe instrument panel, which came in either wood grain or brushed aluminum, and it had full gauges all the way around rather than warning lights on the outer gauge spots. The rest of the interior was the same as that found in the Z84 trim until 1975.

From 1976 forward, carpet trim was added to the lower door panels, as was a grab handle. The kick panels also came in full vinyl.

Those four models were the primary optional trim levels, but other packages were available as well. For example, from 1976 to 1981, the 1/2-ton short-bed trucks in both product lines had a Z77 option, which was referred to as the Chevy Sport or GMC Street Coupe. This kit used the interior trim from the Z62, plus the V22 Deluxe front appearance option and BC2 Deluxe instrument cluster usually found on the YE9. They also included special rally wheels, the N67, which are difficult to find today and highly desirable as a result.

Another option is a bit more rare, depending on your perspective. These were the years of the truck wars, and because Chevrolet and Ford were competing for sales, they often offered year-end promotional packages. For Chevrolet, these were called the Bonanza; GMC called them the Royal Sierra. These trucks were usually set up with the Z62 trim level, but they came with standard carpeting as found on higher models. That promotion ran until 1980, and from 1981 to 1987, you could choose between the Z84 and YE9 interior packages.

Finally, let's talk about the Canadian offering. If you happen to stumble upon a Chevrolet/GMC Wrangler, you've found a truck that was only available in Canada. If you're building it in the United States, you definitely have a collectible, albeit common, vehicle. These trucks have unique paint schemes and exterior decals, both of which were never available in the United States, making them special.

One other interesting note about Squarebodies: From 1981 to 1987, you could walk into a Canadian dealership and order the 350-ci V-8 on a 1/2-ton two-wheel-drive truck. That wasn't possible in the United States.

Special Editions

Chevrolet built several special edition trucks over the years, which are usually difficult to find. They celebrated all sorts of different events and themes and always sold in small runs. Finding information about them is difficult, as it involves digging through magazines from the 1970s. The following are a few examples.

The 1979 GMC Amarillo GT had special badging, custom wheels, and a 454 big-block engine, all in a 1/2-ton truck. It also included the Sierra Classic interior package, but with an additional CB radio.

The GMC Beau James edition had a tonneau cover; custom red, white, and blue "Beau James" stickers on the bed; and the Sierra Classic trim.

The 1979 Chevrolet Big 10 was a 1/2-ton short-bed Chevy with a 454 big-block V-8. This, and the Amarillo GT, were likely produced because of the upcoming emissions regulation changes put in place with the gas shortage of the 1970s.

GMC California Sundancers came in yellow with gray accents and two-tone blue pinstriping. They also had 15X7 Mag Sprinter Western wheels, tube bumpers, a roll bar, and a sunroof.

The 1975 GMC Gentleman Jim was painted in black with a gold strip in the center of the truck and gold accents inside the chrome trim. The dashboard and interior were color matched (a rarity for this time period), and it even came with an eight-track tape player and a CB radio.

The 1977 GMC Indy 500 Special came with custom paint and decals, including a multicolor eagle design that went from the bodyline down-

1975 GMC Indy 500 Special

One of the guys who I refer to in this book is Joe Yezzi, the owner of Squarebody Syndicate. In the course of writing this book, I discovered that he had a new restoration project that just had to be included.

It's a 1975 Indy 500 GMC, which ran in the 1975 Indianapolis 500 (of course), carrying a huge steel bass drum in the bed. Joe found it in the state of Washington, sitting in an overgrown blackberry bush, just rotting away. The owner wanted to get rid of it, and Joe was just the guy to buy it.

The truck, as it sits today, needs a bit of work. There's a ton of rust, particularly in the bed rails and bottoms of the fenders, but, surprisingly, the cab and cab floors are solid.

How to Spot a Fake

Because these trucks have been off the sales floor for more than 20 years, a lot of people have worked on, customized, or modified one of them. That also means that there are a few fakes out there, and it's important that you're able to sort out the good from the bad.

The rarest models are usually the ones that came in the most limited runs and, therefore, are the ones most likely to be faked. The Indy 500 models are one example, but more common are the Big 10 trucks. After all, it's easy to put a 454 in a truck and call it a Big 10, but that doesn't make it so.

Also, the earliest years tend to be faked but for different reasons. In some states, the earlier models are still smog exempt. California, for example, requires smog checks for vehicles made in the 1976 model year or newer, so some owners swap the front ends on their trucks and even go so far as to change the VIN just to appear as if their truck were older. Always make sure to check the VIN in all locations.

When inspecting a truck, check the production date stamped in the side of the frame. If it doesn't match with the year of the truck, say a frame stamped with "76" on a 1984 Silverado, it may be a rebuilt or salvage vehicle.

ward and stood out against the silver paint. A total of 500 of these trucks were made. GM trucks were the official truck of the Indianapolis 500 12 times over the course of this body style's run, so there are other variants of this special edition as well.

The 1976 GMC Olympic Edition was available in Canada only. It had a white base coat with a red stripe that went down the upper half of the body and came across the hood. It also had a custom Olympic emblem on the hood and stickers on the windows, and it came in the Z62 trim with chrome bumpers.

The 1976 GMC Spirit of '76 celebrated the U.S. bicentennial. It was a white base coat with red and blue decals and custom badging on the interior. The seats were also done in red, white, and blue upholstery, with matching blue carpet.

VIN Decoding

The easiest way to sort things out is by decoding the VIN and analyzing what the truck does and doesn't have. If you don't know the year of the truck, there are a few tips on sorting things out correctly.

First, count the number of digits in the VIN. If there are 13 total, and the VIN is mounted on a plate in the driver-side doorjamb, the truck is a 1973–1978 model.

If the truck has a VIN on the dashboard, but it's not 17 digits, it's a 1979–1980 model. And if the VIN has 17 digits and is on the dashboard, it's a 1981–1987 model. For example, should you approach a seller and he tells you that the truck is a 1973, but the VIN is clearly on the dashboard, it may be a 1981–1987 with a front clip swap. That's quite common, as the earlier front ends are considered

Decoding a VIN

The 1973–1987 Chevy/GMC truck line uses a conventional 13-digit VIN system. The VIN system changed three times during the course of the Square-body truck production run.

1973–1978 VIN Designations

First Digit: Division
C   Chevrolet
T   GMC

Second Digit: Chassis Type
C   Two-wheel-drive
G   Light Duty, Forward Control
K   Four-wheel-drive
P   Forward Control

Third Digit: Engine
Y   V-8, 454 ci, 4-barrel carburetor (P Models)
S   V-8, 454 ci, 4-barrel carburetor (C Models)
R   V-8, 400 ci, 4-barrel carburetor
L   V-8, 350 ci, 4-barrel carburetor
U   V-8, 305 ci, 2-barrel carburetor
T   Inline-6, 292 ci, 1-barrel carburetor
D   Inline-6, 250 ci, 1-barrel carburetor

Fourth Digit: Series
1   1/2 Ton
2   3/4 Ton
3   1 Ton
4   Heavy Half/Big 10

Fifth Digit: Body Style
2   Forward Control Chassis Only
3   Cab-Chassis
4   Pickup and Van
5   Panel
6   Suburban
7   Motorhome
8   Utility

Sixth Digit: Model Year
3   1973
4   1974
5   1975
6   1976
7   1977
8   1978

Seventh Digit: Assembly Plant
A   Lakewood
B   Baltimore
F   Flint
J   Janesville
V   GM Truck-Pontiac
S   St. Louis
U   Lordstown
F   Freemont
1   Oshawa
3   GMAD Detroit
4   Scarborough

Remaining Digits
The remaining digits are a sequential serial number, unique to the truck.

1979–1980 VIN Designations

First Digit: Division
C   Chevrolet
T   GMC

Second Digit: Chassis Type
C   Two-wheel-drive
K   Four-wheel-drive

Third Digit: Engine
D   Inline-6, 250 ci
L   V-8, 350 ci
R   V-8, 400 ci
T   Inline-6, 292 ci

Fourth Digit: Series
1   1/2 Ton
2   3/4 Ton
3   1 Ton
4   Heavy Half/Big 10

Fifth Digit: Body Type
3   Cab-Chassis
4   Pickup

Sixth Digit: Model Year
9   1979
A   1980

Seventh Digit: Assembly Plant
A   GMAD-Lakewood
B   GMAD-Baltimore
D   GMAD-Doraville
F   Chevrolet-Flint
J   GMAD-Janesville
K   GMAD-Leeds
R   GMAD-Arlington
S   GMAD-St. Louis
V   GMT&C-Pontiac
Z   GMAD-Freemont
1   GM of Canada-Oshawa
3   Chevrolet-Detroit
4   GM of Canada-Scarborough
7   GMAD-Lordstown

Remaining Digits
The remaining digits are a sequential serial number, unique to the truck.

1981–1987 VIN Designations

First Digit: Nation of Origin
1   United States
2   Canada

Second and Third Digits: Division
GC Chevrolet
GT GMC

Fourth Digit: GVWR Brake System
B   3001 to 4000
C   4001 to 5000 (includes El Camino)
D   5001 to 6000
E   6001 to 7000
F   7001 to 8000
G   8001 to 9000 (includes G Van Bus)
H   9001 to 10000

J   10001 to 14000
K   14001 to 16000

Fifth Digit: Line and Chassis

C   Conventional Cab, two-wheel-drive
    (1981–1986)
K   Conventional Cab, four-wheel-drive
    (1981–1986)
P   Forward Control Chassis,
    two-wheel-drive
G   Van, Sport Van, cutaway,
    two-wheel-drive
R   Conventional Cab, two-wheel-drive
    (1987–1989)
V   Conventional Cab, four-wheel-drive
    (1987–1989)
W   El Camino, two-wheel-drive

Sixth Digit: Series

1   1/2 Ton
2   3/4 Ton
3   1 Ton
4   Heavy Half/Big 10
8   El Camino

Seventh Digit: Body Type

0   Sedan Pickup
1   Hi-Cube/Cutaway Van
2   Forward Control
3   Four-door Cab
4   Two-door Cab
5   Van
6   Suburban
7   Motorhome

8   Blazer
9   Stake/Platform

Eighth Digit: Engine Designation
1981 Models

D   Inline-6, 250 ci
T   Inline-6, 292 ci
G   V-8, 305 ci, 2-barrel carburetor
F, H   V-8, 305 ci, 4-barrel carburetor
L   V-8, 350 ci
M   V-8, 350 ci, Heavy Duty
Z   V-8, 350 ci, Diesel
W   V-8, 454 ci

1982–1984 Models

D   Inline-6, 250 ci
T   Inline-6, 292 ci
H   V-8, 305 ci
L   V-8, 350 ci
M   V-8, 350 ci, Heavy Duty
C   V-8, 6.2, Diesel
J   V-8, 6.2, Diesel
W   V-8, 454 ci

1985–1986 Models

T   Inline-6, 292 ci
N   V-6, 262 ci
H   V-8, 305 ci
L   V-8, 350 ci
M   V-8, 350 ci, Heavy Duty
C   V-8, 6.2, Diesel
J   V-8, 6.2, Diesel
W   V-8, 454 ci

1987 Model

T   Inline-6, 292 ci
Z   V-6, 262 ci, Throttle Body Injection
H   V-8, 305 ci, Throttle Body Injection
K   V-8, 350 ci, Throttle Body Injection
C   V-8, 6.2, Diesel
J   V-8, 6.2, Diesel
W   V-8, 454 ci, 4-barrel carburetor
N   V-8, 454 ci, Throttle Body Injection

Ninth Digit: Check Digit

Tenth Digit: Model Year

B   1981
C   1982
D   1983
E   1984
F   1985
G   1986
H   1987
J   1988
K   1989

Eleventh Digit: Assembly Plant

F   Flint
J   Janesville
S   St. Louis
Z   Freemont
1   Oshawa

Remaining Digits

The remaining digits are a sequential serial number, unique to the truck. ∎

more desirable, so be aware.

The VIN is located in a few different spots, depending on the year of the truck. There's the aforementioned doorjamb plate for pre–1978 models and the plate on the dashboard for 1979–1987 models.

If the dashboard is intact, you can also find a factory options decal located in the glove box. This should help you determine the trim level of the truck.

Once you know the VIN, the next step is to decode the information according to the various generations and designations.

The easiest way to find out if you have a fake is to start with either the sixth (1973–1980) or tenth (1981–1987) digit in the VIN. This tells you the year of the truck, and it's something you can compare against what the owner tells you.

In addition, you can check for VIN locations in other spots on the truck to ensure that all of them match. Compare the glove box number with the one on the dashboard, for example, or the one on the frame (underneath the cab on the passenger

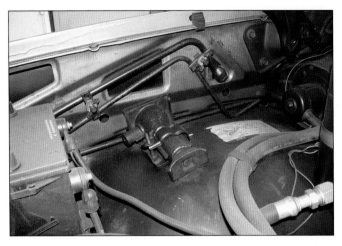

The more factory parts and stickers present on the truck, the more valuable it is. This truck had all of the factory stickers in the correct spots. In addition, the original jack and tire iron were still in the fenderwell.

side between the mounting holes for the forward bed bolts). There is also a VIN stamped on the engine block and transmission, but if the truck is either missing the drivetrain or it has been swapped, you're out of luck.

The next thing to look for is sheet-metal changes. As previously mentioned, some eras of front clips are preferred to others, and it changes based on taste. It's entirely likely that you find a 1981–1987 truck with 1973–1980 front fenders, hood, and grille because that was the owner's favorite style. But what's also common is the wrong grille on a specific year.

Another general rule is to gently knock on the metal with your knuckles, listening for differences in tone. If body filler was used, the sound tends to sound much less hollow than metal without bodywork. You can also look inside the fenders and under the hood for paint overspray or dents, both of which indicate either replacement or previous bodywork. Pay particular attention to the area around the lower bed sides on the earlier trucks, as they could have been replaced at some point as well.

Let's say that you find a truck online that you like and go to check it out. The owner tells you it's a 1981

Chevrolet Silverado with the 6.2 diesel. When you look closely, you see that the turn-signal lenses are in the grille, not the bumper, which tells you that it's at least a 1983. Now that your suspicion is raised, you remember that the 6.2 diesel engine wasn't introduced until 1982, so the truck can't be a 1981.

What you do with that information is up to you. If you prefer what the year actually is versus what they're telling you, you can proceed. Just be sure that the title or paperwork for the truck indicates the correct year and model; otherwise, you could be purchasing a stolen truck or one with fouled paperwork.

The Right Truck for You

Here's a very basic two-part question to get you started: Do you like short beds or long beds, and of those, do you prefer a Stepside or Fleetside?

Over 14 years, General Motors produced more than 4.2 million of these trucks (4,206,467 to be exact). Out of those, more than 1 million were 1/2-ton trucks. Thousands of these trucks are out there for you to find. And in contrast to previous generations when short-bed trucks were

rare, this body style has so many options that it's relatively easy to find the more desirable models.

If you need to narrow it down further, the next question relates to trim level. The luxury models are difficult to find, although many sellers claim that they're selling a Silverado, because they assume (incorrectly) that it's a general term used with the truck.

If you're looking for power options, nicer materials, and a generally higher-end vehicle, yes, search for those lines. But if not, or if you're okay with essentially creating a clone by upgrading a lesser trim with the higher end stuff, go for it. If the current owner has all the documentation, it's a strong indication that the truck has been well taken care of.

The engine and transmission are major components to consider when purchasing a truck. If your plan is to buy a new crate engine and move forward, feel free to skip this portion. However, some restoration enthusiasts want numbers-matching trucks. They prefer the original engine and transmission package in the original truck, and they restore or rebuild whatever drivetrain is present. If that's the case, you're going to have a harder time finding your preferred vehicle, particularly if you want a big-block 454 or similar in a standard cab.

Why? Trucks are driven a lot. And some of these trucks became work vehicles that saw more than 100,000 miles in their first year. This means that a sizable number no longer have their original engines, which were long ago replaced. Take a good look at how important that is to your build; you might be causing yourself more headache and heartache in the process.

If you're a novice, and you're not sure how to do a lot of the work yourself, you should look for a truck in better condition. You may spend less trying to elevate the truck to a restorable condition, but you will spend more money on the initial purchase. Conversely, if you can buy a truck for less money that's in poor condition, you may spend more time and money on it in the long run.

Ownership Documents

You're going to find that a lot of trucks come cheap with the caveat that they're missing the most important part: ownership documents. With older vehicles, there's always the chance that one owner lost the paperwork and sold the truck to someone else with just a bill of sale. Although that's legal in some areas, if another person finds the original title or pink slip, he or she has every right to put the paperwork into his or her name and claim the truck as stolen. And that's another reason that the paperwork is missing: The truck was stolen.

Another scenario you may run into is salvage titles. A salvage title follows the vehicle for the rest of its existence. Because it's a salvage title, the resale value is dramatically lower than a truck without one. That saves you money, sure, but it also costs you on the back end once the truck is repaired. Buyers always wonder exactly how far gone the damage was, and what you had to do to fix it. That's enough for many to just walk away, and you should probably do the same before starting such a project (although you could use it as a parts truck, which I discuss in chapter 2).

Every state has different rules on how the ownership paperwork is handled. Whatever your situation is, make sure you have all of it and that there is no lien or other issue hanging over your head. That paperwork needs to be free and clear, 100 percent, or you risk losing the truck entirely. And if you've already finished the build when one of these issues surfaces, you're in for a world of hurt.

Customized Versus Stock Trucks

Many trucks have been customized to some degree, and they're often for sale. It can be difficult and expensive to bring the truck back to stock condition. You could buy that truck and be happy with it, and that's fine. But will it be perfect for your next restoration project? Probably not. This book focuses squarely on performing a stock or near-stock restoration.

You're better off in the long run avoiding customized trucks. If the truck has been customized, stock body parts and panels often don't fit correctly. You never truly know what's causing the problem. In addition, you never know how far the customization extends into the project until you buy it.

Let's say you find a truck that's lowered, and all the work looks good, so you get it for a steal. Once you strip it down, you notice that the rear frame has a C-shaped hole in the frame above the rear axle

This 1981 Chevrolet Cheyenne was my first step into the world of Squarebodies. It wasn't a good purchase because, even though it didn't appear to be modified, it had quite a bit of work done to it. The engine wasn't stock, I never learned what the keyhole in the fender activated, and the tailgate, well . . .

The tailgate wasn't even a real tailgate. Instead, it was a custom piece. In the end, even though I saved money on the purchase price of the vehicle, I spent a ton more on buying replacement parts.

Buying someone else's abandoned project often isn't worth it because there are too many missing parts that are expensive to replace. This is my old two-wheel-drive Blazer, which is missing a frame and multiple parts, and it didn't even roll. Because there was so much to find and assemble, plus I didn't do any of the disassembly, I ended up abandoning the project and giving it to a friend who needed a donor truck for parts. Usually, if someone abandoned his or her project, there's a good reason.

Here's a great example of the type of rust you find on some trucks. This is in the rocker on a 1973, as well as the lower portion of the door. A little bit of cleanup work has already been done. (Photo Courtesy Lonnie Thompson)

Notice the bubbles around the perimeter of the holes in this door skin? That's how rust can look at first, before it does major damage. If you see this on a panel without holes, there's likely more rust underneath. (Photo Courtesy Lonnie Thompson)

to allow the axle to travel farther, thus improving the ride on a lowered truck because the axle isn't hitting the frame. Fixing that C-notch is not easy and, depending on the quality of work, may require you to buy either a new back half or an entire new frame.

Or, let's say the truck has a custom paint job. Once you have the truck down to bare metal to refinish it, you find that most of the bodywork is backed by duct tape and fiberglass. Always assume that there's more customization done to the truck than is readily apparent.

One other thing to note is that unless you've built one before, don't buy someone else's abandoned project that's now in parts. This is a guaranteed way that you never discover where something is supposed to go, how it's supposed to fit, and so on.

Rust Versus No Rust

Rust is one of the single most important factors when assessing a restoration. Extensive rust substantially increases the cost of any restoration. For 40-some states and all of Canada, rust is a real issue for older vehicles, and something to watch out for, particularly in the 1973 and 1974 models. Some of those years had major rust issues in the bed.

Common places to find rust include the cab corners, rockers, fenders, and wheel arches. These are the spots that are prone to leaks when window rubber fails or that take the brunt of the impact when driving on a salty road in the winter.

In general, rust starts where water settles inside the body. This means that the common areas previously mentioned are good places to start, so walk around the truck and get up close with the metal. If there are obvious signs of rot, holes in the body, and so forth, you know there's a potential repair in your future and can plan accordingly.

Another thing that you can do is perform the magnet test. It goes pretty much the way it sounds: You place a magnet on various areas of the truck, including the wheelwells, rockers, cab corners, and so on. If the magnet doesn't stick, which indicates that there's body filler (typically a sizable amount) underneath the paint, that tells you that the truck has been repainted and/or repaired. You should, of course, ask the truck owner's permission before you stick a magnet all over the finish, but if he or she is okay with it, go for it. You might be surprised at what you find.

Less obvious signs of rust are small bubbles in the paint or even tiny pinholes. With bubbles, you're looking for clusters of imperfections in the paint. They may not have broken through the surface yet, but

Many trucks of this era may have had a camper shell on them, and some of those have used a rubber gasket between the shell and the cab. If so, they may have a telltale rust line outside the normal boundaries of the rear window. (Photo Courtesy Lonnie Thompson)

The cab corner on this truck is obviously damaged and needs to be replaced. But how about the rocker just forward of it? In this case, it seemed fine, but it's always good to look for damage if adjacent panels have issues as well. (Photo Courtesy Jefferson Bryant)

it makes the metal look similar to the surface of the moon. By rapping lightly on a metal panel and surrounding area with your knuckles, you can listen for tone differences. If it starts to sound different from the rest of the body (particularly in a usually rust-free area such as the center of a door), you know that's likely where the rust begins.

If the body part has an area that you can move for more access, open it. The tailgate, for example, may have rust in the lower corners near the hinges. Open the tailgate and take a look, pulling it away from the body if possible. Open the doors and inspect both sides of the door skin, plus the bottom of the door itself. Look behind the rocker panels and the lower areas of the bed. Just because rust is not obvious on the outside, doesn't mean that it's not on the inside.

The bottom of the cab is a bit more difficult. Assuming that the truck is stock height, stick your head underneath and look for areas that are red in color. There may or may not be bubbles in the finish, as some regions used rust proofing on their vehicles right off the dealership lot.

Rust on the cab floor is usually hidden on the inside by carpet, but you should be able to see any obvious patch panels or repairs from previous jobs. If the welds look like peanut butter or the work looks sloppy, prepare your offer accordingly.

The bed is another spot where rust can rear its ugly head. In the early years, Chevrolet had some problems with premature rust, which, depending on your source, was either from poor metal choices or a faulty primer. This rust showed up on the fenders as well, as both the bed sides and the fenders used the same materials. This was mainly a problem in the early years of 1973–1975, but depending on the truck, you may find it in later models. To know if these trucks have the

bed sides that were replaced early on, look for the color of the primer on the inside of the bed; gray is the original primer color, and black is for the replacements from the recall. Some also have obvious patch panels.

Now, rust isn't a deal breaker. It's likely that you will find it no matter where your truck has lived during the previous few decades. Finding excessive rust is when you realize that you're going to have to replace more than 50 percent of the sheet metal, and it could be worse than that. The first rule with rust is to always assume there's at least 20 percent more of it than you can see; it might be lurking under paint and bodywork.

That 50-percent number may seem low, as you may enjoy or have experience doing metal repair. To others, that may seem too high because they don't want to do any metal work if they can avoid it. It all comes down to experience. Just know that you need to keep that other 20-percent figure in your head because you always find more rust than you expected.

Engine and Transmission

You can take your truck to an ASE-certified mechanic, have him conduct an inspection, and uncover any problems. He can hook the truck up to a scope and identify any readily apparent problems. At a bare minimum, you should take your Squarebody on a test drive to evaluate the current condition of the engine and drivetrain. Drive it around the block a few times before you hit the freeway.

Does it sound like it's misfiring? Can you smell excessive amounts of gas? Does it blow out white, blue, or black smoke? White smoke indicates coolant in the oil. Blue smoke often means that it has worn valve seals and seats. Black smoke is a telltale sign that the fuel injection or carburetor is not correctly calibrated. Each one of these questions helps you determine whether or not the engine is worth keeping or if it needs some work.

The same goes for the transmission. If each automatic shift feels clunky and it sometimes misses a gear, that transmission needs to be inspected thoroughly. If it's a manual and the clutch barely grips and it grinds into every gear, it also needs work.

It's difficult to know if you have a cracked block, but one very basic test is to try to turn the crankshaft. Using a long-handled ratchet and socket, turn the crankshaft bolt (in the centerline of the engine, toward the bottom) to move the pistons. If they move, it's a good sign. If they don't, or if they require a serious amount of force to get moving, there are likely other issues, such as a seized piston, bent pushrod(s), bent crank, and so on. No matter what they are, it's likely that the engine is pretty well damaged, so you might want to consider it a wash. Worst case is that you have to buy a new engine; best case is that it needs a mild rebuild.

Performing a leak-down test and a compression test are two other ways to determine the condition of an engine. A leak-down test is used to test pressure retention on each cylinder. Two- and single-gauge models are available, but for more accurate results, use a two-gauge type.

With the engine warmed up and turned off, remove the spark plug on the cylinder that you're testing. Turn the engine over to top dead center (TDC), using a ratchet on the crankshaft, and put the air fitting adapter into the spark plug hole. With the gauge at zero, connect the air line from your air compressor to the other end of the tool. Now check the gauge to see how much air is leaking. If the number is between 8 and 12 percent, you're fine; the engine should be great. Test the rest of the cylinders; a variance of up to 5 percent among them is acceptable. If the numbers are between 15 and 20 percent, it's time to figure out where the leak is coming from.

With air pressure in the engine, listen to see if you can determine the source of the leak. If it's coming out around the dipstick tube or valvecover breather, it's leaking past the rings. If it's out of the carb, it's past the intake valves. If it's leaking out of the exhaust valve, you may hear the noise anywhere in the exhaust, including the tailpipe.

If the leakage number is higher than 20 percent and it's past the rings, it's time to move on. The engine needs some work, and although it's drivable, you may experience some horsepower loss. If the leakage number is more than 30 percent at the exhaust valves, pass on the engine. If it's more than 20 percent on the intake valve, you're there as well. Granted, these aren't hard and fast numbers, and the decision is ultimately up to you. But consider your options.

A compression test is similar to a leak-down test, but it uses an older technique. Remove all of the spark plugs and then pop the coil lead off the coil. Connect a compression tester to a spark plug hole. Crank over the engine using the key and starter, and count how many engine revolutions it takes for the gauge to top out at maximum pressure (you may want to have a helper turn the key while you check the gauge). Do this for every cylinder, taking notes along the way, until they're all checked.

You're looking for consistent pressure in each cylinder, and to ensure that the numbers are within 10 percent of one another, give or take. If your gauge reads less than 30 percent, the engine has a compression leak, and you may want to move on (or negotiate the price of the truck lower accordingly).

If you're not good at these types of mechanical projects, consider paying a professional mechanic to give the truck a once-over. Many mechanics can check out a project for you on the side, depending on the price you offer. If you don't know or trust any mechanics (or you don't have the extra cash), maybe one of your experienced friends could do it. Either way, it's always good to have a second opinion, particularly if he or she has more experience than you do.

Take your time when looking over a potential project's drivetrain. What you find could determine whether or not it becomes your next project or the next guy's.

Chassis, Suspension, and Brakes

The chassis, suspension, and brakes are similar to the drivetrain, in that it's handy if you can drive the truck. Cruising at slow speeds, it's easy to listen for squeaky bushings or go over a bump to notice how the steering wheel feels. Giving the truck a series of basic braking tests at various speeds and seeing how the truck handles overall is a huge help to decide whether to buy it.

If you do not have the opportunity to drive the truck, grab a flashlight and get down on the ground to check things out further. When it comes to the suspension, look for worn bushings with obvious cracks. If you can pull on a tire and hear the suspension clunking, you likely have poor bushings or bad ball joints, both of which can be dangerous if not fixed (that said, ball joint replacement is something that most home mechanics can do themselves).

Be sure to consider the suspension of the truck. Up front, upper and lower control arms, tie-rod ends, coil springs, and so on should be straight and free of any wrinkles or major bends. If you see a problem, the truck has likely seen some kind of impact or maybe a *Dukes of Hazard*–style jump. Coil springs that look like limp noodles were likely heated at some point, the result of an inexperienced person's attempts to lower the front end.

As for the leaf springs, look for any obvious cracks, twists, or other damage in the steel. There should be a few individual leafs in the pack; if there's just one, the truck has been lowered. Also, make sure that the axle is located underneath the leaf springs. If there are only two or three leaves in the pack, you have to decide whether or not a new set of leaf springs is worth the purchase.

Brakes are obviously a critical component on a truck, and if they're seized, there's not much to

Inspect the brake fluid when you check out a truck; that could point out more clues, too. This particular truck was very well cared for, but the brake fluid was grimy and full of dirt and rust. It meant that the entire braking system should be gone through, so that new fluid could be flushed through the system. It wasn't life threatening or dangerous, but it was another cost to add to the overall project.

test. You have to break them free before you can determine how well they work, but you could also make the argument that if they're frozen, they need to be replaced entirely.

Look for holes or leaks around the brake lines, cracks in the rubber hoses leading to the calipers, and rust inside the master cylinder. Brake lines are made of rubber and the rubber stretches, fades, and cracks over time. If this is the case, all of the lines may need to be replaced. Remember that your brakes are a safety device, and safety must never be compromised. If it looks abnormal, it likely is, and that's obviously a problem.

The chassis of the truck needs to be solid, unless you plan on purchasing a new one for the project. Look for rust spots and note if any of them penetrate all of the way through the frame. Although fixing a chassis is doable, it can be a big project, and it may be going further than you want to attempt.

The bushings on this project truck worked, and the truck drove fine, but they didn't last for much longer. The cracks visible along the edges of the bushings were pretty substantial, and the bushings needed replacement soon, anyway.

Beater Options

A "beater" is one of those friendly terms for a truck or car that's had a hard service life. These vehicles are often in such poor condition and need such substantial restoration that it's not worth the investment. However, a beater could be used as a parts truck. The thing is, you have to assess the truck as it stands and see what you can realistically fix. A truck that's been lowered may be easy to raise back up to stock height, but was the frame cut to drop it? Does it have drag marks on the frame? Is anything bent or tweaked? A lot of times a cheap truck is one that has a bunch of problems, so be wary.

Yes, you could, in theory, rescue a beater truck. And when you check it out, it may seem that it's not beyond repair, and that you could give it a new home. In the process, however, you will probably spend thousands of dollars trying to get the truck back up to specs. And who knows what other problems you might find.

Believe me, it's better to save your money and get something nicer to begin with, rather than hoping that a cheap beater will work.

Determining Your Skill Level

The key is to find a truck that fits your needs, budget, and skill level. The argument could be made that this is the hardest step of the process. How do you know what you're capable of before you take on the project?

Let's assume that if you've purchased this book you're not an expert in the field. You may be a skilled bodyman, painter, or welder, but these specific trucks aren't your bread and butter. Many owners have done some kind of mechanical work, so you have the expertise to rebuild the engine, brakes, rear end, and suspension.

You could be the one who installed a new top end on your last small-block engine. If you've done brakes before and know how to tear apart a suspension the right way, or you've made any number of mechanical improvements or repairs to a vehicle before, chances are that you have the mechanical skills necessary to restore a truck.

Think about what you can and can't do. The simplest way to do that is by making a list. Skim through the following chapters and try to figure out what it is that you can do. Jot down the tasks that you feel confident about, then make another column for things that you're iffy about, and a last column for tasks that you have zero confidence in at all.

If the list of things you can't do outweighs the number of things you can or are iffy on, you could be farming out a lot of this work, which is fine as long as you can afford it. Alternatively, you could also spend the time to learn how to perform the procedures. At the end of the day, it comes down to how much time you want to devote to the project, including learning (and fixing mistakes) in the process.

If your "can't do" list is virtually everything, don't let it get you down. First off, there are many automotive restoration projects that pretty much anyone with patience and time can handle. It doesn't take a genius to clean up and install tailgate latches for example, or learn how to do some basic wiring, either. The main thing to remember is that many of the projects are simple mechanical restorations. It went together years ago, and all you have to do is make sure it goes back together the same way. If it helps, think of trucks as big LEGO blocks, just with a lot more components.

My 1981 Cheyenne was a beater, and I knew it. But my theory was that I was going to redo the truck anyway, so why spend the money on something nicer? The interior was a great example of the problem. It was past the point of restoration, which meant that the only option I had was to replace everything.

My 1981 was equipped with a 305, but my goal was to find a 350-equipped truck that had more performance potential. After owning the truck for a short time, I decided to sell it.

GETTING STARTED

Take an organized and methodical approach to truck restoration; it saves you time, money, and frustration later on. Restoring any vehicle is a massive undertaking, and without proper preparation, it can quickly become an absolute nightmare. Starting off randomly and arbitrarily pushing forward is no way to accomplish anything, let alone a restoration project. Before you actually start the restoration, you need a solid plan as to how you're going to tackle the entire restoration, estimate cost, accommodate a cost overrun of 20 percent, and set a budget. Within a restoration plan, you set specific tasks and accomplish them in a timely matter. Before you start, create a list of what you need; that way, you can make sure that your budget is on track. Remember, you also need the correct tools to perform high-quality work.

Organizing Your Process

The key, as it is with any big project, is to plan out major sections beforehand. Divide each portion of the project into individual components, then work it down from there. For example, you could organize by area: cab, bed, engine, etc. Or you could organize by the type of work you're doing: rust repair, bodywork, paint, mechanical. Whichever method of organizing your restoration you choose, it's absolutely critical that you have a consistent and methodical system to keep it on track. If not, you can squander time, parts, and money. Often, it comes back to haunt you in the end.

One of the easiest ways to sort things out is to list, in detail, exactly what you plan to do to the truck, something like a mission statement. If you're doing a full restoration, plan out the project. Some things can be done simultaneously, particularly if you're farming out the work; the interior (at least some of it) can be done while the truck is being painted, for example, but others must follow a very specific sequence, otherwise they aren't done correctly, if at all.

You're still in the early planning

Before you dive into your restoration, you need a complete plan and budget so you can save time and money. Without one, it's easy to lose your way and the truck restoration becomes a decades long project.

stages here, but the system sequence generally goes like this:

1. Disassembly
2. Rust repair
3. Bodywork
4. Paint
5. Engine/transmission
6. Suspension, brakes, steering
7. Interior
8. Electrical
9. Final Assembly

Of course, some things can be done whenever you want. If you're experienced at engine rebuilding, you could do that at any step of the process, and just wait to install it once the truck is painted. The interior, again, is a matter of timing. In theory, you can do it right away but keep it stored safely somewhere until final assembly. You don't want to have that nice, new finish ruined with body filler dust and overspray.

The key (and let me just hammer this one home) is taking the time to dial in exactly what you want to do and how you want to handle it. To do that, you must be organized; I can't stress that enough.

Spreadsheets and To-Do Lists

You need to comprehensively organize all the procedures and parts required to complete the restoration. This is a mammoth undertaking, so it's not going to be cheap. But if you're not organized as you go about the restoration process, you spend more money in the long run. With Microsoft Excel, Apple Numbers, Google Docs, or another program, you can build a spreadsheet that tracks your process.

For example, each component can have its own line on the document, with a checkmark as it goes through each phase of restoration. Or each phase of the restoration can have its own line, and the components receive a checkmark. It's up to you how it's organized; just make sure that it is.

In case you don't have any idea where to begin, here's a starting point: Set up a basic spreadsheet that has columns for priority, task, budgeted cost, budgeted hours, actual cost, and actual hours. Before you begin the work, fill in the first four columns; that add up the budgeted cost at the bottom of its column, and add up the budgeted hours at the bottom of its column.

This gives you an idea of what you expect the whole project to cost and how long it will take. Then, as you go through the build, you can track your actual costs and actual hours. When you're finished with one phase, you can compare the two columns, which should give you an idea of where you are at in relation to the next phase.

Using a spreadsheet has a number of advantages for organizing your restoration, but one of the main ones is tracking cost. Over the course of your project, whether it takes years or months, you're going to pick up parts here and there to fix things. Those parts cost money, and it's easy to forget all of the little things that you buy along the way. Nuts and bolts, for example, are often just a few dollars here and there, but they do add up. Having each purchase and part, no matter how small or seemingly insignificant, on a spreadsheet allows you to see the running total of the actual costs involved in the process. If you put together this spreadsheet before the build begins and include estimates of what you need, you can compare notes later to see how much (more or less) you

spent. That information will help you with future projects and budgeting them properly.

Another popular option is to use David Allen's book *Getting Things Done* as a guideline. The phrase, "getting things done," or GTD, is a way to determine what you need to do and when. Depending on the level of granularity that you want to use, your project list can have multiple nested projects and tasks, with estimated times also included. By the time you have things mapped out, you should have a solid idea of how long your project will take to do. If a day arrives when you want to do something but only have a set amount of time, you will know what you can and can't accomplish.

The key to the GTD system is that granularity, so don't be afraid to really dig into things. Although the resulting to-do list is quite large, it allows you to budget your time efficiently and ensure that you don't forget anything along the way.

Several computer applications are also available for both mobile and desktop devices that you can use for GTD, so search around to see what suits your needs best.

Choosing the Level of Restoration

Determining what kind of restoration you want to perform depends on the type of vehicle you purchase. On the low end is a daily driver restoration. For these types of rebuilds, you're not worrying if the tires are from the same manufacturer as they were in 1973 or if the seats are of the exact factory material that the dealer ordered. You just want to restore the truck to stock or near-stock condition, and maybe you include bolt-on

Choosing a Build Type

The following is a quick rundown of the various types of build you may want to consider for your truck.

A daily driver is just that: a truck you drive every day, say, to the office. It's relatively reliable, all the parts are in good working condition, and you could park it anywhere without concerns about it starting when you return. The paint job, although nice, won't be worth tens of thousands of dollars because you're going to be driving it, and that can bring chips and scratches into the mix. This type of build also means that the interior is in good shape, but you may not have used the highest quality materials. And if something breaks, you don't feel weird about heading down to O'Reilly's to grab the parts.

A show-quality truck is slightly different. The goal here is to build something that doesn't look out of place at a car show, which means that all of the finishes meet higher standards than for a daily driver. The paint job is flawless, or close to it, with little to no orange peel and everything from the engine bay to the doorjambs is covered. The bodywork is straight as an arrow, the interior is spotless, and the number of overall flaws is minimal, at best.

Now what kind of show you're planning to attend changes things from there. If it's a custom car and truck show, your truck might have a few custom touches. If it's the local cruise night at the mall, you could probably spend less money. The point is, you have a wide range of choices.

A concours restoration is a whole other ball of wax. The term comes from the Concours d'Elegance, a show that has gone on for centuries (back to the horse and carriage days), and at which only the highest of standards are considered worthy. Typically, the goal is to imagine that your truck was bone stock, just rolled off the line, and was being judged on that basis, but better. So if the bumpers were chrome to begin with, they're chrome now, but the quality of the overall finish is higher. Long story short, a concours restoration can involve tens of thousands of dollars in costs, which, if I'm super honest here, is not something you should do to one of these trucks. That is why I focus on the daily driver and show-quality aspects in this book; not one that requires you to take out a second mortgage on your home. ∎

upgrades, such as brakes and ignition. These types of builds tend to be focused on drivetrain and comfort features because how the truck looks may not be as critical as how it functions. You may simply like older trucks, and having one that's able to haul an A/C unit across town for you comes in handy.

At the top end are concours-style builds. These trucks are 100-percent authentic and are virtually identical to the way they rolled off the assembly line. When entered in a show, they score the proverbial 100 points because they are just perfect. These trucks take years to build, and, although the results are immaculate, it's just like any other car or truck restoration, which means that they're worth a lot of money and shouldn't be driven excessively.

It's likely that your build will sit somewhere between those two extremes. You may want a super-clean truck with a varnished wood floor, immaculate paint, and a killer interior, but you may upgrade to disc brakes for drivability and put an LS engine under the hood to keep things modern and more reliable. Maybe you purchased a base-model 1982, but you prefer a V-8 and the front end of the 1973 model, so you bolt one on.

Let me make one thing clear: This book does provide the tips and tricks you need to restore a 1973–1987 Chevrolet or GMC truck to a reliable and correct weekend driver, but it does not cover a concours restoration. I discuss all of the pertinent procedures for disassembly, component repair, parts installations, and assembly so you have a faithful stock restoration.

Set your goals according to personal preference, budget, and level of restoration. Some people restore vehicles for the resale value, and they expect to invest a lot money on the front end to get the results right later on. Others don't care about the money; they just want a truck that works. You decide what you want.

Setting a Budget

Whatever type of restoration you plan to perform, it's a major investment. If you're going to do a low-budget restoration, you can get away with buying a lot of parts second-hand, online, and at junkyards. You're going to sink a decent amount of cash into the project no matter how shallow the build. Unless you're a painter, paint and bodywork can be one of the more expensive costs in the process, and if your project needs paint, be prepared to pull out your wallet.

The level of restoration determines the budget of the restoration. Depending on your situation, you may feel that spending $25,000 on rebuilding a project is ridiculous, and $5,000 seems more in your price range. But if you're going for that 100-point winner, $25,000 is on the low end for sure.

Ultimately, the budget of your restoration is going to include the cost of your parts, materials, and time. Most hobbyists don't factor in their time as a cost, but you probably should; the hours you spend on your truck are ones you're not spending with your family, friends, work, etc. After you do a thorough inspection of the truck and create an inventory of what you need, you can start pricing out a budget.

Project Component Pricing

There are some basic numbers that you can discern by doing some groundwork before you pick up a single tool. Start by breaking down the process into the individual components, bodywork, paint, interior, etc. Then determine what you can do yourself and what you need to farm out. When it comes to the work you have to rely on others to do, visit local shops for some general estimates. Don't worry about the specifics; get some broad ranges of prices so you know what you will be dealing with.

Your carpet should run a few hundred bucks with installation. The headliner and door panels are inexpensive in the aftermarket, so expect to spend a few hundred dollars there. If you want stock seats, you can either buy a refurbishment kit for $200 or so, or take it to an upholsterer who charges anywhere from $500 to $1,500, depending on the material used. (Even though vinyl is stock on many of these trucks, many restorers go with leather for the quality.)

Basically, stock seats, carpet, headliner door panels, and related parts could cost anywhere from $1,000 to $5,000, and that amount varies based on the amount of stuff you have to purchase new and what materials you use. On average, however, you're probably looking at around $2,000 in materials and parts. Alternatively, find a shop that gives you a firm estimate, and go with it.

Paint and bodywork make up the lion's share of restoration expense because both can widely vary. Often, you find a project truck that appears to be perfect, but by the time it's down to bare metal and the layers of paint and bodywork are stripped clean, you discover a world of rust repair that you may or may not have budgeted for.

To do a faithful restoration, you need to cut out all the rusted sheet metal. Some restorers prefer to retain as much original sheet metal as possible and install patch panels. Other restorers replace entire body panels. I don't recommend a cheap fix-it job with a quick coat of body filler and some primer. Those types of results often don't last, and the problem is that sometimes what you think you're paying for isn't what you actually get. There are many show trucks out there that don't pass the 10-foot test (where you can't see a flaw from 10 feet away), or ones that look great today, but don't last because of the poor build quality.

Body Shop Estimates

When it comes to finding the right body shop for your project, research its history and past work thoroughly. Find out what jobs they've done in the past, and ask what was included in those prices.

For example, during the research phase of this book I spoke with one person who was having his truck repainted the stock color. The interior was fine as-is, so he didn't want to spend the cash on spraying the door-jambs and dashboard, just the exterior. Even so, hours of bodywork ended up going into the doors and body, but he ended up spending $6,000 to get the truck sprayed. I also know someone who paid $10,000 to have his truck painted in time for the SEMA show, and not only was it done within 14 days, but it still looks flawless a year or so later.

So how do you figure out your price? The easy way is to ask for an estimate. If the truck is drivable, take it to a few shops and ask for quotes. If it's not, either pull it on a trailer or take some detailed pictures and show them to the shop (obviously that last one isn't ideal, but it might put you in the ballpark). Also ask them for their hourly rates.

Once you have a few quotes, add another 10 to 15 percent to each of them in case of disaster, for example a bedside that needs to be replaced instead of patched, the cab floor is rotten and you didn't know it, etc. That's a good place to start.

Reality Sets In

Regardless of what number you pick, it's important to understand that the total cost of the project will be more than what you expect. In the process of building your truck you will find more than a few problems that were completely unexpected. What started off as a small rust repair patch job turns into new cab corners and floors; you get the idea. As a result, consider your desired budget to be a starting point, then add 10 to 20 percent. It may seem excessive, but it's better to plan for the worst and be significantly under your budget.

Almost more important than setting a budget is making sure that you adhere to those numbers. After all, it doesn't make any sense to come up with some number guidelines and then not follow them.

Preparing Your Workspace

Whether it's a rental shop or your home garage, the space you use for your truck's restoration project must be well organized and well stocked. Otherwise, you're doomed to failure before you even start.

The first step is to make sure you clean your workspace thoroughly. Obviously, there are a few caveats here, as you will likely spill oil or something similar on the floor, so keeping it spotless may not always be possible. However, by having your tools and parts clearly labeled and sorted, you save time in the end. Why? Because you're not losing minutes or hours hunting down stuff that you need; it's all right where you put it.

One way to keep the area tidy at all times is to stop about 10 minutes before the end of your day and clean up. I like to go through the room with a broom and dustpan, possibly some degreaser if I've tackled something heavy. By doing it at the end of each workday, you find yourself having fewer excuses for not going in the following day because there's nothing stopping you from finishing tasks.

Give yourself as much space as you can for things you don't know you need yet or parts you remove during disassembly. It's likely that you have several piles to sort through, and with the cab, bed, engine, transmission, and frame removed from the truck, you quickly learn that they take up a large amount of space, and often you can't overlap them at all. Plus, you always need some kind of area to clean parts, so you can never have too much free space.

Evaluating What You Have and What You Need

With a truck in hand and a plan to do the restoration, you have to figure out what you have and what you still need. But how the heck do you do that? Truth is, you're not going to always know what you have and/or what you're missing, but if your work area is organized, you can come up with a pretty good list.

Although you may have done a "walk through" when you purchased the vehicle, a key step in the restoration process is to revisit every component to find out what you need. Your list should also specify which parts need to be restored or replaced.

The gas tank is a good example: Some can be repaired so that it looks and functions like stock but doesn't have the details of a fully restored or replacement tank. Or it could be replaced cheaply with an aftermarket or salvage unit. And then there's restoring it, which is different than repairing it, you're taking the good, existing materials, and bringing them back to their original specifications.

This evaluation process also helps you figure out how much money you're going to have to spend to sort things out.

NOS Versus Reproduction Versus Aftermarket Parts

With your list in hand, find the parts that you need to get started. For the most part, the types of parts that you use fit into two categories: new old stock (NOS) and reproduction.

NOS parts are, in this case, original components made by General Motors (or one of its subsidiaries) that you would find at a parts store of that era. You can buy these types of parts online on eBay, Craigslist,

or other sites. Specialty dealers buy old stock from defunct or closing dealerships, although those are hard to find. You can also try junkyards, because their trucks could also have the parts you want; they just may need some reconditioning to function perfectly. On the downside, these parts are more expensive, are more difficult to find, and are in limited quantities, so the cost increases accordingly.

Reproduction parts are intended to be just as good as NOS parts but built today using modern production facilities. In theory, reproduction parts fit and perform exactly like stock, and there's no functional difference between them. In practice, however, reproduction parts vary widely in quality, depending on where you purchase them. There's no bulletproof method for finding out who sells the best parts, so be wary of sheet metal from thinner stock than usual, misaligned body lines, and so on, as those can cause problems for you later. On the flip side, they are cheaper to buy, but I do not recommend them because it isn't worth the time required to adjust sheet metal simply to fit properly.

A few companies that offer high-quality and consistent product include Classic Industries, Goodmark, Dynacorn, and AMD. Any of these are a good place to start the selection process.

If you want to build a 100-percent period-correct truck, your only options are NOS or restoring what you have. That makes for a more expensive build, mainly because you'll be spending both time and money on finding what you need, but the result could be worth more than a truck restored with aftermarket parts.

If you are building a weekend

truck or daily driver, or the part you need is perishable, such as a rubber brake line, a third parts source is available: the aftermarket. These are similar to reproduction parts in that they are not original materials, but they're not supposed to look or function like originals, either. Typically, the part is designed to improve upon a flaw. Stock hood hinges, for example, have mammoth springs that can cause sheet-metal alignment issues, and therefore have been redesigned for better performance.

What this comes down to is deciding what is more important to you: authenticity or the overall appearance. If it has to be authentic, you should use NOS parts. If you want the look but don't care about whether a part is original or not, aftermarket and reproduction parts are the way to go.

Purchasing a Parts Vehicle

In the course of searching for a vehicle, you often stumble across a truck that has one or two perfect components but is too far gone to be a viable restoration project. Maybe it's missing an engine, bed, or cab, or it's a long bed and you prefer a short bed. Whatever the problem, if the truck is affordable, and the total value of its parts could be worth more than what the seller is asking, you're looking at a parts vehicle.

Parts vehicles allow you to use the same business model as your local wrecking yard. In their case, they purchase hundreds of vehicles for low prices. As a vehicle sits in their yard, people (like you) come in and buy parts from it, making money for the yard. As soon as the vehicle makes more money than the original purchase price, every additional component is sold for a full profit.

Now apply that to your project. There are lots of reasons for missing parts, such as if you want to take a base-model truck and turn it into a higher trim level, or possibly because of a component that would take too much time and money to repair rather than replace. Parts vehicles are the perfect way to solve those issues in an affordable fashion. But what makes them so cheap?

Parts vehicles almost always have some kind of major problem, and therefore are not worth restoring, but they have many excellent parts. Common reasons are that it has a salvage title, missing paperwork, or no title at all. A vehicle with a salvage title means that at one point the vehicle was in such disrepair that it was no longer considered to be safe to drive; therefore, it was given a salvage title. Although you can buy a vehicle like that and restore it, a salvage title can seriously depreciate the value. But you don't need a title if you just want to strip the cab of the parts, so it still has some value, just not as much as a project vehicle.

There are many possible reasons that a truck may not have a proper title, and theft is high on the list. You should be wary of purchasing any vehicle that comes without paperwork, because it may cause a problem for you later on. In addition, purchasing a cab with the intent of using it as a replacement for your current cab requires that you swap the VINs, which is illegal in most states.

Organizing and Cataloging Your Parts

With a full restoration, one that involves blowing most of the truck apart, you'll need lots of storage.

Small bags such as these by Ziploc make organizing small parts a ton easier than just tossing them into a coffee can. (Photo Courtesy Lee Hurlbutt)

Keeping parts organized speeds up the reinstallation time and makes the entire process run more efficiently. (Photo Courtesy Lee Hurlbutt)

Generally, parts can be divided into three categories:

- Small parts: something tiny enough that it could fit into a resealable plastic bag. Bolts, fasteners, and small engine parts fit into this category.
- Medium parts: bigger than the average bag could hold, but a box works just fine. Think moldings, gauges, etc.
- Big parts: the ones that can either fill a shelf by itself or need a dedicated area in your workspace. For example, fenders fit on a shelf, but the cab is ideally stored on a rolling cart.

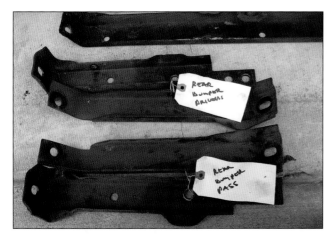

If the part is too big for a bag but not needing a huge shelf, use tags to label them properly. Make sure they're secured to the part tightly, so you don't risk losing the tag while the part is stored. (Photo Courtesy Lee Hurlbutt)

Because most of these components need shelving of some kind, you want lots of industrial-grade metal shelving units for your workspace. Many home supply stores offer inexpensive options that hold hundreds of pounds, and, unless you're trying to fit an entire bed on one, they are fine for the majority of your components. Shelving is critical, and it needs to be dedicated solely to the restoration project so there are no mix-ups.

There are both inexpensive and expensive options for storing small parts. The cheapest way to go are resealable freezer and sandwich bags, such as the ones available at any grocery store. Some name-brand versions have an opaque white area so you can label the contents with a permanent marker. They work great. Although you can use a twist tie and call it done, resealable and lockable bags keep the contents more secure.

Another option is cloth bags made specifically for restoration projects. These are made of canvas and include a paper tag that also ties the bag shut. They're not cheap, but they are durable.

Regardless of the bag option you choose, also buy a few packs of 3x5 index cards. Sometimes the markings on the outside of a plastic bag can fade, and with cloth restoration bags, the tag can tear. To avoid those issues, write the contents of the bag on the index card, then store the card in the bag. It's double security.

When it comes to labeling, make sure that the label on the bag is an accurate description of what's inside. You may run into a problem if you don't know what the part is called technically, or where a certain bolt should go. Be very specific with your labels, and even write a short description if necessary. It could read "Left upper corner of bumper bracket, holds bracket to frame," for example. There's nothing wrong with being more detailed than necessary.

Other indispensable tools to have in your kit are a good digital camera and a printer. If you're restoring your truck to resell it, taking copious numbers of pictures always helps the resale value. It proves to the buyer what's underneath the paint and gives evidence of what's been done. But the camera serves an even more important part during teardown. As you disassemble a component (the door, for example), take pictures of each part before it's taken apart, during, and after. Take pictures of the bolts once they're loose, too. Print out the pictures and put them into the bag with the parts (or tape them onto a larger part, if necessary). That way you know what they are, where they go, and what it will look like when it's properly reassembled.

This book provides step-by-step instructions on how to do various things. If you take the time to do the same steps with your project, you have notes on the unique peculiarities of your project. Because these trucks are more than 25 years old, it's likely that someone along the way has adjusted, tweaked, or changed some component to meet his or her own specifications. Having a record of how those parts go together comes in handy when you try to sell the truck, as well as when you're putting it together.

You need boxes in a variety of sizes to house parts of varying size. Individual bags for different parts of the same area can be stored together in one box. That allows you to have one "zone" covered in the box, with multiple bags to allow for unique descriptors.

Boxes come in all shapes and sizes, and if you've ever moved your home, you have a good idea of what they cost. Some options have cardboard divider trays to help segregate your stuff.

One way to approach parts organization that's worked well for me in the past is sorting (or grouping) by component or region. For example, I have a shelf or an area dedicated for the engine, and that holds everything from the original carburetor to the motor mount bolts (minus the engine). Another shelf holds the bed parts, another the cab, etc.

You also may want to sort things further, from front to back on the truck, or create zones for each part showing where it goes. It's important that you maintain all of your parts in one area and keep things there for the duration of your project. Once you start shifting locations, things inevitably become lost, costing you time and money in the process. Before you begin, figure out where the shelving and parts will be stored, and then keep the parts there.

You also need to "catalog" your parts. To keep beating a dead horse, a spreadsheet can come in handy. In different columns, write down what the part is, where it goes, and what it's used for. That quick reference should make it easier to sort things out later.

Tools and Equipment

It goes without saying that sometimes you want to focus on the basics. These are the hand tools that any enthusiast likely already has. I recommend home stores such as Lowes and Home Depot; they have their own brands, Kobalt and Husky, respectively, and both have lifetime warranties. Those stores have most of the general tools that home repair shares with auto mechanic work.

You may also consider using Craftsman tools. My father introduced me to the brand when I was a kid, and once I started "sharing" his toolbox, many of his Craftsman tools made their way into my own box. The great thing about Craftsman tools is that they have a killer warranty: the company stands behind its tools and guarantees them forever. If your ratchet should break a tooth, contact the company for a new one; the same goes for any of the hand tools. Granted, they don't typically fail, so you should be fine. But it's good to know that if it does happen, you're covered.

A basic socket set, both standard and metric, deep- and shallow-well, 1/4-, 3/8-, and 1/2-inch drive, are going to be your best friends, so invest in a quality set that has the features you prefer. Six-point sockets fit bolts better in some situations, but for others, a 12-point connects more quickly (and sometimes better), saving you time. Having multiple sockets in different drives helps when you have rusty bolts to remove, plus they're handy if you have clearance issues with fitting a ratchet in a tight spot. The point is, you want a lot of sockets.

The ratchet that fits those sockets is also crucial. You want ones in different drive sizes, and possibly different lengths. You should invest in a high-quality set of hand tools if you have not already. Although Snap-on, Matco, Mac, and others are exceptional quality, an enthusiast restorer does not need tools of this caliber. You would be just as well suited using tools from Craftsman, Husky, Rigid, and other similar brands that also have a lifetime warranty.

You need a digital or regular click-type torque wrench for critical components, particularly for the engine, and a matching set of torque sockets. Wrenches are also required, so buy both standard and metric; these trucks use both formats. You also need both box- and open-end wrenches.

Ratcheting wrenches, including reversible ones, are available from many manufacturers, but they are a bit more expensive than standard versions. These come in handy while trying to remove a part from an area where a ratchet and socket don't easily reach. Ultimately, they are not critical; it's a matter of how much time and money you're willing to spend.

A good screwdriver set is required as well, both Phillips and flathead.

Fortunately, there aren't too many odd-shaped heads on screws on these trucks, but you want varying lengths and head sizes. Also available are ratcheting screwdrivers and ones with removable tips. Both work just fine.

A dead-blow hammer is a good investment, particularly if you're working on the suspension. You might consider a 5- or 10-pound sledgehammer, too, again, for the suspension or other pieces of hardware that don't come out easily.

Safety Equipment

As someone who has had a few close calls, I can't say this often enough: Always protect yourself properly when working with tools. Eye protection is first on the list. When doing almost anything, wear safety glasses. You can buy versions that fit over your regular eyeglasses. They're cheap, usually less than $5 a pair, so buy several in different styles. Find ones that you like and keep them handy at all times.

When glasses don't cut it, look into a face shield. This is a clear piece of plastic that's designed to protect your entire face from harm, including sparks, flying metal debris, and so on. They're not indestructible, but they do

I recommend keeping these types of gloves handy in your shop, as well as two forms of protection for your face. You should use safety glasses every time you work on your project. You can never have too many options.

provide more protection than glasses, and they help to keep your face scar free.

When working on most jobs, I wear latex gloves (or non-latex alternatives) to keep grime off my hands. They break, but they often keep sparks from damaging my skin while still giving me a tactile feel. When I need more protection, mechanics gloves are a good option. These usually have knuckle protection and are made of cloth or a stronger fabric. They can wear out and usually aren't as inexpensive as a box of latex gloves, but they are necessary for many tasks. Finally, thick welding gloves are best for, well, welding. Because they're so thick, you lose a lot of your normal tactile feel, but you don't want welding spatter to sit on your skin. It hurts. A lot.

Basic clothing needs start with good shoes. Many wear work boots with a steel toe because of the protection they provide and ankle support they give. They can handle welding spatter, grinding sparks, and the occasional dropped part. The right brand also has insoles that help prevent fatigue.

Long pants made of denim or heavy canvas material are important. Although you could wear shorts in the summer, the problem is that hot or painful items inevitably make their way to your legs, and then you're in a world of hurt. Long pants also keep liquids away from your skin, and that makes showering and clean up a lot easier. They should go over the heels of your boots for extra protection.

For your torso, long sleeves are ideal, but short sleeves can work in hotter temperatures. Make sure your clothes fit and aren't too loose. You certainly don't want to catch a piece of cloth in a spinning part, putting

you at risk of breaking a bone or worse.

Other general rules include making sure that all of your electrical cords are free of frays or cuts, having fire extinguishers handy, having drinking water to keep yourself hydrated, and making sure you weld away from anything flammable. Common sense will take you far, so think before you act.

Lifts and Jacks

If you have the money and space to buy a lift, go for it. A hydraulic or pneumatic lift can make your life a lot easier, although they do take up a lot of space. It's not necessary by any means, so if you want to do the job with regular tools, buy at least two floor jacks, 1/2-ton or larger, and 8 to 12 jack stands.

The need for jacks seems obvious at first because, of course, you will be lifting the truck in the air at one time or another. But why so many jack stands? The more stands you have under your truck, the less likely it is to fall off. Don't just put one under each corner, support the cab and front of the bed with another four, and maybe four more if you have the space. Also, if you're doing detail work during assembly, you

can always wrap a terrycloth towel around the top to protect the fresh paint or powder coating.

Electric Tools

The number-one tool on your electric tool purchase list should be a reciprocating saw, often referred to by the brand name Sawzall. The reciprocating saw is an infinitely flexible tool that allows you to cut wood and metal quickly and easily. When you become good at handling one, using the tool becomes second nature, making it easy for you to cut the most delicate path in tricky metal.

During a restoration, you may have to cut up a large portion of metal (frame, cab, the front end of your parts truck) and form it into smaller pieces. Reciprocating saws are sometimes used by first responders to open cars after a wreck, which means that if the pros use it to get people back to safety, it will work just fine on that 1974 you bought for parts.

Cordless and corded, impact and traditional, 3/8- and 1/2-inch chuck. You can never have too many drills, and it's likely that you will be working on one component with a larger drill, and another with a cordless. You could get by with just a corded

You need the right tools and equipment for safely and professionally restoring your Squarebody truck, or any vehicle for that matter. A set of wheel dollies allows you to quickly and conveniently move the truck around your workshop. In addition, a two-post lift allows you to safely work under the truck. While four-post lifts are handy as well, they take up more room and are more expensive.

The cab and box have been separated from the chassis so a complete restoration can be performed.

These 4.5-inch grinders come in handy, and if you have multiple tools, you can save time by switching devices, not sanding/cutting discs.

impact and a 3/8-inch cordless, but give yourself some options.

A good 4.5-inch grinder is important to have for welding and metalwork. A cordless or corded impact wrench is valuable when your compressor is filling up with air and you just need to finish a quick procedure.

Specialty Tools

Many times you need a tool to do just one specific task. Here are a few tools that you may need over the course of your build, with the assumption that you're purchasing a crate engine or using what's existing.

An engine hoist is a must to pull the engine, whether you rebuild it or not. Find one that has features and more than enough capacity for your engine to be pulled from your particular truck. Torin makes a full line of industrial tools, and its 2-ton Big Red engine hoist is rugged, reliable, and an excellent deal at about $300. Sunnex International makes a 1⅕-ton foldable engine crane that provides rapid rise for lifting the engine out of the engine bay easily. If you're working out of your home garage, the vertical folding feature allows you to tuck it away after you've finished using it. The OTC 4,000-pound-capacity folding floor

crane is also an excellent option because it has the capacity to pull a gas or diesel engine from the Square-body line up.

A coil spring compressor is available from a variety of auto tool suppliers, including Summit, Jegs, and Classic Industries.

Eastwood, AutoZone, and many others offer OEM and trim molding removal sets, which are available with nylon construction, so they don't mar or gouge the trim.

Torin, Orion, Jegs, and others make excellent engine stands. Be sure that your engine weighs less than the capacity of the stand. You don't want it to collapse from overloading; your engine may be damaged and you may be injured. Most enthusiasts use a stand for rebuilding an engine and not simply for storage. Therefore, be sure it has a rugged mounting arm, so you can rotate the engine into the desired position while rebuilding. Stability is another factor in choosing a stand; be sure it is wide and stable enough so that it does not tip over when moving.

Other specialty tools include a steering wheel puller and a steering column spring compressor. You also need the following: camshaft installation tool, feeler gauges, compression tester, straightedge, calipers, microm-

eter, and piston-ring compressor.

You can check Craigslist and eBay for sales from retiring mechanics. Many quality tools are available that way for pennies on the dollar.

Air Compressors

An air compressor is not absolutely required for rebuilding a truck, but it certainly can come in handy. Air saws, D/A sanders, and impact wrenches run off an air compressor, and although many have electric equivalents, it's nice to have the air power on all the time. If you purchase a new air compressor, make sure it is rated at 5 scfm at 90 psi on a 20-gallon tank. You can always go bigger, and the more tank space you have, the longer it runs.

You can also rent an air compressor from local home supply stores, but if you plan on doing work on your vehicles in the future, you might as well buy one now. The 240-volt models are a good buy because they run efficiently and are usually more heavy duty with a larger storage tank. You want this because a smaller compressor isn't able to keep up with the demands you put on it with a tool such as an impact wrench.

Some consumer-grade compressors use Teflon rings on their pistons.

A top-grade high-capacity compressor of 60 gallons or larger is worth its weight in gold. Also, larger capacities mean that you can run more tools longer. If you are going to paint your truck, you need a large compressor. Nothing is more frustrating than having to wait for the compressor to kick on while you're in the middle of a project.

This keeps them quiet and doesn't require a ton of external lubrication, but if it's used in a painting environment, the rings are eaten up quickly. The result is a compressor that doesn't compress air, and you are without the air power you need. A good tip to remember.

Pneumatic Tools

A pneumatic impact wrench and an air ratchet in 3/8- or 1/2-inch diameter are vital tools. The tools run solely off the pressure from the compressor, and, assuming the compressor can keep up, they run forever.

A plethora of tools can be used with an air compressor. For general use, you want an impact wrench, air ratchet, air saw, and die grinders in both straight and angled forms. You can remove almost any bolt with the impact wrench and air ratchet, particularly the stubborn ones that seem to be rusted on permanently. They're also good for assembly, and

Pneumatic tools, such as an impact wrench, air saw, air ratchet, and air file (shown), help you keep the job going and are quite efficient. Sanding with an air file is a huge help during the bodywork phase.

even though I wouldn't use them for torquing bolts to spec, they are nice to have, particularly when you're blowing apart a truck. Also, note that you want special impact sockets to use with the impact wrench. Regular sockets can explode when the force of an impact wrench is applied.

An air saw works well for cutting out rusty panels, and die grinders are great for cut-off wheels and sanding discs.

Be sure to buy good-quality equipment. Many cheaper tools use inferior seals and often develop leaks or are not able to keep a consistent pressure. Spend the money on a decent tool that lasts, and you will thank yourself for it later.

Air Tool Precautions

Use caution when using air tools during assembly or disassembly. Air tools can apply more pressure than you need and strip or break a bolt that seizes in place. When using hand tools, you can feel when a bolt is tight prematurely or is not threading into the part correctly. Do not rely on air tools for the proper torque on a bolt. During assembly, air tools should only be used for running bolts into the threads. The final fas-

tening should be done by hand with a wrench, ratchet, or torque wrench.

Welding and Metalwork

If you would know how to weld, you probably already have a good welder. If you would like to take up the skill, you should start with a simple and flexible model that's easy to learn. For that, I recommend a MIG welder.

A MIG welder uses a metal inert gas to shield the arc as you're welding. They are often affordable, and you can even purchase one at a local home supply store for a few hundred dollars. By taking your time and learning how to work with different types of steel, your resulting welds will be good enough to handle anything. MIG welders create a nice, clean weld and they are easier to operate than TIG welders.

Typically, MIG welders have a wide range of operating capabilities, features, accessories, and prices. Although there are many MIG welders to choose from, Lincoln, ESOB, and Miller offer models that are ideally suited for automotive restoration. When shopping for a welder, first determine whether your garage has 110V or 240V wiring. That said, some machines have the flexibility to use either voltage, but it's still good to know if you have access to 240V power or not.

You also need to know the maximum thickness of metal you're going to weld on the project so you can select the welder with the proper capability. A welder operates in 10-minute duty cycles, so a 30-percent-efficient welder operates for 3 minutes within the 10-minute cycle. You need to estimate how much you will use the welder because that determines duty

A MIG welder is essential for any patch panel installation or replacement of any large panel. This is a Millermatic 180 that I've used for welding everything from sheet metal to frames. Although there are more powerful models, this one is affordably priced and small enough to work in tight spaces.

cycle. Heat-overload protection is a useful safety feature because it prevents a welder breakdown or fire in the workshop. Make sure the welder uses the desired size and type of wires. Most automotive welders use ER70S-3 and ER70S-6 wire for welding body panels.

The Millermatic 211 features high-quality construction and reliable operation, giving it capabilities that offer an excellent value. It operates on 120V and 220V input, 30-percent duty cycle, output range of 30 to 120 amps, and can weld metal up to 3/16 inch thick. Another welder with an impressive duty cycle is the Lincoln Power MIG 180. It has input voltage of 208V/230V, amp range of 30 to 100 amps, duty cycle of 30 percent at 130 amps, and welds metal up to 3/16 inch thick. Other similar units include models by Hobart and Miller. For example, I own a Millermatic 180. It's an older model that I picked up a few years back, and it's been a workhorse for me. It can create a nice, clean weld that is easier to do than a TIG weld, and strong enough to handle most restoration jobs.

Once a part has been welded, you grind the weld flat to the panel. A variety of grinders and types are available to do this. One is an electric angle grinder, usually a 4½-inch model. These are great to use with flap-wheel grinding discs (they use flaps of variable-grit sandpaper to wear down metal), as well as for cutting and grinding. If you buy a bigger grinder, it becomes more difficult to finesse with smaller components, and because it has more torque, it heats up the metal quickly. That, as you will learn later, is the enemy.

Another type is a pneumatic die grinder, in both angle and non-angle forms. Ingersoll Rand, Sunnex, DeWalt, and others offer mid-level consumer versions at reasonable prices. Most die grinders operate up to 25,000 rpm and accept a 1/4-inch air inlet. A 1/4-inch model allows you to use all sorts of cut-off wheels, attachments for sanding discs, and more, which makes them versatile. Eastwood offers a complete accessory kit that provides all the abrasive wheels you need for a restoration project. You can use them for cutting, shaping, and working into those deep pockets that a larger tool just can't handle.

If you find yourself in a situation where you have a dent in a panel and you can't gain access from the other side, you can use a stud gun. This welds a metal stud directly onto the metal panel that you can then attach to a slide hammer to pull out the dent. You then cut or break off the metal stud and grind it to clean up the metal. The results can be quite nice, and you save on body filler.

For more metal fine-tuning, various metal shaping tools are perfect, including body hammers, dollies, and even a sandbag or two. Metal shaping artists use these, and they can become indispensable during your restoration. By using a hammer and dolly, you can flatten and shape everything from door skins to bed sides. The more metalwork you do on your own, the less time you need for doing bodywork. It's always best to metal finish the body as much as possible before adding filler; you often achieve a better result.

Consumable Materials and Supplies

Sanding discs, welding wire, welding gas, and so on are items that you "use up" during a restoration. You need to budget for these consumables because nothing is worse than needing one to finish a job and not having it. Unfortunately, coming up with an accurate estimate is nearly impossible. But if I were to hazard a guess, I'd say budgeting $250 to $500 for consumables is a good place to start, knowing that it varies widely.

The debate with consumables comes down to cost. On the one hand, you don't want to spend so much money on consumables that you can't finish the project, but buying those that are too cheap become dangerous. It's a fine line.

Again, I go with name brands for the most part, including 3M and Eastwood products. If I'm in a bind, I check with my local welding shop for their opinion (Praxair, for example, here in Arizona), because they often have first-hand knowledge of what works and what doesn't.

Take cut-off wheels, for example. A metal cut-off wheel typically comes in packs of three or more, and they are usually made of aluminum oxide. This consumable is a safety concern; their spin speeds are around 20,000 rpm. If they crack or fail, you have a disc spinning at something going very fast. If that "something" is your head, neck, or other vulnerable body part, you could be in for a trip to the hospital. By all means, you should consider the cost of consumables when you make your purchase, but don't take short cuts when it involves your safety.

I like 3M products, so I use them for everything, including abrasives. Eastwood also carries an excellent line of abrasive discs and cut-off wheels. And if I don't know what brand to go with, I ask the sales team which ones are of the highest quality.

Making Your Own Tools

If no one sells it and you need it, sometimes you have to make your own tool or modify one you already own. For example, I once needed a very large crow's-foot wrench to remove a bolt in a spot that wasn't easily accessible. The fix wasn't cheap, but I purchased a wrench from a local supplier, then used

a torch and a bench vise to bend the tool into a "Z" shape, making it usable for my application. Now I have a tool that's not as effective for its original purpose, but works great for certain situations.

The cab and bed are two large parts that you may want to move around your workspace. Both components require multiple people (or a hoist or a lift) to move them, and you likely want to work on, under, or around them as you go. The easiest and best way to do this is with a cart. Various companies sell bed and cab carts (often called body carts). Innovative Tools and Technologies sells a sturdy bed dolly that's completely adjustable and folds out for around $600; Northern Tool sells a PBE model for around $230. If you want one that can move a cab and a bed at the same time, DJS Fabrications sells a simple, straightforward cart that uses four 1,000-pound casters.

If you're handy, you can build a cart of your own in a few hours. If you chose that route, make sure you're good with a welder, buy

some heavy-duty casters designed to roll on your type of flooring, and measure everything twice. The end result is a cart for this project and many other projects in the future.

There are hundreds of options for building your own tools, and I can't discuss all of them. But when a tool from a manufacturer doesn't quite do the job, don't be afraid to make something yourself with a little creativity and some sweat equity.

This simple bed cart was built using an old piece of shelving and a few casters. The casters were welded to the shelving, and, using the holes already in the shelving frame, the bed was bolted to the new cart. Now the bed can be moved around the garage easily and quickly.

Working with limited garage space is tough, but the owner of this truck had a great idea. He made custom carts for his bed, cab, and front clip so he could swap out the chassis. Now they roll around on the floor easily, giving him access to whatever he needs whenever he likes.

BODYWORK

The goal of this book is to give the guidance and instructions to properly disassemble, repair, and replace parts and reassemble your truck into a sound, reliable, factory-correct vehicle. You can perform all these restoration steps with some competent skills, tenacity, the right tools, and time.

Bodywork presents a different set of challenges than mechanical work. Bodywork is an art, but it's also a skill, which can be learned. In most cases, you go through lots of sandpaper, body filler, and time, but you can do this all yourself if you have the resources. You must be patient, but you can do this. If you've never operated a welder or used basic metal working tools, you can take a class or have a skilled technician or friend show you how. You need to be reasonably confident that you can complete good- to high-quality-level bodywork because you won't be able to fix poor bodywork once the truck has been painted. Without proper bodywork and prep, your paint job is going to be flawed or flat-out horrible.

I say this because the bodywork process is difficult, meticulous work that requires consistent attention to detail, and you shouldn't feel any shame in farming out the work to a qualified professional. Understand that going that route is expensive, but you get professional results.

That's what the bodywork of your truck comes down to: patience. If you're a novice, you may burn a lot of time and money sanding away on your truck and looking for a perfect finish. The more time you spend, the better the results are likely to be. As long as you're willing to do that, feel free to load up on sanding blocks and sandpaper because you will need them. But again, if you feel that it's too much work or not worth the return on investment, start looking for a professional who can do the task for you.

Installing New Cab Mounts

Before you start the actual bodywork, you may need to perform some repair and disassembly procedures. After a few decades of use, the rubber cab mounts underneath the cab of a Squarebody are likely dry-rotted and drooping. This can cause the doors to misalign, fenders to tweak, and the bed and cab to be mismatched; replacing them is important. Fortunately, you can either replace the

Bodywork is often the most expensive and time-consuming aspect of a restoration project. If a professional shop performs the bodywork, you will have considerable expense for its completion. If you choose to do it yourself, you need to invest time, patience, and a lot of materials. But you can and will develop the skills for completing specific procedures.

Four mounts are underneath a standard cab truck; six under a crew cab. It's easiest to swap these out if you have the front sheet metal removed from the truck. Unbolt one side's cab mounts using a ratchet, then use a floor jack with a wood block between the metal and the jack to lift the cab slightly off the mounts. Lower the truck back down, then loosely install the bolts on the new mounts. Do the same on the opposite side. When the cab is back on the frame, double-check your measurements. Once they match the original specs (or the specifications in a Chevrolet manual), tighten the cab mount bolts with a ratchet.

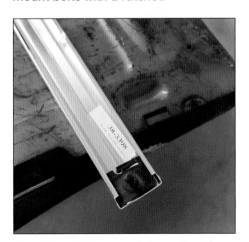

The clips slide up and down the trim for easy installation. You just cinch them to the truck after the screw is installed.

If you have a tiny nick in the edge of the trim, you can remove it with a hammer and wedge-shaped dolly. Use the top of the dolly to form the edge, and strike the trim with the hammer to get it back in shape.

You might have to do a bit more work on the areas that are scuffed up, such as hammering directly on the panel without the dolly. When you're done, all it needs is a quick polish and it's ready for the next step.

stock mounts with rubber mounts or with high-performance polyurethane mounts. Should you go with the latter option, you can expect the mounts to be firmer and last longer. They're also affordable.

Before you start the process, make sure to take measurements from the bottom of the cab to the frame so that you're able to verify aligning the two parts correctly.

Body Trim

Squarebody trucks had a 14-year production run, and during that time, body, trim, and hardware evolved significantly. The 1973–1979 trucks typically carried chrome trim on the cab and bed sides, and it was fastened to the body with various compression clips. You need a trim tool kit to pry off these various trim pieces during body restoration.

Always exercise patience when removing the trim because you want to minimize any breakage. You have stainless strips down the sides, taillights, grille, and the like, but not a bunch of needless accessories. Fortunately, that makes removal a little easier.

From 1981 to 1987, things became a tick better, depending on your perspective. Most of the trim was held on by tape, with the exception of the molding underneath the back window and the tailgate. So, on the one hand, it's easier to remove, which is nice. But putting it back on may mean buying replacements, which isn't quite as cool.

After the old trim is off, determine whether to repair or replace it. Ultimately, this depends on the condition of the pieces. Most of the time, stainless trim can be refurbished; a bit of metalwork and cleaning can return them to like-new condition. In those situations, some paint and some new clips make things go smoothly. But if they came off in poor condition and have tons of dents, you should replace them.

Stripping the Finish

The 1973–1987 Chevy or GMC that's taking up your workspace has likely seen quite a few dings and dents over the years. It may have even been repainted with the tools and standards of its era. But today, it's ready for a new finish, and that means getting down to the bare metal.

You have several ways to remove the existing paint. One option is to use a brush to apply the jelly-like aircraft stripper onto the surface that you want to bring down to bare metal. You spread it around thoroughly and let it sit for about 45 minutes until the paint bubbles up. Then, you use a metal scraping tool to remove the paint until you're left with the raw finish of the metal.

I've used a few different brands of aircraft stripper over the years, with varying results. Klean-Strip Aircraft Paint Remover worked well in the spray form, but I preferred POR-15 Strip Gel Aircraft Paint Remover on most other surfaces. I felt as if I were able to get a more even consistency that way, and the gel just seemed to perform better.

Using aircraft stripper is fine for most tasks, and it can be applied to an entire vehicle if you wanted to, but it is a caustic chemical. You need to wear proper safety gear, including eye protection, rubber gloves, long pants, and long sleeves. Working in a well-ventilated area is also crucial.

Using aircraft stripper is also excessively messy, which is why you may want to use it for smaller areas or ones that you can't remove through other means.

Another option is to remove the bodywork with either mechanical or pneumatic tools and then use a lot of sandpaper. Although it's one of most cost-effective methods for removing paint, it is also one of most labor intensive.

Your approach to stripping the body should match the amount of paint it is wearing. If you have many coats of old paint, you can start with 24-grit sandpaper and work your way up to lighter abrasive discs. In most cases, you should start sanding with 80-grit sandpaper on a D/A sander or even a sanding block. Be careful not to sand one area for too long and create too much heat, which will deform the sheet metal. And be careful not to remove the paint too quickly because this gunks up the sandpaper and wastes material.

Stripping accomplishes two things. First, it removes the old material, and second, it creates a clean surface for the body filler and primer to adhere to the truck. This is a long process, and a D/A sander is not always the best tool for tight curves or small spaces. For those areas, you have to work manually, which also takes time.

A third option is media blasting. This method is quite common, and you can buy media blasting guns and

tools at most major auto parts stores. You can also find them at most online and local retailers. Eastwood supplies a wide range of media blasters, media, and related equipment. Once you have the equipment, you also need the correct safety gear.

The next step is to pick the media. Many online tool retailers (including some that sell media blasters) also sell sandblasting media. Sometimes it's recyclable, so make sure to spray your product in an area where you can recover the media, such as over a clean tarp.

Again, be sure to use the appropriate respirator, eye protection, and clothing.

Media Blasting Option

A media blaster strips rust from almost any part or panel down to the bare metal. You must select the right equipment, air compressor, and media to achieve the desired result. If the media is too aggressive, you can pit, warp, or even blow through good metal, and that's something you want to avoid. Use a high-capacity 60- to 80-gallon air compressor that runs at 90 psi with 9 cfm of airflow. Next, select the correct media for the particular parts you're stripping. For most body panels, a media of 60 grit is appropriate for hoods and trunks; 30 to 60 grit is suitable for fenders, doors, valence panels, wiper grilles, and quarter panels.

Aluminum oxide, silicon carbide, and glass bead are the most common types of abrasive media. For stripping most body panels, glass bead and aluminum oxide are preferable. You can test the abrasiveness on a small, inconspicuous part of the body before proceeding. If you suspect that the media is too abrasive, choose walnut shells or corncob because these are mild abrasives and don't etch the metal. They also remove paint and bodywork from your truck, but they don't build up as much heat, so they're less damaging in the process. Walnut shells, however, are tough to clean up because they get into every nook and cranny, which can add time to remove.

Glass beads feature medium abrasiveness. Glass bead can be reused up to 30 times.

Plastic beads are made of acrylic, polyester, melamine, and urea. They provide aggressive stripping performance but do not produce a lot of heat, so panels do not warp.

Aluminum oxide comes in small grains. It is not biodegradable and must be disposed of carefully.

The correct media blasting technique is essential for achieving the best result. The following are a few tips to help you to strip the body panel to the bare metal and avoid damaging it.

First, do not use more than 35 to 45 psi. If you use too much pressure, the panel pits and may possibly warp. If you blast the media onto one panel for too long, the sheet metal can warp and be damaged beyond repair because of the excess heat that's built up in the panels (as with welding). You must also completely strip the truck to use them, meaning no rubber, chrome, or plastic anywhere in the vicinity of where you want to remove the finish, unless you mask those parts off heavily.

You need to strip parts consistently and methodically. Position the nozzle at a 45-degree angle at a distance of 9 to 10 inches from the panel or part. Work in a consistent pattern, such as front to back, so you don't lose track of what has been stripped.

Painted parts typically have a clear coat, one or two layers of base coat, and primer coat, so you should strip one layer at time.

A wide range of portable sandblasters are available, and many units are extremely affordable. Campbell-Hausfeld and other blaster tanks with 20-gallon capacities can be purchased for $200 to $300. All-Source's Rollout Abrasive Pressure Blaster is suited for at-home restoration projects, and with the right media, easily strips metal surfaces. It has an 80- to 110-psi operating range and requires a minimum air volume of 6 to 20 cfm at 80 psi. Unitec's Speed Blaster Sandblast Gun is a gravity-feed gun that uses a typical air hose, and you also have media adjustment control. Campbell-Hausfeld's AT1226 Sandblasting Kit can spray almost any available media. With the right air tank and setup, it efficiently and effectively strips off paint and cleans off rust to reveal bare metal.

Soda Blasting Option

Soda blasting is considered one of the better options available today, but it is certainly not as abrasive or aggressive as media blasting. Therefore, soda blasting is ideally suited for removing paint and a light amount of rust. Most Squarebody trucks have been exposed to moisture and experienced serious corrosion and, therefore, have significant or heavy rust. As a result, media blasting is often the preferred method for stripping the cab, bed, and many body panels.

Soda blasting can be used on steel, aluminum, plastic, or fiberglass. You can spray around chrome without damaging it, and the resulting finish has no texture. When you're finished spraying your truck, there will be a thin film of soda over the vehicle. This stops the truck from rusting (at least temporarily). When you do decide to lay down that first coat of primer, you can rinse off the soda with water; it's that simple. The downside is that you can't use it to remove heavy rust or body filler.

Eastwood offers a dual-purpose soda/media blasting unit called the Master Blaster Dual Abrasive Soda Blaster. The dual-tank setup features a wheel axle and grab handle. Each tank has a 100-pound capacity for media and flows as much as 10 cfm at 120 psi. With this setup, you can start with mild soda and gradually transition to more abrasive media. It allows you to determine the best media for any job. You can strip almost any part without the risk of damaging it.

What's best for your application? That depends on your particular project. If your truck has heavy rust and lots of body filler, be prepared to choose from walnut, aluminum oxide, silicon carbide, and glass beads. If it doesn't, go with soda. Remember, you can always start with soda and then use stronger media if necessary.

Body Shop Option

You can also use a local body shop to perform high-quality media or soda blasting. You can call around town to find people who work with lots of different media so they can physically show you their results. You want to find out what their downtime is like, particularly if your project needs to go through faster. Also, check out their facility to be sure that your truck doesn't just fall to the wayside or that it's treated poorly. Yes, it's there to have the paint stripped, but you don't want it damaged in the process. Finally, there's cost. It's always a factor, and I try to find a happy middle ground between what I'm spending and the quality of the job performed.

Acid Dipping

You can take a completely stripped Squarebody chassis and body to a shop that specializes in acid dipping, although in recent years, many restorers have preferred to use media blasting. Acid dipping is an expensive option, and most chemical dipping procedures range from $1,000 to $2,000.

Similar to sandblasting, chemical or acid dipping involves taking your truck to a specialist's shop where the entire vehicle (usually one piece at a time) is dipped into a vat of chemicals. The chemical treatment process has several steps. First, a solution strips paint and grease and then fresh water removes any residue. After the body has been cleaned, it is immersed in the acid tank to remove the rust; the next step neutralizes the acid. Some chemical dipping companies also spray the bare metal with a self-etching primer afterward, because the oils from your skin cause the metal to rust.

This is an efficient method, but the downside is that it strips everything, including hidden areas in the cab, inside the kick panels, and behind the dashboard. These spots are difficult to spray with a paint gun and that means they could stay bare metal for an extended period of time. That could lead to rust down the road. It isn't the end of the world, and it is something that you can work around. Just be aware of what you're getting into before you drop off your truck.

Process Combination

What is likely to happen is that you will perform a combination of these processes on your truck. For example, you might choose to sand the fenders and hood yourself, then take the chassis for a chemical dip while you sandblast the inside of the bed. Or you could use an aircraft stripper on the doors and a D/A sander to remove bits of paint that just weren't coming off otherwise.

Whatever method(s) you choose, be sure to take your time and do it correctly the first time. It's critical that everything is as clean as possible before you start the actual bodywork.

Inspecting for Rust

Although the 1973–1987s have a strong chassis that's resilient to corrosion, the cab and surrounding sheet metal is susceptible to rust. Unfortunately, water likes to collect in many places, and that means that there can be lots of rust on your project.

To note where there is rust, use a permanent marker and draw circles and arrows around the points on the body that need rust repair, feeling free to write on the finish if necessary. Don't worry, it's all coming off anyway.

You often find rust on the cowl right by the windshield and near body seams. The rockers are also common spots for rust, as are the floors, lower portions of the fenders, core support, lower areas of the bed sides, cab mounts, cab corners, and tailgate.

Two locations where I see rust all the time are underneath the battery tray(s) and on the passenger-side floorboard. The first is because of leakage from the battery, which makes sense. But the second is one that you should check out before you buy a truck. Often, the heater core leaks, and when it does, it does so on the inside, right into the carpet. Because it's on the passenger's side, the driver doesn't always notice it. Plus, removing the heater core isn't fun, so owners put off the repair as long as possible. As a result, the carpet collects water (and mold), and, because it's always pressed against the metal, it forms rust. Make sure to peel back the passenger-side carpet and check for damage prior to buying.

Before you rush out to buy new panels, you need to assess the damage. You may find one or both kinds of rust: surface and severe.

Surface rust resides mostly on the surface, and has not had a chance to invade the metal. This causes the panel to have a rusty tint to it. The rust area can become larger and still not have penetrated the metal, in which case it's referred to as "scale," based on its similarity to lizard scales.

Rust can lurk and fester in many different areas of the body. With this particular Squarebody, the carpet was pulled back to reveal that the floors were rusted significantly and were starting to rust through.

Replacement Panel Sources

At some point, you may have to buy a replacement part or two. Fortunately, there are tons of options for these trucks.

Dynacorn is probably your best first call, for both pricing and flexibility. It sells rocker panels for around $30 for the inner and outer skins, and it has everything from bed kits to cab floors.

Brothers Trucks is another source for pretty much anything you need for these trucks, sheet metal in particular. It has inner cowl panels for around $40, and both full and small rocker panel replacements for under $25. Lots and lots of options here for sure.

Classic Industries has a cab corner for $15 and inner door panels for $20. It doesn't have quite the quantity as Dynacorn and Brothers, but it is another option.

When the rust has been forming for years, you likely find holes in the metal. The metal is weaker than it should be, often having thinned out at least a few steps down in the gauge chart; 10-gauge sheet metal may be as thin as 14-gauge, for example as gauge number increases the thickness decreases. The thinner it is, the weaker it is as well, which means that you should replace it.

Severe rust can be so bad that there is no panel at all. Rocker panels on the cab often suffer severe rust corrosion, as their proximity to salty roads in snowy areas can accelerate the rusting process. In this situation, you have no choice but to replace the panel entirely because there is no panel to salvage.

Fixing a rusty panel can be a quick job when there are just a few pinholes to patch, or it can require extensive fabrication and new panels. Although smaller areas can be tack welded and fixed, often you have to buy either sheet metal or replacement panels to fix the area. If you go with the former, make sure that the metal that you buy is the same thickness as the metal you're replacing.

To do that, use a sheet metal gauge tool, which you can find online. Eastwood sells one for around $15, and General Tools sells one on Amazon for $20. If you're buying replacement panels, make sure that the manufacturer lists the gauge of the pieces, and double-check that it's the same as what you have. Running thinner metal is cheaper, but it is also easier to dent later on.

To determine whether to install a replacement panel or if it's something you can fabricate yourself, take a look at the original area. If it has many compound curves that require special tools and/or machinery to make, it will take considerable hammer-and-dolly or English wheel work to create a finished piece. You need to possess advanced metal-working skills to create a patch panel with compound curves. Therefore, in this situation, an enthusiast restorer is better off replacing the panel.

To help you decide, ask yourself a couple of questions: Is the area difficult to access to create templates for a patch panel? What's best for my budget? For example, if the floor on your truck has a few weak spots, buying an entire floor kit might seem like overkill. But if the cost of many small panels runs over the cost of the entire floor, go with the floor and save a few bucks. You just have to cut it up yourself to the sizes that you need.

Panel Replacement Procedures

The first thing to do is to cut out an area around the damaged metal using a die grinder with a cut-off wheel, angle grinder, reciprocating saw, or air saw, depending on the thickness of the metal and access for the tool. Then clean up the metal around the edges with an angle grinder with a sanding disc or a D/A sander. The goal is to make sure that the metal on the edges is straight and free of any paint or rust. Do the same thing on the replacement panel so that any areas that will be welded are free of paint.

If you have access to the inside of a panel, such as when you are replacing the outer skin on a rocker panel, you may want to sand off any rust that you see there as well. To protect it in the future, spray a weld-through primer on the surface, then proceed. This allows you to weld in the area if necessary, and parts still stay protected from future harm.

You have a few options when welding in a replacement panel, and they depend on its location. If the panel is in a large flat area, such as the floor or door skin, you may choose to "flange" the replacement part so that the new metal sits just under the original metal.

To install the new sheet metal on the truck, drill holes in the original metal, fit the replacement piece, then place tack welds through the holes and onto the replacement piece. This type of weld is stronger than a butt weld, and ensures that the panel stays in place. If you have no room for a flange, you can fit the two panels as close together as possible and tack weld them, which is a butt weld.

Most people use a MIG welder for this job because a TIG welder is typically more expensive and more difficult to use. You should opt for a MIG welder with a shielding gas, and you should avoid flux-core wire. When welding 18- or 20-gauge sheet metal, the ideal metal wire is .023 inch in diameter, but you can use .030; be careful with the heat settings. The shielding gas is a 75-percent-Argon/25-percent-CO_2 blend, which is common for this application.

When installing patch or complete panels, tack welding the panel in place with a MIG welder means that you're not moving the torch of the welder. Instead, you're just applying quick heat and welding material. The goal is to use enough heat so that the welding material is able to fuse with the metal, but not so much that you build up excessive heat. A typical tack weld lasts less than a second in duration.

Space the tack welds along the panel as far apart as possible. For example, you could tack a door-skin patch in place by applying a quick weld in each corner, then allowing the panel to cool to the touch. Next, you weld at the halfway point between your previous welds, allow those to cool, and repeat until you have one solid weld around the perimeter of the panel. If you do this correctly, you will have minimal distortion around the replacement piece.

Cleaning up the welds requires care also. Using an angle grinder with either a 40-grit sanding disc or a hard-grinding disc, knock down the welds, but do not go so deep that you press into the level of the surrounding sheet metal. Again, take care not to build up too much heat, or you could warp the panel there as well. Switch to an 80-grit sanding disc and then sand down the welds so that they blend into the metal. If you find any holes or gaps, apply tack welds, grind them down, and clean them up.

Although tack welding takes time, you want to take the time to do it right. If you go too quickly, you will warp the panels and that will eat up time and materials in fixing the metal. If you take your time, you find that the resulting panels require minimal bodywork and filler, and that gives you a better result.

Cowl Panel Repair

1 The lower part of the windshield, right around the cowl area, tends to attract moisture, and therefore, rust. This particular truck had three small rust spots in this zone, including this one on the driver's side. You start by cleaning the area; use a wire wheel attachment on a die grinder to remove all of the surface rust. The goal is to have to clean metal; then you can assess the extent of the damage.

2 Use a permanent marker to indicate the area that you want to remove.

3 Here you can see the entire area to be removed. It goes beyond the rust spots and into the good metal, which provides a good spot to weld the new panel.

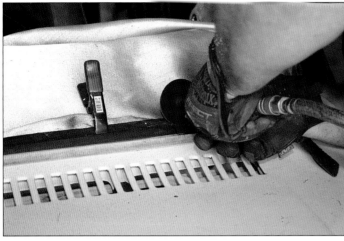

4 Use a die grinder with a cut-off wheel and an air saw to remove the offending metal. Once it's out, you hammer it flat and use that piece as a template for replacement metal in the same gauge.

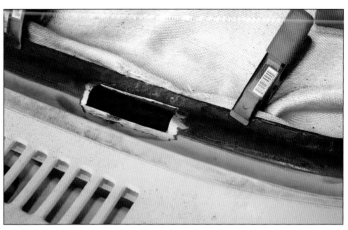

5 With the rusted piece out of the way, use a 100-grit sanding disc on an angled die-grinder to remove any paint that might be in the area. Be sure not to grind in one area for too long because it creates excessive heat and warps the panel. This ensures that you have a clean weld.

6 Use a MIG welder on a low heat setting. Do not apply too much heat to the panels when placing the tack welds. Alternate placing tack welds on one side of the panel and on the other to mitigate the heat. The replacement metal is now tacked in place, but you'll notice that it's not bent to fit the cowl. That's because you first tack it in place at the bottom, then use a hammer to bend it into shape. Were this on a visible panel, you might shape it beforehand, but this is next to the windshield; rubber and trim will cover it up.

7 After the patch piece is solidly tacked in place, tap it down and into shape with a body hammer. You need to work the metal patiently into the correct curved profile. You use small moves and many taps to get it into shape. By tacking and hammering as you go, you can achieve a solid result.

8 Place the tack welds around the perimeter of the patch panel and the windshield frame. Here it's welded in place and correctly shaped according to the profile of the windshield frame. There are just a few welds left to go.

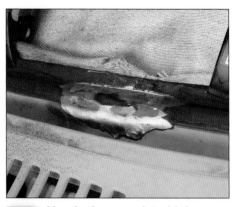

9 Once all of the gaps are filled with weld and the piece is solidly in place, grind the welds flush with the surrounding sheet metal using a 60-grit sanding disc on a die grinder.

10 Here's the completed job, ready for the next stage of the process. The patch panel looks as if it's a part of the windshield frame. That's key to ensure that the windshield fits, and so the windshield seals correctly and does not leak.

11 Usually you perform bodywork and move on, but not so in this area. Because it sits under molding, you apply POR-15 to keep any remaining rust in the area encapsulated. It also protects the new sheet metal. After it has 24 hours to cure, the area can be painted.

Repairing Bed Rust Damage

The beds on these trucks are particularly susceptible to rust. From what I've heard, Chevrolet used an inferior primer on the inside of the bed sides for the first few years, causing the beds to rust from the inside out. Regardless, 40-plus years of salty roads and poor weather conditions can take their toll on the bed's metal, which means that sometimes you have to resort to patching some panels.

Quarter Panel Patch Installation

1 To repair bed side rust, buy a patch panel for the affected area so you can replace the original steel. Then use an impact wrench to remove the bed side support bolts because they will be held together pretty well with rust. (Photo Courtesy Jefferson Bryant)

2 With the patch panel laid in place over the original bed side, mark the area using a permanent marker. This is where you start cutting, so it's important that you draw this outline correctly. There are also a few vertical marks showing where to put the vertical cuts because you might not need the entire lower rocker. (Photo Courtesy Jefferson Bryant)

3 Even though you have a patch panel that's big enough to fix most of the lower rocker, you don't need all of it. After all, there's no point in replacing good sheet metal. Instead, use a Sharpie to mark a vertical line on the replacement panel at a 90-degree angle to the edge. That's where you cut. (Photo Courtesy Jefferson Bryant)

4 The lower mark on the panel designates the position of the flange on the edge of the bed so that the replacement panel fits nicely; you also don't want to distort the curves near the fenderwell. The vertical mark matches the tick I mentioned earlier; at this location, you just cut straight across. Also mark for the flange at the vertical edge of the panel. (Photo Courtesy Jefferson Bryant)

5 You can cut the panel using a pneumatic sheet-metal shear, following the inside track for the flange first. You could also use a rotary tool with a cut-off wheel. (Photo Courtesy Jefferson Bryant)

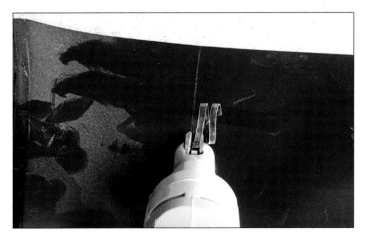

6 Use a sheet-metal shear to cut the replacement panel to size. Take the width of the cutting blade into account and stay within the line. These shears are great because they're quick and efficient. However, the metal that's removed curls up and can be in the way as you move, so it can also be a hindrance. (Photo Courtesy Jefferson Bryant)

7 Use a cut-off wheel of 40 to 60 grit on a die grinder to cut the horizontal portion of the panel. (Photo Courtesy Jefferson Bryant)

8 Closely follow the lines when making these cuts. Here is a closer look at the z-shaped cut in the metal. Notice the vertical jog; that's where the soon-to-be flanged area ends. (Photo Courtesy Jefferson Bryant)

9 After removing the exterior sheet-metal panel, a significantly rusted inner fender was exposed underneath. You can see that it has plenty of rust, but it has solid metal beneath, so it can be cleaned up and does not need to be replaced. (Photo Courtesy Jefferson Bryant)

10 Grind the paint off the edge of the cut with a sanding disc on a 1/4-inch angle grinder. Then, to ensure a strong seam, use a pneumatic flanging tool to set a lip on the edge of the cut-out bed side. This way, the new panel sits on top of the old one, allowing you to spot weld the panel for extra strength. Or you can give it two weld points, one inside and one outside. (Photo Courtesy Jefferson Bryant)

11 Drill out the patch panel, so you can spot-weld it along the seams. (Photo Courtesy Jefferson Bryant)

12 Once the patch panel is correctly lined, use Vise-Grips (or other locking pliers) or body-panel clamps to secure the patch panel in place along the fenderwell lip. Take your time to make sure the patch panel is properly aligned on all sides because you don't want to have to cut out the panel and re-adjust it. (Photo Courtesy Jefferson Bryant)

13 To make sure that you're going in the right direction, place the new panel on top of the old one. This is a close-up of the area where the flange transitions to the cut area on the panel. If you have a gap, it can be filled in with careful welding. (Photo Courtesy Jefferson Bryant)

14 Clamp the sheet metal patch panel securely in its proper position. All of the metal that you will be welding has been sanded down to be void of paint. The gaps should be tight and the panel clamped in place so that the body lines match up. (Photo Courtesy Jefferson Bryant)

15 Use a Sharpie to mark spot-weld positions in the fenderwell. Place a spot-weld about every 3 inches so the patch panel is welded securely to the bodywork. (Photo Courtesy Jefferson Bryant)

16 You may need to remove the old spot-welds that joined the inner and outer bed sides. A spot-weld remover is a great tool for drilling out the weld cleanly with minimal damage to the outside metal. If you don't have one, use multiple drill bits. You drill a pilot hole and then increase drill bit sizes usually to 3/8 inch. Make sure you only drill through one piece of metal at a time. (Photo Courtesy Jefferson Bryant)

17 To remove any surface rust, use a 1/4-inch angle grinder and a sanding disc. Work down to the bare metal because you don't want any rust to come back. (Photo Courtesy Jefferson Bryant)

18 If you see small pockets of rust in the panel, apply a rust encapsulator so that the rust doesn't progress any farther. POR-15, Eastwood Rust Encapsulator, or a similar product keeps the corrosion at bay. (Photo Courtesy Jefferson Bryant)

19 The process begins with tack welds in the corner to anchor the patch panel. Use medium heat on a MIG welder so that the panel does not warp. This locks down the sides but also keeps things solid. A solid and reliable tack weld that has good penetration is round and consistent and rises slightly above the sheet metal. If your spot-weld has spatter and is oblong in shape, it's a poor tack weld. You want to apply the spot-weld hot and fast, so you have good penetration and, therefore, solid and sound installation of the panel. Many welders like to use a hot setting that's close to blowing through the sheet metal so they have the ideal weld penetration. If you operate the welder on a cooler setting, you have poor penetration and the weld could fail. Make sure that the extension of the wire is about 1/4 to 3/8 inch. If it's longer, the shielding gas doesn't cover the tip and the weld is poor. You can use a wire cutter to cut the welding wire to length. (Photo Courtesy Jefferson Bryant)

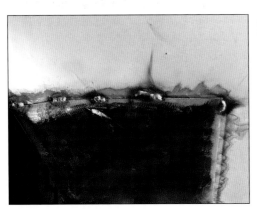

20 Work from the end to the middle, moving around the panel as you go. The goal here is to connect all of the welds with a series of tack welds, but not weld them solidly with one fat bead. You want to minimize the amount of heat put into the panel; too much warps it out of shape. Slow and steady is the idea here. Be sure that the welder is on a high enough heat setting for good penetration. There are two schools of thought regarding how to quench the welds, and I've heard arguments for both strategies. If you quench a weld with a damp rag or use compressed air, the heat stops immediately, minimizing the damage. Other professionals prefer to let the weld cool naturally, which takes more time but achieves (to them) a better result. Weigh both methods and use what works best for you. (Photo Courtesy Jefferson Bryant)

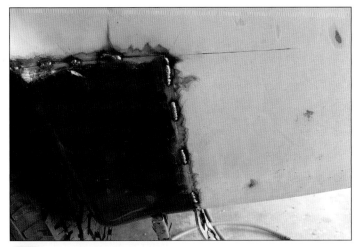

21 *For autobody panel welding, use .023- or .030-inch-diameter wire. You also have a choice of silicone grades of S2, 3, and 6; this comes down to your preference. Repeat the process on the vertical edge of the panel. Again, space out the tacks so that too much heat doesn't build up, and take your time. (Photo Courtesy Jefferson Bryant)*

22 *When your stitch welds have connected all the tack welds, the entire perimeter of the patch panel has been welded to the original sheet metal. When performing this step, you need a medium heat setting on the welder, and you must alternate from one side of the patch panel to the other so you are not applying too much heat to the sheet metal and warping it. (Photo Courtesy Jefferson Bryant)*

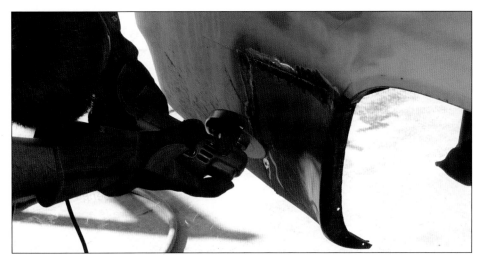

23 *Use a die grinder with an 80-grit grinding wheel and grind down the stitch welds carefully so the patch panel is flush with the rest of the panel. Be careful and do not grind on one area for too long and apply too much heat. (Photo Courtesy Jefferson Bryant)*

24 *Once the stitch welds have been ground flush with the entire panel, the job should look like this. At this stage, the panel is ready for prep and primer. (Photo Courtesy Jefferson Bryant)*

Repairing Cab Rust Damage

The cab has its own share of problems with rust. Typically, you find it on the fenders, rockers, cowl, and cab corners, but sometimes the windshield surround and doors are victims as well. Fortunately, LMC, Classic Parts, Brothers Trucks, Dynacorn, and other companies sell replacement and patch panels.

Cab Corner Rust Repair

1 With the bed lifted and pulled back slightly (and then supported on wood blocks on top of the frame), you can see the rust damage to this cab. It's substantial on both sides, so it needs to be patched. (Photo Courtesy Jefferson Bryant)

2 Identify where the original spot-welds are on the cab. Often, you can run your finger across the surface of the metal and feel a small divot or impression. This is likely an old spot-weld. You can use either a plasma cutter or spot-weld cutter to remove it. When using a spot-weld cutter, align the center pin in the middle of the spot-weld and make sure it stays in position and does not walk. Some technicians use a titanium drill bit and drill out the center of the spot-weld so that the guide pin on the spot-weld cutter is held firmly in place. Drill out any spot-welds on the bottom of the rocker and inside the doorjam. As with the bed, you don't remove the entire portion, just the affected area. (Photo Courtesy Jefferson Bryant)

3 Use a plasma cutter (shown) or die grinder with a cut off wheel to cut off the top of the panel. You typically use a 25-amp machine for 18- to 20-gauge sheet metal. Most machines need to operate at 35 psi or higher. Be sure you wear gloves, correct clothing, and a welder's helmet. Hold the torch at a 15-dgree angle as you cut through the top of the panel. Obviously, that throws a lot of sparks, and working near the gas tank can be a problem. In this case, the tank was empty and had been de-fumed months before. You can also use a cut-off wheel to make the horizontal cut through the sheet metal. (Photo Courtesy Jefferson Bryant)

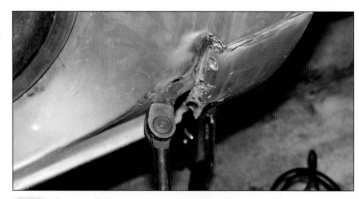

4 Once all the spot-welds have been drilled out the infected sheet metal is cut at the top. A pry bar comes in handy to access underneath the sheet-metal panel. A few gentle pulls with a pry bar removes the corner from the cab. (Photo Courtesy Jefferson Bryant)

5 Using the old cab corner as a guide, mark the replacement panel with a Sharpie or a scratch awl for cutting, and then cut it out using pneumatic metal shears. (Photo Courtesy Jefferson Bryant)

6 Once you've cut out the patch panel, it's time to mock it up to see if it fits correctly. If it does, you can proceed. (Photo Courtesy Jefferson Bryant)

7 Use a pneumatic air punch to knock a few holes in the doorjam and rocker area for spot-welds. Place a spot-weld hole every 3 to 4 inches in the flange of the patch panel. Typically, the spot-weld holes are 1/8 to 1/4 inch in diameter. Grind the paint off the replacement panel with an angle grinder and a sanding disc. (Photo Courtesy Jefferson Bryant)

8 Before welding the piece in place, the inner cab corner areas need to be treated with weld-through primer. It can be applied by spray can or brush, but be sure to apply enough to inhibit rust from forming. This keeps it from rusting at the new welds, plus it keeps the rust from expanding onto the panel. (Photo Courtesy Jefferson Bryant)

9 With a MIG welder, tack weld the panel in place. Make sure the spot-weld has good penetration. If the spot-welds are too cold, they puddle up and often look irregular. If the tack welds are too hot, you can burn through the metal. Again, you want to spread out the heat on the panel, so tack slowly and away from the previous tacks as you go. (Photo Courtesy Jefferson Bryant)

10 All that is left to do is to grind down the welds using a grinder and a sanding disc. Be patient, and smooth out the welds slowly. By moving the grinder around and not focusing it on one place for too long, you make sure that the panel doesn't warp from excessive heat. (Photo Courtesy Jefferson Bryant)

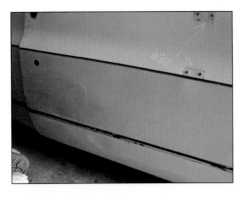

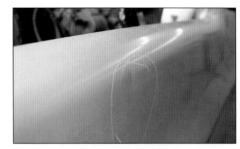

Sight down the side of your truck (as done here by Troy from Borne Kustoms). Also inspect the bodylines of the truck. Use chalk to circle any dents or dings in the body. The original owner didn't want the mirrors that were on the truck because they weren't period correct, which meant that the holes on the doors (marked as "weld") would have to be welded closed.

It may be subtle, but there's a ding inside that chalk circle, and it needs to be repaired.

Repairing Dents and Dings

When working on a new project, I recommend looking down the side of the vehicle to mark (with a Sharpie or chalk) low and high spots in the metal. Make sure the mark encompasses the entire area. Take lots of pictures of the whole truck, making sure to show all of the dents and dings.

If you're simply touching up small areas, you still need to get the area down to bare metal. You don't have to do the entire area, however, if the paint is in good shape. Sand it down to an 80-grit finish using a D/A sander, and make sure to work wide around the affected spot. This is your starting point.

Whether you have a high spot or a low spot in the metal, one method is to make it as smooth as possible using a body hammer. When you use a hammer to pound in a nail, you drive the head of the hammer as hard as possible onto the head of the nail. Metalwork is the opposite. You start by lightly tapping on the panel, working your way from the center of the ding or dent toward the outside. You smooth out the sheet metal enough so that you can apply less than 1/8-inch of body filler because anything more than that has the chance of shrinking and cracking, causing all of your work to be for naught.

If you have access, another method is to use a dolly on the other side of the panel, which gives you a hard surface to strike against. This sandwiches the metal between the hammer and the dolly and can be used to good effect by a skilled person.

Either way, the goal is to smooth out the metal, not pound the panel into submission. Be gentle and apply more pressure only when necessary, otherwise you cause yourself more work than needed.

Collision Repair

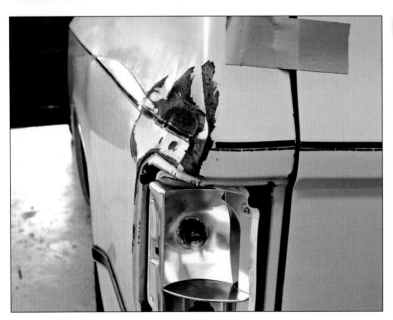

1 *When you have substantial damage like this, you have to decide whether to repair it or replace it. Dents like this are difficult to work on and require a lot of time to repair. It's a compound dent that reaches across the entire corner area of the bed. Cutting out the entire taillight housing and surrounding area is an option, but it's not ideal. If the damage also goes down the side, all the way over the fenderwell, you will probably need to fix it.*

2 With collision damage, other areas nearby were also likely impacted by the initial hit. Spray some black guide coat on the side of the truck so you can assess the extent of the work required. Hold the can 6 inches from the surface and at 45-degree angle. Spray the black paint across the area of concern evenly. The black guide coat always settles in the low spots on the body, highlighting what needs to be pulled. In this case, it revealed a large gash that went across the bodyline; maybe the side of the truck scraped a fence or something.

3 The guide coat allows you to identify the damaged area. Use a rotary grinding tool with a sanding disc to knock all of the black guide coat areas down to bare metal in preparation for metal repair. For most other bodywork, use 80-grit sandpaper on a long block to sand the guide coat down to identify the low areas. Often, you can finish guide-coat sanding with 200-grit paper.

4 If the damage happened a long time ago, there's lots of surface rust to remove. You can pull this dent using a combination of tools, and some of them require welding. Grinding the surface down to bare metal gives you a solid surface for welding, which is important because what you weld on helps you pull the dent.

5 To start the repair, you weld on a piece of metal with a special lip on the end. To fix the damage, you start with the lowest part of the dent and work your way out from there. This should begin to get the metal back in shape, which is the first part of the process. The severe dent to this bed corner required more than a simple dent-pulling rod, so a large metal tab is welded to the bodywork.

6 An attachment comes with the slide hammer kit that you can use to pull the dent. Hook the slide hammer onto the hole of the attachment, and then use the hammer to pull the dent out. Once it's as far out as possible, cut off the metal piece, weld it to the next lowest spot, and repeat. This entire process takes a good three hours to complete, and then another hour or so the following day. In a difficult location such as this, it's better to work with what you have than to try to weld in a replacement panel.

7 The first step in the process was to install the large metal tab to effectively pull out the dent as far as possible. Then, smaller metal studs were welded in place. You can use a stud gun and puller effectively for smaller dents in certain areas. The metal must be bare. Use the larger 3-mm stud, place the stud into the top of the gun, and press it into place. After 2 to 3 seconds, you release the trigger, pull back the gun, and your stud is now ready for the slide hammer.

8 After welding the studs and tabs, move on to a hammer and dolly. The hammer was precisely and patiently used to reform the corner profile of the bed. I also frequently reinstall the taillight during the process to ensure that it fits correctly.

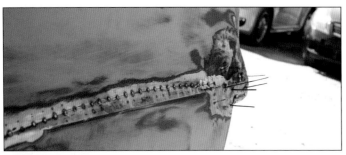

9 Place the slide hammer over the welding stud and turn the wheel at the end of the slide hammer to grip the stud. Work the metal, pulling the slide hammer several times until the dent comes out. With extensive damage (as seen here), you may need to work the metal for some time. Once you have pulled the dent completely, you can simply break off the studs by hand or use a rotary cut-off wheel to grind them off.

10 The material around the taillight may look like ordinary filler, but it's not. It's fiberglass-reinforced body filler. Use it on panels where a lot of metal work has been done, and you need a more solid base. If you just used body filler, it could shrink back excessively, whereas fiberglass-reinforced body filler doesn't shrink.

Mixing traditional body filler is fairly straightforward, so follow the manufacturer's instructions. Use a metal or plastic mixing board that doesn't absorb the filler. Place a 3-inch-wide by 1/2-inch-thick scoop of filler on the mixing surface and then run a bead of hardener across the top of the filler. Using the spreader, thoroughly mix the filler and hardener until it is one uniform color. If you're using 3M filler, the properly mixed filler has a slight pink or salmon color. Be sure to keep air bubbles to a minimum.

Applying Body Filler

Once the panel is close to straight, the next step is to determine the kind of filler to use. Very small imperfections (the kind that look like a slight wave in a panel) can usually be worked out with a thin coat of sanding putty. But in most situations, the best way to start is with a lightweight body filler.

Although most fillers work the same way, you want to check the manufacturer's instructions before you lay it down. The general process is simple. First you apply the amount of body filler that you think you will use onto a mixing board. (You get better with practice.) Then, mix a small amount of the hardening agent with the body filler using a body knife or spreader. These two components are usually different colors, so it becomes obvious when they are mixed evenly.

My personal preference when it comes to body filler is Evercoat Rage Gold, but I use the traditional Rage

It's easy to be afraid of putting on too much filler, but don't be. Apply even pressure and pull it down from a bodyline or swipe it across the surface where your dent is, and then work the surrounding area. Make sure to keep it as smooth and air-bubble free as possible, but otherwise, lay it on. The filler begins setting up in a few minutes, so you need to work quickly.

Dura-Block is one of the most popular long boards available. Use a long board the size of the panel you're working on, so the surface is flat and not wavy. In an even motion and applying consistent pressure, draw the long board across the surface of the panel, working in an X pattern. Most of the filler is sanded off anyway. Use a long block and start with 40- or 80-grit sandpaper to knock down the high spots in the filler.

At some point it makes more sense just to buy a new panel, particularly if it's one that unbolts easily (fenders, hood, and doors come to mind). You have to weigh a few factors to make the decision on your own. Will it take you more time to repair the panels than is reasonable? Are quality replacement parts readily available? If you feel comfortable with replacing the part instead of repairing it, you have to know your options. (Photo Courtesy Lonnie Thompson)

in a pinch. It's easy to sand and produces a consistent, level product. I haven't used the Rage Extreme or Ultra yet, but I've had great experiences with every other Evercoat product (including Kitty Hair and Metal Glaze), so I'm sure those also work well. They're common enough that you can find them at most paint stores and are usually well stocked.

Once the mixing has been done, you quickly apply the filler to the dent by scooping a small amount onto the spreader or knife, then hold it tightly against the panel. While the spreader is at a sharp angle to the body, push it firmly against the panel while dragging it across the dent. This does two things: it removes as many air bubbles from the body filler as possible and it spreads out the filler so that it stays as low as possible. Apply more filler until you have covered the area of the dent, as well as a few inches past the dent. Make multiple passes if necessary.

The goal is to cover the dent and have enough coverage so that the filler sands down to level. Once the filler has been applied, stop and wait until it is hard, usually around 10 minutes or so. Then start sanding.

To sand down the filler, you want to use strips of sandpaper designed for sanding blocks. My preference is an adhesive-backed sandpaper that I use with a block designed to hold that type of sandpaper. For me, this works out better because I can change paper quickly when it gums up, but some prefer using sandpaper that snaps into place on a sanding block with mousetrap-like closures on each end. A Dura-Block seven-piece sanding block set retails for about $60. You can find a properly sized block for almost any body-filler sanding job on your truck.

You typically want to use the longest block possible for the panel. This ensures that the metal is straight over as much of the panel as it covers, and there are lots of big, straight panels on these square trucks. You also want to sand in an X pattern, working your way across the panel diagonally.

Ideally, you make a matching number of passes, but don't feel obligated to count your strokes as you go; it all works out in the end.

For the first pass, you can use 40- or 80-grit sandpaper. The 40 grit is pretty abrasive and should only be used as a quick initial pass to knock down the obvious high spots and remove as much material as possible. Then switch to 80. Sand until the filler is smooth and level with the surrounding metal. You can usually tell when it's in the right area when the borders of the filler seem to have a soft edge. Depending on the size of the dent, you may have to apply a second layer of filler.

I'm a fan of 3M sandpaper for a lot of reasons, but the main one is consistency. I've tried a few other brands, but the 3M stuff sticks to my boards and always puts out the type of pass I'm expecting. That's not always the case with some off brands, so I stick with what I know works.

Knowing when a panel is "done" is difficult to verify. Many pros use

Sand the panel vigorously to remove much of the coat. After a rough pass, these are the typical results. All of the high spots show to either bare metal or paint, and the low spots still have filler, but are feathered out nicely

Here's another example. This dent work was down by the fender. You can see how the filler almost melts away. That's the goal.

their hands and rub up and down the panel to feel if it's straight or not. That's a skill that takes years to perfect, and a good body person is worth his or her weight in gold. If you're a novice, go for as smooth as you can, working your way down to 120-grit sandpaper on the filler.

Once you think the area is done, it's time to apply a lightweight glazing putty onto the panel. This is mixed in the same way as body filler, but it's designed to fill in sanding scratches created in the first steps, as well as any pinholes that may have formed in the filler. You start sanding this with either 180- or 220-grit sandpaper, which should be fine enough to go on to the next steps. If you want to, you can go to finer-grit papers, although it's not entirely necessary.

This process applies to one dent, but your area may have multiple spots on the same panel. Spread filler on multiple dents if they're close, or take your time and do each one individually, taking care not to sand over a previously worked area.

A dent under the taillight only needed a small coat of filler. (Photo Courtesy Jefferson Bryant)

The first step in the gapping process is to assemble all of your panels and align them as best as possible. It's not unusual to use shims to get things lined up correctly, particularly with aftermarket sheet metal, as is the case with the front fenders on this particular truck.

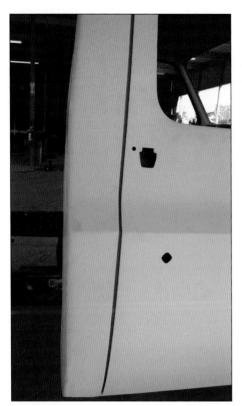

Gapping correctly starts with the doors toward the back of the cab. You align them with the cab manually, then the fenders to the doors, hood to fenders, and so on. This gap is a bit off just above the bodyline below the door handle because it hasn't been worked on yet.

Gapping the Panels

One of the issues that you will grapple with over the course of your build is the fitment of the panels. You should have consistent and evenly spaced gaps between the body panels. You get that consistency by "gapping" the panels.

When these trucks were built, it wasn't critical to have nice, clean gaps, in general, and for a truck, it was even less so. Today, having that consistency is more difficult when you add aftermarket sheet metal, which is notoriously difficult to fit.

Many people skip this step entirely. It's laborious, and because

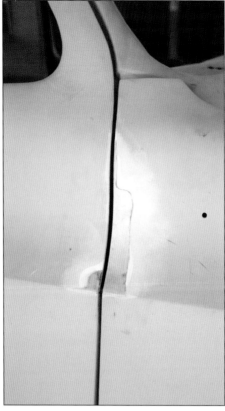

You have two ways to fix a gap. If it's tight, you can grind off the excess sheet metal on the side with the tighter edge, and then bodywork it accordingly. If it's wide (shown), you can weld a thin piece of rod onto the wider portion and blend it into the panel with a grinder and then do the bodywork.

it's not always appreciated after the fact, some don't think that it's important. The best restorations, however, always have perfect gaps, so if you want your truck in that arena, you should definitely consider putting in the time.

Fixing Factory Issues

One common problem with these trucks is with the hood. Two things happen: First, the hood hinge springs become stiff, either with age, corrosion, or a break in the coil, making it difficult to close the hood.

Second, because of the first problem, the hood doesn't shut properly, and tends to buckle in the middle. That's because there's a factory crease point in the hood that was designed to crumble the hood upward in the case of an accident. Because you apply pressure to the front of the hood when you close it, however, the damaged hinges cause the hood to flex at that crease point. The end result is that the hood bows upward and doesn't align properly.

LMC Trucks sells a hood brace kit that's super cheap ($20 plus $6 for silicone sealant). If you want to prevent your hood from bending in the first place, you should definitely consider it or a similar product.

Prep for Paint

Once all of your bodywork has been completed, you can prep the body for paint; it's one of the crucial steps in the entire restoration process. In the end, no one is going to care if all of the screw heads are aligned in the same direction or if the engine is period correct down to the stickers if the paint job is horrible. The easiest way to kill a paint job is to skip the necessary steps for prepping the body the right way.

This prep work is also important for the overall cost of the restoration. Prep time eats up a lot of hours, and if you're paying someone to do the job for you, you're going to spend some serious cash. But if you can do the work and save yourself that cash, it's more money that you can devote to the paint job or to the supplies. Plus, prepping for the paint job is more time consuming than it is a skill set, meaning that you are perfectly able to do this job yourself; you just need to get after it.

Initial Body Prep

Although you've likely stripped your truck down to the bare metal already, that doesn't mean that your cleanup is perfect. Now that the bodywork is done, you need to scuff and clean the entire surface so you can lay down your first coat of primer.

To begin that process, use a fine Scotch-Brite pad to scrub every surface on the truck. This includes the interior, engine bay, and anywhere else that you plan on painting. If you've replaced portions of the floor, scrub it as well, top and bottom.

You will build up a "tooth" that the primer can bite into, so make sure

that you scrub in all directions with the pad, on every surface possible.

1 *One area that is often overlooked is the rain gutter located above the side windows. They collect rain that can turn into rust if the sealant below (sometimes caulking) isn't in top-notch condition. And that can screw up your paint job.*

2 *If you were to paint over random flecks of paint and a bumpy surface like this, you'd have a horrible result. In addition, you may find old sealant applied with lead or a chemical that can react with your paint job, causing fisheyes and the like.*

3 *The easiest way to remove old caulking is usually with a wire wheel on a die grinder. The goal is to make the resulting metal smooth.*

4 *Sometimes, as was the case on this truck, lead was used as a body filler. Use a propane or oxy acetylene torch to heat the lead, but be sure not to heat the body panel too much. Once you have applied enough heat, the lead should bead up and roll off. This trick also works on regular caulking, particularly when it's so deep in a crevice that you can't access it effectively with the wire wheel.*

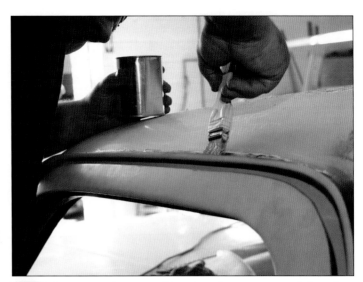

6 Once all of the caulking has been removed, brush on some POR-15 to protect the area from future rust. You lay down new caulking before the area is ready for paint. New caulking covers up any imperfections in the POR-15, so you don't need to bodywork it. If you prefer to bodywork the area, just as with any other panel, you can apply filler directly over the POR-15 and then down the new caulking.

5 Irregular metal lies underneath the caulking, which came from the factory's welding process. These areas can become little pools of water and start the rusting process. You need to prevent that from occurring.

8 Whether you're painting or priming your truck, you want to protect the wheels. Typically, you need to keep the truck mobile, so you still need a method of rolling the truck in and out of the workspace. You can either use car dollies to do that, replace your aftermarket wheels with ones that can be damaged, or just cover the wheels with big bags (shown). You can also find canvas and paper versions of this same setup, or just tape them up yourself. (Photo Courtesy Jefferson Bryant)

7 With the surface scrubbed clean, you need to clean up the surfaces that you're about to spray. Use a lint-free paper towel with wax and grease remover to remove any sanding residue or dust. Be sure to hit all of the areas. Then go over everything with a tack cloth as a second line of defense (shown). (Photo Courtesy Jefferson Bryant)

9 *The more time you spend on the masking process, the better the results will be in the end. The idea is to cover every surface with tape and paper that you don't want painted, using the edge of the tape to cover the seams. Use 1½-inch 3M yellow tape around the perimeter of the area to be masked off. Use a high-quality masking paper to cover the vital components before you spray. Be sure that the paper has as few wrinkles and flaws as possible. Use a single-edge razor blade or utility knife to trim the paper. (Photo Courtesy Jefferson Bryant)*

10 *You want to make sure that the paper is as flat as possible. If you see a crease or wrinkle in the paper, tape it back down so paint does not bounce off the paper and onto a nearby area of the body. (Photo Courtesy Jefferson Bryant)*

A Word About Masking

In the priming stage, because of the heavy nature of the product, you don't have to mask thoroughly, and you don't have to use a paint booth to do your work; a relatively dust-free environment is fine. However, when you're masking a panel, there are two ways to work: creating a hard edge and creating a soft edge.

Hard edges are when you tape the masking paper onto the panel and the tape creates a hard line where the next layer of product appears. When you peel off the paper, you have a thick edge that you can feel. In some cases, this is unavoidable, but acceptable; a two-tone paint job might have this, for example, particularly in cases where the stripe is in the center of the side of the body. But, with careful planning (and/or trim and pinstriping), you can avoid problems.

A soft edge is created when you back mask a panel. This involves flipping the masking paper in essentially a 180-degree arc from where you want to mask. You pull the paper back over the masking tape so that the sticky side of the tape is partially exposed. This slight curvature of the tape allows the spray medium to dissipate a bit more, creating a softer edge. It's not ideal for blending panels every time, but in the primer stage it might come in handy.

The best strategy is to select the entire paint system before you start any work because a primer, paint, and clear coat system from one manufacturer is complementary and you get the best results. If you mix and match from several paint manufacturers, the results may be disastrous. For example, the paint may react with an incompatible primer.

The currently available primers include etch primers, wash etches, and high-build primers. Most etch primers are phosphoric acid and help reduce corrosion. Wash etches can be applied by sprayer or brush and are thin. A high-build primer is thick and difficult to apply, but it can be used for filling in bodywork.

I suggest laying the primer by working from the inside out. Start by spraying the floor of the cab, working your way up the firewall and back to the cab wall. You don't have to tape anything off because the overspray will be scuffed and covered in the next step anyway. Make sure that you're able to access as much of the area as you can; you can lean into the cab and spray.

You have two options for working with bare metal. The first is to use epoxy primer, which coats the metal and provides corrosion protection. You can also top it with a primer surfacer that you can then sand down to be straight. A self-etching primer does the same job as an epoxy primer, and you can also apply a primer surfacer on top of it. So what's the difference? You can apply body filler on top of an epoxy primer, but not onto a self-etching primer.

If you took your truck to a professional chemical stripper or a media blaster during the initial phase of the project, they may have laid down an epoxy primer to make sure that the metal was protected. You can sand that down to bare metal if you like, or you can apply body filler on top of it. If they (or you) used a self-etching primer, you must take the body down to bare metal before doing any repairs. In the end, it's up to personal preference.

The goal of the epoxy/self-etching priming stage is to prime every part of the body in one solid coat.

Next, you want to lay on enough sandable primer material so that you can use it to smooth out and level the panel. You may do this several times to achieve the best results.

Mixing and Applying Primer

1 *You start with an epoxy primer, mostly because you will to be doing (and redoing) bodywork. It's thick stuff and helps protect the body from future rust. Follow this with a primer surfacer that you can block sand to keep the body as straight as possible. This isn't necessary in some places (the inside of the cab or underside of the bed, for example), but you may want to do it just to be thorough. It's important to mix the primer according to the instructions on the can. The primer mix ratio is listed on the can or container. Often, acrylic enamel is a 1:1 ratio for primer and reducer. If you don't mix thoroughly, you risk wasting materials and time. (Photo Courtesy Jefferson Bryant)*

2 *Give the truck one last pass with a wax and grease remover. Make sure everything is as clean and masked up as possible. (Photo Courtesy Jefferson Bryant)*

3 After you lay down a coat of epoxy primer, all of the bodywork is protected. You can either apply another coat or two or move on to the next stage. (Photo Courtesy Jefferson Bryant)

Once you have the sandable primer laid down and the surface is dry, you can then spray or dust a contrasting color over the surface. It's called a guide coat. The purpose of the guide coat is to give yourself a visual guide of the high and low spot locations in the panel. While you sand the panel, the high spots turn gray (or the color of the primer), and the low spots show up as black. The goal is to sand until everything is the same color as the primer.

If a spot is still low after extensive sanding, you have to add filler to fill in the gaps. Whether you use a spray or dry guide coat is up to you. In a pinch, you can use spray paint.

The goal is to sand until the guide coat is removed and the surface is even. However, sometimes that doesn't happen the way you want it to. If you see low spots, but you're now sanding bare metal with a block, you have a low spot that needs to be filled. If it's shallow, you can use a glazing putty and sandpaper to level it out. If it's deeper, you may want to go back to the body filler stage and get the panel back to a starting point.

The next step is to remove the 320-grit scratches in the panel. To do that, use a D/A sander and 500-grit sandpaper, making sure to keep the sander flat against the surface. Work your way around the truck and/or panel until all of the surfaces are worked evenly. If necessary, you can also sand by hand in tight spaces.

Clean the panel again with a wax and grease remover, then use a gray Scotch-Brite pad to scuff everything to the same point. If you see shiny spots on the panel as you clean, those areas aren't scuffed enough. Go over those again with the Scotch-Brite pad.

Once the truck is in full prime, you have a few options. Some people prefer to let their project sit for a bit. The logic is that any body that has seen lots of filler has some issues with shrinkage. Once the filler has set for a period of time, it can shrink back a bit, causing a slight wave. Other people feel that you should start with a base coat right away. Their logic is that they've done enough work to ensure that shrinkage isn't a problem.

I usually err on the side of caution and let the truck sit for a bit, maybe two or three weeks. It's not crucial, but it allows you to focus on other tasks. You can then block it down one last time prior to paint. It's up to you.

This cab belongs to a 1976 GMC long-bed Stepside that had seen better days. The rockers and most of the floor were replaced, plus some of the windshield area. But now it's in full prime, and on a cart, which makes it easy to move around a shop.

PAINT

The paint job on your truck is arguably the most important component of the restoration process. It is the first thing that people see when they walk up to the vehicle, and it protects the sheet metal of the body. It can also be the most expensive part of the process because of the extensive costs of the paint, labor, and materials. As they say, a good paint job isn't cheap, and a cheap paint job isn't good.

At the end of the restoration process, this is just another component that you need to check off your list as you put everything together, but it is a very important one. Go into the process being aware of the costs ahead of you, the time that it needs, and what you want the end results to be.

For the highest quality results, most owners opt to hire a professional shop to do the paint work because exceptional paint jobs demand a very clean spraying environment. If you opt to paint in your garage, you need the proper tools and accessories, including a temporary paint booth, paint guns, and a large high-volume compressor. You also need the knowledge and skill to do it properly.

DIY Versus Paying a Professional

The paint job is a key part of the build, and it needs to be done quickly, cleanly, and correctly. If it's not done correctly, you may not be happy with the results, or, worse yet, you may have to do it over or pay to have it redone.

With that in mind, you must decide if you want to take on this job yourself. The answer is influenced by the kind of results you want.

Choose the Level of Result

A simple paint job can be accomplished by laying down a coat of primer, a single-stage paint, and a quick buff job. The results can be nice, and single-stage paints are not bad by any means. However, they don't have the depth of a base

The dashboard area has compound curves and many nooks and crannies. Therefore, take your time and be sure to apply the paint evenly to all surfaces of the interior. It's a good idea to double-check your work.

coat/clear coat finish. That said, it may be exactly what you want, and for that level, you can likely take it on yourself.

On the other end of the spectrum, you have candies, pearlescent additives, and other complicated hues, all of which require an extra layer of complexity and skill. A novice could attempt this, but the results would likely not be up to what a professional can do, or they could be much worse. However, you probably fall somewhere in the middle. You may want a paint job using a factory color, possibly a factory two-tone, and prefer a two-stage paint over a single-stage. Once buffed, you then have a nice paint job that can last years, and not a spot in your truck will be missed in the process.

Keep Budget in Mind

With those possibilities in mind, I recommend that, unless you have some experience with paint work, you have a professional paint your truck. That choice, however, does not make the job easier or cheaper to do. A quality painter or body shop can be difficult to find. Paint jobs typically range from $3,000 to $10,000 for a competent but not flawless paint job.

Painting requires skill or extensive practice to do properly, and it can legitimately take a long time. In some cases, various industry pressures and factors come into play. It also means that traditional tradesmen and shops often have to take on more jobs than they can handle, causing them to juggle multiple projects simultaneously. That means a paint job can often take much longer than anticipated or forecasted.

You need to consider both types of budget: money and time.

Research Potential Shops

It is absolutely critical that you do your research before you trust your project to any paint or body shop (or private laborer). You could make the argument that this is important with any step of the process, but with the paint job, the entire truck is in their hands and if it gets screwed up in any way, you could find yourself without a vehicle.

I've been involved in scenarios in which the painter promised one thing and delivered another and then expected additional payments. Finding a good painter is a bit like catching a unicorn in a field of money trees. When you find one, latch onto him or her and hold on tight. They're worth their weight in gold.

The following is a quick list of tips for evaluating a paint and/or body shop.

- Your friends have personal experience with them
- They have a track record of producing high-quality results on time
- They have multiple show awards
- You've seen the quality of their paint jobs in person
- You've spoken to other customers at a show who've had their vehicles painted by them, and they recommended them highly
- The shop is clean and organized (cleaned daily)
- The shop has its own paint booth(s)

That is not to say that there aren't outliers in this process. The best paint job I ever received came from a friend of a friend who rented a shop at a local boat dealership and sprayed the car overnight. That paint job was phenomenal and earned me heaps of praise by both the media and my friends. But I only found that painter because my previous choice, the guy with a professional shop and paint booth, had attempted to panel paint a candy finish that resulted in a zebra-striped car.

I cannot stress this enough: Do your research and make sure that you find a painter who can do the job you want him or her to do. Don't be afraid to pay highly for a good job. Always follow this maxim: A good painter is not cheap, and a cheap painter is not good.

Equipment

Part of the reason that a quality paint job costs as much as it does is because of the materials and equipment needed to do a thorough job. There are many consumables that you use in the process, and you want to have some on hand so that you're prepared in case of a time-critical scenario (which can happen a lot when painting).

Paint Booth Versus Clean Painting Area

In an ideal world, you would have a paint booth in your backyard that makes everything more convenient. But if you're only planning on doing a paint job or two, the expense doesn't make as much sense. Instead, you can rent a paint booth from a local body shop. Sometimes there are places set up in your area dedicated to the shade-tree mechanic. Some of them have paint booths to rent as well.

Should neither of those options work out, the next best choice is to create a paint booth of your own. You will never achieve the same results that you will with a professional booth, but you don't have the

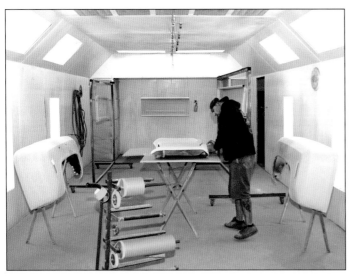

A clean paint booth is critical if you want to keep your paint job free of dust and dirt. Any dirt, debris, or contaminants left behind often wind up in the paint, so make sure the booth is as clean as possible.

costs, either. To build one, however, is not a quick process.

Painting is a tricky subject because, depending on your local laws, you may or may not be allowed to spray paint in your garage or work area. Even if you are, do you want to lay down that immaculate finish in the same space where the day before you had two quarts of oil on the ground from pulling the engine? If you can, keep your bodywork space and your dirty work space separate from each other. If that's impossible, make sure to do a ridiculously thorough cleaning *before* you paint; otherwise, you're sure to have problems with the finish.

Air Compressor

You need a large-capacity air compressor. I currently use an 80-gallon compressor, which is more than enough for the jobs that I do on a regular basis. You want a 240V, two-stage compressor, which is typically the kind that has a belt connecting the engine to the compressor. It looks a bit like a Harley-Davidson V-twin, complete with big fins. If you don't already have a 240V connection in your workspace, you should install one.

If you use the same compressor for painting that you do for general tool work, you're going to want to set up a separate hose system just for paint. A lot goes into putting one of those systems together properly, but the basic premise is to remove the water and condensation that builds up in a compressor from the paint lines through multiple driers and desiccants. Also, if you oil your tools (as you should), the painting lines must be free of said oil. That can also mess up an otherwise great paint job.

Air-Handling Equipment

Depending on where you live (and frankly, it's still a problem in desert climates), water forms in the compressor and air lines. If that water comes out with the paint, you may toast your paint job, and that can ruin your day. In addition, traditional pneumatic tools require regular oiling to function properly. If that oil feeds back into the air lines at all, it can atomize with your paint as well, laying down oil with your color. Again, a problem.

The idea setup is to have a completely isolated system that is disconnected from the compressor and sealed when not in use. You can mount various air-handling components to a wall (or the outside of your booth), meaning that they're always out of the way. These include multiple dryers, pressure regulator(s), water separator(s), desiccant system, and dedicated air lines just for painting.

It all costs money, but the less you protect your lines, the higher risk you take of something fouling your paint job. Most of the paranoia about clean air lines is justified.

Spray Gun

Although I've only done a few paint jobs, I have multiple paint guns, with one dedicated to each task. I have two good-quality HVLP gravity-feed guns that I use for both color and clear. You want to isolate those two components for two reasons. First, there is a window of time after the base coat is laid down in which you can start to lay down the clear. You don't want to be still cleaning out your gun in the middle. Second, keeping the two components of the paint job separate just keeps things cleaner, and that's nice.

I also have an HVLP gravity-feed gun for primer, but it has a much larger tip because it sprays a large amount of solids.

Professional painters typically use at least three guns.

By having so many options for laying down virtually any material onto a vehicle, you can clean and prep each one individually, which makes the process more efficient. Alternatively, if you either don't want to or can't afford to purchase multiple spray guns, get a high-quality gun and buy multiple tips and liners for it. This makes the cleaning process

Constructing a Temporary Paint Booth

A professional body shop with a permanent paint booth produces exceptional results. Painting at home is a painstaking, meticulous process that requires attention to detail. Many owners may opt to paint their trucks on a budget at home. But before you buy all the materials, be sure it's legal to paint a vehicle at your residence. Some states have banned residential automotive painting, and you don't want your truck to put you on the wrong side of the law.

If you choose to paint at home, the painting space must be clean and that means devoid of dust, contaminants, and debris. If you plan to paint a truck in your garage, you need the cleanest environment possible, and that means constructing a negative-pressure temporary paint booth. If dust, dirt, and any other contaminants reside in the painting area near your truck, they often wind up in the paint and you have flaws of a poor-quality paint job.

Squarebody trucks are available in a range of styles and lengths. A regular-cab short-bed is a little more than 20 feet long. Thus, be sure that your garage has enough room to accommodate your booth, which should have 3 feet of space between the truck and wall, and the booth itself. In theory, a 22 x 22-foot or similar-size two-car garage gives you enough room to construct a paint booth and enough room to spray the entire surface area of a short-bed truck. A crew-cab long-bed is nearly 21 feet long, so a 26-foot-deep garage is ideal.

Temporary paint booths can be relatively easily and simply constructed using 2 x 4-inch wood beams or PVC pipe. Many prefer to use PVC pipe because it's easy to cut, prime, and glue together for a secure joint. You just need to ensure the design, size, and ventilation are adequate for your particular project.

The first rule is to design a paint booth that fits your needs and size of the truck. Begin by sketching the paint booth's measurements before you start construction.

For the booth sides, you can use 1-inch PVC pipe in 20-foot lengths, or multiple sections to extend to 26 feet. Next, select 12- to 14-foot-long pipes for the end sections. You can install as many lateral support pipes as necessary to make it sturdy. Some have tied the PVC pipe to the ceiling and walls of a garage for extra reinforcement.

Once the PVC framework has been constructed, enclose the framework with polyethylene or sheet plastic. Drape the plastic over the entire length of the enclosure and then cover the 8- to 10-foot walls plus 6-foot (or taller) sidewalls. You should have enough plastic left over to cut and use later as a strip below the fan. There should be enough plastic around the front of the booth to fold over and dangle to catch excess overspray (6 inches should be fine). Also hang plastic over the rear of the paint booth to cover it.

Be sure to allocate enough room for a fan. You can use clamps to secure the plastic in place around the fan. Use duct tape to create secure seams. The plastic should rest tightly against the PVC frame because it needs to be airtight.

Next, properly position drop cloths inside the paint booth. Some 4-foot-wide cloth needs to be placed so that the corners reach the paint booth's legs. Pull the drop cloths taut and work out any unevenness. Then, lift each of the paint booth's legs, one at a time, to push the drop cloth edges underneath. If it doesn't fit right, or it doesn't line up under the paint booth's legs, step back and visually inspect the legs. Each one should be nearly perpendicular to the ground.

Mount a furnace filter and box fan to the side of the booth so they can vent paint fumes. Position the fan outside the paint booth and halfway up from the floor. Place it on a stepladder for support and about an inch or two from the side legs. This gives the fan and ladder the necessary support. Use duct tape to attach the furnace filter to the outside of the sheet vinyl. ∎

Even if it is legal to paint in your state, you may have to use water-based paints or be restricted by your equipment. Verify the local and state laws regarding performing a paint job in a residential area. Be sure to contain your paint project to your property. You don't want paint to escape your garage and damage your neighbor's house or cars.

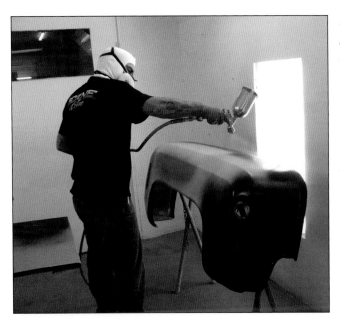

Having multiple HVLP guns allows you to keep contaminants out of the process. No matter how well you clean, a bit of material from a previous coat may make its way into your base or clear, causing extra work.

go a little more smoothly, and with multiple tips you avoid issues with spraying the wrong material through the wrong orifice.

Many brands and grades of paint guns are offered in a wide range of prices, and as the old adage goes, you get what you pay for. Most entry-level guns are plastic; higher-end guns are stainless steel. DeVilbiss, Badger, Iwata, Binks, and others offer excellent paint guns that deliver exceptional results. My recommendation is to buy the highest quality paint gun you can afford because it directly impacts the quality of the paint job.

Everything being sprayed has a dry time, and having multiple guns allows you to work more quickly and more efficiently. Primer can clog up a nozzle quickly. If you don't want to stress about it, buy a cheaper primer gun to lay down that finish, then clean and reuse it if possible; otherwise, toss it.

Mixing Equipment

Mixing paints often requires adding a catalyst or reducer. If you're mixing a color yourself, you definitely want to know how much of what you're putting in. Buy mixing cups at your local auto paint store with marks indicating different mixing ratios and measurements. You want to buy lots of these, because you use them at each stage of the process.

You can also never have too many stir sticks and filters.

You should agitate every mixture before you pour it into the gun, so you want a filter between the mixing cup and the gun. This is cheap insurance to keep sediment and dirt out of the process.

Cleaning Products

You need to make sure that everything is perfectly clean before you lay down the next coat of primer, paint, or clear. Tack rags come in handy all the time. These are pieces of white cloth that are designed to pick up sediment and dirt that may be present after wet sanding the primer. You can also use reducer and high-quality paper towels (usually blue and sold in large boxes at auto paint supply stores) to wipe down the truck.

Safety Gear

Always wear some kind of face protection that either incorporates a respirator or a fresh-air system. Think of a gas mask, essentially. Keep it in a sealed bag at all times, and change the filters before you do a paint job. It will save your lungs.

Inhalation of paint fumes can lead to serious injury or death. The Sunstrom H01-2021 uses a filter cartridge that provides excellent protection for up to 40 hours. 3M offers a full line of respirators for painting and industrial work. The 7500 Professional Half Facepiece is a conventional respirator that features soft, comfortable plastic and holds two organic filters. The 3M GVP-PSK Paint Spray System is a Positive Air Pressure Respirator that uses a fan to direct air to the mask rather than drawing the air through respirator cartridges. This makes it easier to breathe and particles are not pulled into the mask.

Clean suits are made of either a lint-free cloth or a composite material such as Tyvek. You put them on over your regular clothes, then seal yourself up and use protective booties. This is another way to keep contaminants out of your paint. Disposable and reusable painting suits and booties are available from paint suppliers and online sources.

Latex or nitrile (the material used if you're allergic to latex) gloves are also very important. The oils on your hands can transfer to your truck, and if you're not careful, you can cause fingerprints to show up in the final coat. Latex or nitrile gloves also protect your hands from the paint itself, and, because they're easy and cheap to change, you can swap them out for fresh gloves regularly. Tuck your clean suit into them to make a complete body seal.

Abrasives and Sanding Equipment

At this stage of the process you should have already prepped your truck, but you may need to touch up an area before painting. A soft sanding block and 400- to 600-grit sandpaper come in handy. You also want a small bucket of water or access to a hose. Scotch-Brite pads are also useful for scuffing up small spots before paint, so have some of those nearby as well.

Masking Materials

Masking paper and automotive painter's tape in various widths are very useful. I typically use the green painter's tape made by 3M that you find at an auto body store. A paper stand/dispenser makes the masking process much smoother. They're set up to mate the tape and the paper simultaneously. Slick.

Paint Types

Now, before you get all excited about the possibility of painting your truck, I've got to break some bad news. Once you pick a type of paint you must keep with it the entire way through the build. You may think that you can mix any paint with just any old kind of primer, but you'd be wrong. Paints and primers are chemicals, and they need to work together in harmony.

If you mix one with a wrong type, the chemical reaction may be bad enough that you have to start all over, going all the way down to the metal, until there's none of the offending substrate left.

Scared yet? Don't be. You don't have to be a chemical engineer to understand how paints function, you just need to have a basic idea of what the different types are and how they affect your build.

For instance, if you have a color in mind at the start of your build, whether it's the factory shade or something different, you want to know what brand and type of paint it is. Now that seems silly to think about when you have a rust-eaten truck in your shop and paint is the furthest thing from your mind, but it shouldn't be. Paints come in systems for a reason, so you should consider that from the jump.

Here's a good example. A few years back, I had a car painted by a good friend of mine. I knew that I wanted a House of Kolor shade, Limetime Green. So with that in mind, he bought the appropriate primers, sealers, and base coats to match. When I started the bodywork, everything was done in those materials, and it all came out flawless. To this day, it's one of my favorite paint jobs. But it almost didn't happen.

A year before, I had sent that same car to another painter to do essentially the same job. Instead of following a system, he mixed and matched however he liked, sometimes from panel to panel, and the results showed it. Not only was the color different on the bumper, doors, trunk, and body, but there were reaction spots all over.

Yes, eventually the car received a solid paint job, but first, everything had to be taken down so that all those spots were eliminated. It was a lot of work (and money). It could've all been saved if the first guy had just used one paint system for the entire job.

My painter friends say that you can mix and match some paints, particularly if they are the same brand (Valspar and House of Kolor, for example). But they've learned all that from years of experimenting on

Many types of paint are currently offered, including acrylic enamel, urethane, and water-based paints. You need to determine the best type of paint for the type of restoration you're performing. This particular paint is Omni MBC (made by PPG), which is an acrylic urethane, and therefore can be sprayed over other Omni acrylic urethane products.

other people's rides. You have only *your* truck to play with. I don't know about you, but I'd rather just paint my truck once and be done instead of becoming an amateur chemist.

Another of my painter friends knows how paints work on another level. That's because while he planned on playing pro baseball, and even made it to the minor leagues, he first earned a degree in chemical engineering. After an injury sidelined him, he started a paint shop. And if he tells me not to mix my brands or only mix the ones he *knows* works, that's what I believe.

Which brings me back to the start: What kind of paint should you use for your truck? Well, the following are the basic types.

Lacquer

Let me get one thing out of the way: You're not going to paint your truck with a lacquer-based paint. The durability of the product isn't great, as the longer it's out in the sun, the more it dries out. It's usually more expensive, often it's illegal to spray, and it requires meticulous maintenance. Yes, you can achieve a stunning paint job with a lacquer finish, but it's often not worth the drawbacks.

I bring this up because your truck may have been painted with lacquer previously. My personal project, a 1981 Chevrolet Silverado, had been repainted sometime along the way. The truck now has faded and peeling paint, and I can tell that it's lacquer because it's cracking and peeling away from the truck. When the time comes for me to paint it, I'm going to try to remove as much of it as possible so that down the line I don't have issues with a new finish (although you can spray over lacquer with some products; more on that shortly). If your truck is in a similar situation, you might want to consider the same.

Waterborne

Prior to 2010, it might've been hard for you to find waterborne paints at your local paint supply store. And even though Auto Air Colors has been around for decades, the concept of using this style of paint wasn't popular. Then its use became the law in some states, and now it's standard in many automotive paints.

So what is it? All paints use solvents of some kind to carry the pigment to the surface; once the solvents break down, you're left with the color. In waterborne paints, most (but not all) of those solvents are replaced by water. The result is a drastic reduction in volatile organic compounds (VOCs), which makes sense for the planet and your health. Even so, you still want to use a mask when spraying.

The transition to waterborne paints hasn't been overwhelmingly popular, and I can remember a time when people using those paints were the rebels, stepping out of the norm to try something new. Today, it's pretty common, and you shouldn't be surprised if your options are more limited in other fields.

The biggest issue with waterborne paint was how to work with it. After all, you want to keep your paint types within a system. Urethane paints with urethane primers, for example. Fortunately, waterborne paints work well with urethane primers and clears, so you have a bunch of options. On top of that, the only thing water-based in the system is the base coat. Everything else that you use, from the primer to the clear, still has solvents. That means that if you've painted anything before, this process is very similar, other than laying down a base coat.

Let's tackle that process now. You want to use a stainless-steel spray gun, otherwise you risk having rust in your finish, and nobody wants that. The main disadvantage is the amount of time that the paint takes to "flash," which is the process by which the solvent evaporates and you're ready to apply the clear. You're now drying water, so you want to use a fan or other type of blower to, as PPG's website puts it, "promote the flow of air over painted surfaces." As with all other paints, you must have a clean and oil-free air system so you don't inject any other problems into the base coat.

With today's products, the end results with a waterborne paint can be just as stunning as they are with a traditional solvent-based system, and there are other advantages that the professionals who use it in production love as well. Is it right for your truck? Soon you might not have an option. But for now, it's certainly one of your better ones.

Urethane

When it comes to urethane and acrylic enamel finishes, I'm talking about the resins that make up a paint. Urethane paint uses urethane resin, and you can spray it over pretty much anything, including lacquer. Urethane paint is super durable, so you don't have to worry as much about chips and flakes down the line. Sounds perfect, right?

Well the downsides here are pretty significant. Urethane paints can be pricey, particularly when compared to acrylic enamels in the same colors. Also, when they spray out, depending on the color, sometimes they can look a bit more plasticky, which is not what you're going for, or at least you shouldn't be. Oh, and it's super toxic, so using a respirator is a must when you apply this stuff.

Acrylic Enamel

This type of paint is also durable and dries with a nice, hard shell, but to achieve that finish you should consider baking it with professional heat lamps made for the task. They take longer to dry, which also means that they take time to harden fully, so keep that in mind. Acrylic enamel also creates orange peel, which is the slightly textured look that you find on most new cars today. It requires some extra time for wet sanding and buffing later.

Another downside is that acrylic enamel paints don't often cover as well as their urethane competitors.

What that means to you is that it will likely take more material for the same results, particularly because the size of the droplets that acrylic enamel paints produce is smaller than those of urethane. So basically, even if the enamel saves you a bit of money on the front end, you might be paying more in the long term with more coats and time spent in the finishing stages.

Paint Colors

If you're looking to re-create the original color, you need to do some research on what color your truck was to begin with, which isn't always easy if you bought it in rough condition. To sort things out, find your Regular Production Option (RPO) number. It's on a blue and white decal that's located inside the glove box. Listed at the top is the Serial No., Paint code, and SE No. It details what custom things were done to the truck at the factory, and the all-important paint code tells you what color (or colors) your truck was originally painted.

Paint codes, however, come in many variations. There's a "regular" code, a GM code, a Ditzier PPG code, a DuPont code, and half a dozen other alphanumeric sequences that mean something to somebody. Even if you were to have a handy chart of what color is what code, there's yet another aspect to consider: two-tone paint jobs.

Chevrolet had quite a few paint combination options available at the dealer. Some trucks had white or ivory roofs; others had a white stripe either down the center of the sides of the truck or at the rockers. There were special colors for limited editions, which also had special trim levels. Point is, there were a lot of options.

Take a picture of your RPO, and ask your local auto body shop what it

This is Chevrolet's color chart. Dealers used it for customers to pick their truck's color(s). If you took a color sheet like this to a body shop with a color-analyzing machine, they could match the color for you perfectly. One great online source for this is paintref.com. Every 1973–1987 Chevrolet truck's paint colors is listed, including swatches and codes. It's a wealth of information.

means. They have access to the codes for all of those two-tone variations and can provide you with answers. If you can't do that, such as if your RPO isn't on the list anymore, or you don't have the original glove box, consider taking one of your smaller body parts (such as the gas door in later models, or possibly a fender) to have them match it in house. Most paint supply stores can determine what the paint color is or was using various tools, so they should be able to help you out.

If you don't care about what the factory offered, feel free to paint your truck your favorite shade of blue or green or whatever you like, but it won't be a factory-like paint job.

Priming

With all of the bodywork out of the way, it's time to lay down some primer so that you can move toward paint.

Apply Primer

1 The first thing you want to do is to hang any removable parts. You can either use a cart for this purpose or screw some eyelets into the studs in your workspace's ceiling and then hang the parts by chains (shown). Either way, the point is to hang the parts in such a way that they're oriented the same way as they are seen on the truck. (Photo Courtesy Lonnie Thompson)

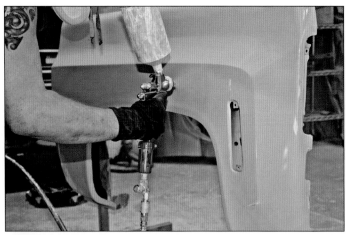

3 This panel had already been sprayed with primer; you can still see the bodywork underneath. A good final result requires multiple coats of primer. Once the primer is dry, wet sand it to a consistent finish so that you're sure it's straight. If it isn't, add glazing putty/filler as necessary, and repeat. By adding layers of primer and block sanding it out while wet sanding, you will have a smoother finish. (Photo Courtesy Lonnie Thompson)

2 The key to spraying primer is to keep the gun consistently 6 to 8 inches from the surface as you move. Also make sure you keep the same pace as you pass the gun across the surface. When you spray a body panel according to this technique, the paint is evenly applied to the surface. (Photo Courtesy Lonnie Thompson)

4 After you have applied the primer to the body panels, install all the panels on the truck. Once everything has been reassembled, roughly gap the panels, and make sure to lay down a layer of guide coat, either in spray or powder form. This is a contrasting color to the primer (typically black). Lay it down evenly on the body. During wet sanding, the guide coat is sanded away. Any high spots in the panels still have guide coat, and low spots don't. This helps tremendously while you work out the kinks, and is handy to do after a panel is primed. (Photo Courtesy Lonnie Thompson)

5 Some make the argument that, "it's just primer," and they don't mask off their truck before they start laying it down. The problem is that overspray happens, and if your chassis is clean and rebuilt, you have just wasted all that time and have to repaint or, at a minimum, detail your chassis all over again. Do yourself a favor and mask off everything before you lay down any kind of spray material. (Photo Courtesy Lonnie Thompson)

6 *If you're doing a full restoration, you end up with a primed truck that looks something like this. Notice that the entire firewall and the inside of the truck is done. That last part (the primed interior) is important. If you've replaced the floors or any sheet metal at all in the truck, you need a coat of primer on both sides of the surface. In addition, a good portion of the dashboard is exposed, and because it typically is painted the same color as the body, it needs to be bodyworked and primed as well. (Photo Courtesy Lonnie Thompson)*

7 *Between coats, you may notice that one of the pieces needs to be prepped again. You can do that with primer. Here's one of the finished panels, complete with guide coat. In this case, it's spray paint, but you can do all sorts of fancy things with guide coat if you want.*

Sealing

Once the bodywork is 100 percent complete, everything is wet sanded flat, and the truck looks ready to go, the next step is to lay down a sealer coat or two.

Why? Well, a sealer does a few different things. For one, during the wet-sanding process you likely sanded through the primer and into the metal. That happens, but if you were to spray the base coat over the metal immediately, you'd have issues with the end result. Because you're in the home stretch, you don't want that.

Second, sealer can help extend the coverage of the base coat. Sealers come in a variety of colors, and if you're using a translucent base coat, it can affect the end result. For exam-

ple, if you sprayed a white sealer underneath a translucent green base coat, the green would appear brighter than if you used a dark gray sealer. Even if you don't use a translucent shade, having a similarly tinted sealer works to your advantage.

Think about it this way: If you laid down a black sealer on a fence and tried to spray a white paint on top, it would take forever to cover the black. This is essentially the same concept.

Applying Sealer

1 *Clean all areas again before you spray so that the body surface is as clean as it can be. By going over everything with a tack rag and compressed air, you can ensure that most small particles are removed.*

2 Laying down the sealer is the same as laying down primer, although you typically make just a pass or two, or until the panel is covered completely. You won't be sanding, so make sure that it lays down as flat as possible.

3 After the truck is completely sealed, go over everything with a tack rag and compressed air, then lay down the base coat. Be sure you work against the airflow of the booth or apply the paint in the opposite direction of the airflow so you have the best and most even coverage of the primed surfaces. You don't want to use a dry paint spray because it will result in problems that you have to fix later.

4 On top of the peach-tinted sealer here, is a base coat with a copper hue that matched the original truck's interior. A urethane base coat paint often has a 4:1 paint-to-activator ratio. After you thoroughly agitate the base paint in the can, pour some into a mixing cup (from paint supply stores). Then transfer some paint into the gun cup. Test spray the gun on a practice panel and adjust the tip. You can adjust the airflow rate and fan pattern to match the paint type and the application requirements. Hold the gun about 6 to 8 inches from the surface and apply the paint in a 60- to 70-percent overlap. Apply the paint from the bottom of the panel to the top, which works against the air flowing through the booth. Avoid dry spray on any other parts of the car. Here, the copper ended up covering pretty well even though it was fairly translucent, thanks to the extra color "lift" that the sealer provided.

5 Here's a good example of why you want to seal the primer. Even after multiple primer coats and sanding, you may have spots of bare metal. Spraying sealer ensures that the bare metal doesn't cause a reaction during the finish coats.

6 It's always important to prep and clean the panels between coats. Each layer is another possibility for a reaction, and keeping the coats clean is the best way to avoid a problem.

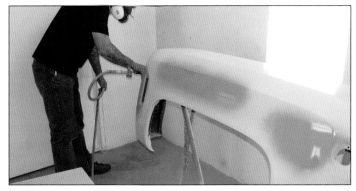

7 Apply small spots of sealer on any bare areas you notice. This gives you just a touch of extra coverage and insurance for later.

8 Inspect the panel to confirm that it is completely and evenly covered in sealer.

Mask Off Areas to Prevent Overspray

1 Proper masking is important. I recommend using a high-quality tape, such as 3M yellow masking tape. Be sure that the surface is clean and dry so that the tape adheres to it. Draw the tape from the roll and apply it under the edges of the area you want to paint. When using masking paper, apply the tape to the edge of the paper and let half the width of the tape extend from the paper and then apply it to the surface being protected. Don't forget the windows. It's always best to go overboard when it comes to masking so that you don't have to redo anything later. (Photo Courtesy Lonnie Thompson)

2 One tricky area to mask, particularly if you apply a two-tone paint job, is the rain gutters. A foam tape is easy to work with. With large components such as the tailgate or hood, use the "push/pull" method: Push the tape into the middle and pull it to the other side.

3 Masking the doorjambs isn't always easy because you can't push the tape against a surface once one side of the cab is taped. If you're patient, you can do it right, which means that there are no visible seams from the outside of the cab.

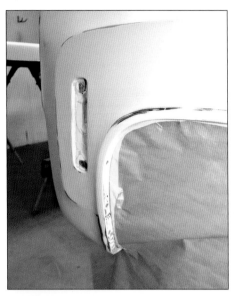

4 *Make sure that all components are properly protected from overspray, and that means taping every component thoroughly. Corner lenses, for example, are taped from behind so that no overspray blows through onto the underlying items.*

5 *If your engine bay has been painted, you mask it off for sealer as you do for primer. Be sure the engine is properly bagged or masked so that no paint slips past the barrier and ruins the engine finish or creates other problems. All of the parts will be removed later for the base coat, and then reassembled for final paint and clear.*

6 *It's important to mask from the bottom of the truck to the floor as well. As you're spraying (whether it's primer, sealer, base coat, or clear), air could kick up dust from under the truck and onto the wet substrate, ruining the finish. Taping from the floor to the bottom of the truck prevents that from happening, or at least it minimizes the risk. Don't forget to mask off details such as the VIN, labels in the doorjam, and so on. Attending to those details makes the difference between a professional-looking paint job and a rookie mistake.*

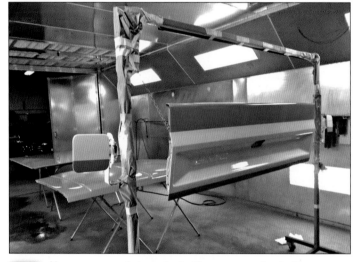

7 *If you can, paint parts in the same orientation as they appear on the truck. For example, this tailgate is hung vertically and the tonneau cover (an aftermarket accessory that covers the top of the bed) is laid flat. This ensures that the paint falls on the body the same way all around, which can help minimize tonal shifts. (Photo Courtesy Lonnie Thompson)*

8 *Your paint job, to a certain degree, is icing on a cake. However, a good paint job can't hide poor bodywork. If your bodywork has problems or flaws, fix them before applying paint. Some colors are more revealing than others. Black is one of the most difficult colors to get right. If the body of the truck isn't perfectly straight, you will see it in the reflection every time. Take your time doing the bodywork. (Photo Courtesy Derrek Ramsey)*

Painting Basics

Now that you've got all of your equipment in hand, it's time to start laying some paint. But before you do, take some extra time to make sure that everything is clean. Double-check that no tape or paper has blown off and exposed a previously masked area, and that your gun is clean. Once all of those basics are covered, you're ready to go.

Mixing the Paint

Mixing paint is actually a chemical process, and you want to make sure that you do it properly. Improper mixing could result in a choppy spray pattern, inconsistent finish, and more, so take your time and do it right.

The main thing to pay attention to is to mix the product using the manufacturer's specifications. As mentioned earlier, you should buy a system of products (such as House of Kolor clear coat, reducer, hardener, etc.) because they go together on a chemical level. If you mix brands, you risk having a chemical reaction in the process, which can show up on the paint job once you've laid it all down. Keeping it in the same system ensures

When adding reducer to the paint, follow the manufacturer's recommended ratios. That paint-to-reducer ratio varies greatly from one type of paint to another, but often it's 2:1.

that you minimize problems later.

Reducers come in different speeds: slow, medium, and fast. Whatever you choose depends on your working conditions and the paint system you choose, but the gist of it is that slower reducers are better for hotter temperatures; faster reducers are better for colder temps. The speed refers to the length of time it takes the paint to "flash off." The combination of ambient temperatures and the speed of the reducer should work out to around

Mixing cups have dozens of measurements marked around the sides, which make it easy for you to figure out how much you need. Reducers activate at different speeds, often influenced by the climate and the time of year. After you stir the paint thoroughly, place the paint gun in a holder, add a filter in its cup, and pour in the paint.

Use a stir stick to better mix the color. This particular shade is an acrylic enamel metallic, which makes it even more critical to stir it efficiently; otherwise, some areas on the finished truck could have more metallic than others. One cool trick that I learned from Troy at Bourne Customs is his method of putting paint into a mixing cup. Instead of pouring paint from the can into the cup, he uses the stir stick to "lift" the paint into the cup and then he drags the stick against the lip of the cup. It sounds kind of weird, but if it's done quickly enough, the paint is in the cup efficiently, with minimal loss of materials.

It doesn't matter how many different guns you have, you always need to clean them prior to running any paint through them. The more thoroughly you clean them, the less likely you are to have issues. That means disassembling them completely. For example, this gun was last used on a black paint job, and it was about to spray a metallic copper color. Were any of those particulates able to escape, they would ruin the finish.

Once you have disassembled your gun, one way to remove dirt or paint is to soak the parts in reducer for an hour or so. Then, wipe everything clean with a lint-free paper towel and reassemble. Next, you need to properly adjust the gun so that it's ready for the type of paint and the project. When you test spray the gun, it will probably emit a round bulls-eye pattern. You can back off the fan to its widest setting, and then turn it down until you have an elliptical pattern that provides a taper on the edges for excellent paint coverage.

You need to be meticulous when cleaning your truck's body panels. Your hands contain oils, and every time you touch a panel you leave a little bit behind. Without using a degreaser, those oils can become fish eyes or defects in the paint, which leaves you with no choice but to start over. Another reason to clean the panels with degreaser is that it gives you an opportunity to ensure that each panel is straight. The degreaser acts like a temporary clear coat, giving you a reflection that you can inspect for waves, dents, divots, or imperfections in the substrate. It's best to catch these things now before paint; otherwise, you just have to do the work over.

the same period of time if you pair the two correctly.

Prep the Paint Area

Before any paint can go down, make sure that you take your time and clean *everything* before you go into the booth.

Paint can dry and creep into every orifice possible on a paint gun; that increases the chance that it can exit the gun with your color or clear coat. Then you have dirt or worse in your finish. At best, you have to respray that panel. At worst, it could be the whole truck.

This is one reason that many painters have separate guns for different materials. For example, even though I'm nowhere near being a professional painter, I have a gun for primer, one for clear, and one for color. I know other painters who have a gun for metallics and one for solids. I have a friend who has one for single-stage and a separate one for two-or-more-stage paints.

How you spend your money on guns is up to you, but you might want to consider having a minimum of three, and keep them all as clean as possible.

Previously, you made sure that your surface was clean before you sprayed primer, sealer, or anything else. It's no different with paint; if anything, it's even more important. Because you've likely been sanding on primer, there are probably a good amount of particulates and dust in the area, and that has to be removed. Every part of the vehicle must be cleaned with degreaser and a lint-free paper towel, then run over with a tack rag and compressed air. Every cleaning detail helps.

Laying It Down

Once everything is clean, the truck is sealed or primed, the gun is prepped, and the paint is mixed, it's time to spray the color.

Techniques for spraying paint vary, but you want to keep the gun 8 inches or so away from the panel, keeping the spray pattern perpendicular to the panel itself, and "walking" the panel as you go. Typically, you overlap the previous layer by 25 to 50 percent, and you don't want to lay so wet a layer that the paint could run. Lots of things can change this process. If you're spraying a candy color, for example, you paint the entire vehicle when it's assembled; otherwise, the color looks different from panel to panel.

Always consult your local paint

Apply Paint

1 A lot of the way you hold a gun is in the wrist. Many painters hold the gun perpendicular to the panel all the way down-ward, and then "flick" it at the end to finish the pass.

2 After a few coats, you may wonder if you have enough coverage. One way to find out is to take a handheld daylight lamp and shine it over the panel(s) in question. The light puts out a color and temperature similar to the sun, which lets you see any light spots in the finish. You can then "dust in" any additional color that's necessary.

3 With a two-stage paint, once you're sure you have enough color down, it's time to mix the clear. You should be fully suited up: coveralls, hood, mask, gloves, and booties. Clear coat is notoriously sticky after it's sprayed out, and any dust or contaminants in the air inevitably find their way into the finish. You can sort that out in the wet-sanding process, but it's best not to make your job too difficult. Before applying the clear, wipe down the base coat for any contaminants. Many paint systems require two or three coats of clear coat.

4 The techniques for laying down clear are pretty similar to those for applying primer and base coat, but this coat is a bit "wetter." Some painters prefer to bury the clear on the panel even if it runs. That way they know that there's enough material to work with for wet sanding. Similar to other steps in the process, properly mix the clear with activator to the correct ratio. Remember that this step is temperature and humidity sensitive, so take that into account. Most painters apply two or three coats of clear so the paint is securely wrapped in a protective barrier. You should work against the airflow of the booth, and position the gun 6 to 8 inches from the surface. Run the gun parallel to the surface of the bodywork, starting at the bottom and moving toward the top. You should have a 60- to 75-percent overlap. Another tip: Tape up the lid on the paint gun. It doesn't happen often, but the first time you tip the gun and the lid pops off, ruining the panel you're spraying, you'll hate yourself for not taping it down to begin with. Having a lot of space to work with is great, whether you're painting a few parts or the entire truck. This allows you to minimize overspray, plus avoid bumping into things accidentally and contaminating the results.

5 Mask off everything that could be affected by overspray. In this case, the cab roof, dash, and back panel were being sprayed one color, hot rod flat black, with the floor receiving a bedliner treatment and the remainder of the cab receiving gloss black. The only thing that needs paint is visible.

6 *Painting the headliner can be tricky, particularly with a gravity-feed gun. You have to figure out the best pattern for you and your equipment, and be consistent. Be sure to cover the various surface areas of the dash and headliner. Pay close attention to be sure you provide enough coverage.*

7 *Three coats of black base paint were applied to this truck before he put down the clear coat. Each time, he'd wait until the paint "flashed off," then tack rag again, and spray.*

supply store for tips. They've worked with professionals for years, and they know what works and what doesn't. They can help you achieve the finish you want.

Wet Sanding

The process of painting a truck is arguably the easy part of the entire thing, but real artistry shows in the wet sanding.

The concept is pretty simple. No paint job ever comes out perfectly flat,

Place the freshly painted door on a sawhorse in preparation for sanding. Use a flexible sanding block wrapped in 1000-grit sandpaper that is frequently dipped in a bucket of water. As material is removed, take breaks and use a rubber block to wipe away the residue to reveal the clear and paint underneath.

and all of them have some amount of orange peel. In fact, most factory paint jobs have some kind of orange peel, but once a vehicle has been restored, the goal is typically to remove as much of it as possible.

The process is the same as during the priming and blocking phases, except with progressively finer sandpaper and using water as a lubricant. By sanding the panel flat, you eventually work the clear to a point at which it's fairly flat, and you can polish and buff the finish. When done properly, this results in the flattest, smoothest paint

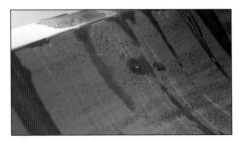

As the water dries, the high and low spots left on the clear are visible, just as with the primer and guide coat. The goal is to eliminate all of the low spots, then move to the next-finer level of sandpaper. Repeat until you're ready to polish.

job you can achieve.

Obviously, you only have so much clear to work with, and if you're using a single-stage paint, you have potentially even less to work with. There's a balance between sanding the panel flat and sanding through the clear entirely, and it takes some practice to do it correctly. Most painters lay the clear on pretty thick with the intention of working out any runs during the wet-sanding process.

When I first started building cars and trucks, this entire concept was lost on me. Why would you spend all this time sanding on a new paint job? Why can't you go straight to cutting and buffing? But then a body man explained it to me, and I understood. Every panel has a certain number of imperfections, and everything is about making sure that it's straight and can reflect a mirror image. Sanding is removing large chunks in the body-work stage to fine particles toward the end. All of those steps are what separate the best paint jobs from the mediocre jobs. It may be tedious at times, but it's important, so make sure you do it properly and take your time.

ENGINE

The engine is the heart of your Squarebody, and General Motors installed a wide range of engines in this venerable truck: the rugged ubiquitous inline-6 small-block, the powerful big-block 454, and the Detroit Diesel. Because these trucks have been around for so long, owners have used them to haul furniture, pull boats, and a lot more. This means that one of these trucks has seen a lot of miles, and maybe a new engine (or three) in the process.

Because many high-mileage trucks may not have the original engine, you cannot restore it to like-new numbers-matching condition. Is that a problem? It is in the world of GTOs and Mustangs.

However, the market for these trucks is very different than the one for muscle cars and other classics. In 1969, the keen eye might have thought twice about just slamming any old engine into a Camaro, because it was a collectible muscle car that would likely appreciate in value. But nobody thought trucks would be worth anything for decades. After all, the clothing store

Old Navy went around the world buying 1947–1955 Chevrolet trucks to use in stores as decoration, and it wasn't as if they paid $20,000 each. Trucks were more-or-less worthless for a long time, so the engine inside just didn't matter.

Things changed with the 1967–1972 Chevrolet trucks. When the value of these trucks started to increase so did the rest of the market, and now all trucks reap the benefits. But now that they've been out in the world for so many years, many of them don't have the original engine. And you know what? Nobody cares. I haven't met a single truck enthusiast who has bragged to me about his or her "numbers-matching truck restoration." No, they go on and on about their new 350 or 454 swap, or their plans for an LSX, but never have they bragged about the numbers matching.

To further prove the point, most owners make sure that the truck has at least a 350; a 305 would be almost a shame on their name. And a V-6? Never. Throw it in the garbage. Not worth their time. So yes, you can build a numbers-matching truck if you want, but don't stress out if your project doesn't meet the

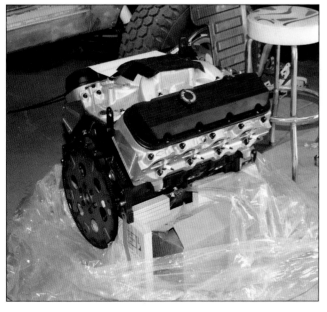

Many trucks do not have the original engine block or transmission because many of these workhorse engines have been yanked and replaced. In these cases, you cannot perform a numbers-matching restoration. If you do have the original engine, you can restore or store it. If you store it, you can swap in a new LS or Gen I crate engine.

Crate Engine Option

Depending on where you buy it, a crate engine can be more expensive. But a crate engine means that you now have a known variable in your truck, instead of hoping that the current engine is going to always work. Some include a warranty, which you also might buy from a quality engine rebuilding shop, but usually only if they do the whole rebuilding job. Plus, with a crate engine, there are usually horsepower advantages, you can find parts more easily (depending on the original engine, of course), and it may just cause you less stress overall. If you want authentic, there's nowhere better to start than your local Chevy dealer.

Period-Correct Crate

Another option is to buy a crate engine that's period correct. If your truck came with a 305, you can buy a 305 from a speed shop for less than $2,000 and then install upgraded heads, cam, intake, and so on. You can also buy an engine and make it look period correct by applying patina, using original components, or mixing and adding dress-up items. That way, it's more reliable but has the same flair as it did stock.

A good friend of mine has built quite a few Squarebodies in his day. The first thing he does when he buys any project is to visit his local Chevrolet dealer (they know him by name) to buy a new 350-ci crate engine. Then he tops it with his favorite intake manifold and carburetor, mates it to a new 700R4, and drops the whole thing into his truck. Every truck he builds, and he builds at least two a year, has the same engine and transmission as the previous. That means he always knows how they're going to install, how they function, and where

they don't perform as well. You might want to consider going a similar route on your project.

Chevrolet LS Series

If you're not hooked on a period-correct engine, let me propose another option. Look at the newer line of Chevrolet truck engines: the LS series.

The LS line of engines can be found in many vehicles, from the 1999–2006 Silverado to the Camaro and so on. Hundreds of performance parts are available for each engine. You can buy a 5.3 V-8 if you want, or keep it low profile with an LS3 that pushes 430 hp. The complete LS lineup can be purchased directly from General Motors, so you know they're factory fresh.

If you don't want to drop that much cash on a new LS engine, that's truly where your world opens up. For less than $2,000, Summit, Auto Zone, and other companies offer 4.8 and 5.3 engines, complete with transmission, computer, water pump, accessories, and wiring harness. They come with a limited warranty, you know exactly how many miles they have, and because they come with a transmission, you can check another thing off your list. This gives you the reliability of a newer Silverado truck, but you can customize it with components from other vehicles as well. Plus, you know, reliability in a 25-year-old truck is something to be proud of.

You have to adapt the engine to the chassis, transfer case, and electrical system. Fortunately, many companies make vehicle-specific wiring kits. Painless Performance and Ron Francis have a wide variety of harnesses that you can work with, and Brothers Trucks has the harnesses for

The LS3 is not an inexpensive engine, but it is one of most powerful and popular crate engines on the market. It's considered relatively bulletproof, meaning that it's very reliable under all sorts of conditions. And because they're so popular, the aftermarket offers replacement and performance parts to customize them to your unique specifications.

Don't think that this engine is so modern that it won't look correct in your square. Companies, such as Delmo's Speed in Prescott, Arizona, make kits to give an LS3 engine the look of an original small-block V-8. Some companies sell carburetor conversions and kits that relocate the original throttle body. Going this route, you end up with a truck with all of the reliability of a modern Chevy truck but with the look of a 1973–1987.

everything from the headlights to the taillights. An engine that complex certainly takes more time to wire, plumb, and diagnose, but that might be worth the extra effort for what you gain. It's a compelling choice.

There is another bonus to doing an LS engine, and that's gas mileage. Even the most finely tuned 350-ci engine barely peaks in the 10-mpg range, whereas you can put LS engines into the 20s, easily.

Many Choices

There are other engines besides the LS that can work, too. The LT1 and LT4s found in 1992–1997 Buick Roadmasters, Camaros, Firebirds, Corvettes, Impalas, and Caprices are popular options. You can find wiring kits for these as well.

Edelbrock offers several crate engines that are either carbureted or fuel injected. Or, if you have a straight-six or

a small-block, you could upgrade to a big-block V-8 and crank that knob up to 11. There are lots and lots of options to choose from.

The point of this discussion is not to veer you toward one engine lineup or another. Instead, it's to make you think long and hard about the options you have for building your truck today. Rebuilding an engine takes a lot of time and money, but so does purchasing a crate. In the end, it's more or less a wash.

You have to decide how often you are going to be driving the truck, and what you expect from it as a result. If you want reliable, you may want to look at newer engines. But if you want that original 1970s to early 1980s feeling, you have to go carbureted; there's just no alternative.

This is one of the more important decisions that you can make in this process, so take your time to do it right. ∎

requirements. You can decode the VIN and determine the original engine type and model. And then you can buy a crate engine or salvage-yard engine of the same type and vintage as the original. Although it is not numbers matching, it provides the same appearance and driving experience as one from the factory.

Again, many owners are not going to perform a strict original engine/transmission restoration, but rather, they go for an *original appearance* restoration. These owners often buy a Chevy Gen I crate engine or another original-equipment engine from a remanufacturer. To take it one step further, you can also buy an LS crate engine.

If your truck has the original engine, you can simply restore it to original condition. But be prepared to dedicate the time, money, and resources required. A complete engine rebuild demands extreme attention to all aspects of engine building, precision measurement, and closely fol-

lowing accepted rebuilding practices. A short-block rebuild requires far less time and money than a complete long-block rebuild.

In this chapter, I cover the assembly procedure after the parts have been returned from the machine shop. When it comes to engine rebuilding, enthusiast engine builders usually do not have a machine shop in the garage. Therefore, the at-home rebuilder disassembles, measures, and delivers crank, heads, block, and other components to a machine shop for machining. After the machining has been completed, the enthusiast puts all the pieces together.

I'm just going to highlight the rebuilding process; if you want to tackle an engine build on your own and want more in-depth information, I recommend *How to Rebuild the Small-Block Chevrolet* by Larry Shreib and Larry Atherton. It provides comprehensive instructions for performing a complete rebuild. Tony Huntimer's *How to Rebuild the*

Big-Block Chevrolet also provides thorough and detailed coverage of the disassembly, inspection, measurement, parts selection, and assembly of an engine.

If you don't feel comfortable performing an engine rebuild yourself, find an engine shop that can perform the entire job. Cost will obviously be a factor, but you want to consider a few other things as well. For example, does the shop offer a warranty on the rebuilt engine? Will they rebuild it to factory specifications? How turnkey will it be? Will you still need to install the heads, intake manifold, and carburetor? Will the block be tested and run on a dyno before you get it back?

Analysis of Work Required

If you rebuild your existing engine (assuming that it is the engine that came with the truck), you could have a period-correct numbers-matching vehicle that's been restored flawlessly. If your truck came with a non-running engine, you have no idea what kind of sur-prises may lie in store when you tear it apart. You need to disassemble it, inspect it, and identify the problems that led to its failure. Some prob-lems may be terminal and require the purchase of new components. If you have a crack in the block, for example, you may have to purchase a new block. If the engine is running, do a compression test along with a thorough test of the engine. If com-pression is somewhat down, you can rebuild the top end and install new heads, a cam, and a rebuilt carb for improved performance.

If you decide to go through the engine rebuild process, and do so correctly and completely, the engine should run for years and be as reli-able as they get. But just know that this job on a small-block engine typically costs between $1,000 and $3,000. The same job on a big-block costs between $2,000 and $4,000. A complete small-block engine rebuild includes disassembly, inspec-tion, measurement, machining, pre-assembly fitment, and final assembly. You can disassemble the engine, buy parts, coordinate machining with a machine shop, and assemble it in your garage. Typically, a complete engine rebuild involves new pistons, rings, connecting rods, lifters, pushrods, and rocker arms. It also includes block line honing and decking, crankshaft truing, and sev-eral other procedures.

On the other hand, if you choose to simply do a minor tune-up, your investment in time and money will be much less.

Engine Removal

You have a couple of options when it comes to pulling the original

Placing this crate 454 back into the frame was easy with a hoist. You usually want to mate the transmis-sion with the engine first, but in this case the shop did a test fit to ensure that everything fit correctly. Although these aren't cheap, the reliability of a new engine rather than rehabbing your old one is pretty nice, and it is certainly less time intensive. Any new crate engine comes with break-in instructions, as well as other tips for making it run properly. This was installed in a C20 chassis, and the brackets were for a C10. Unfortunately, it took a lot of digging around and junkyard calls because people going to junkyards (or the yard owners themselves) unbolt the engine from the frame via the engine brackets because it's easier and quicker. Another common reason is that it's a part that breaks often enough that restorers remove them for their own projects. Either way, it's not a difficult fix, they are just hard to find.

C10 versus C20/30 Motor Mount Brackets

Two brackets that sit diagonally between the top of the frame and the front cross-member hold the motor mounts in place. These are cracked, ripped, or broken because of the torque of the engine, age, or just general deterioration, so the thought is that it's best to just toss out the old part because it should be easy to replace. Well, it is, but only if you know what you're looking for.

As it turns out, these brackets came in two different sizes: one for C10 mod-els and one for C20/30s. Because the C10 has a taller frame than the C20, that bracket is about 1 inch longer. The C20/30 frame (also known as the 3/4- and 1-ton models) has a *shorter* frame, which means that C10 brackets don't fit.

drivetrain from the frame. If you've already removed everything else around the engine, such as cab, fend-ers, core support, etc., pulling the engine is pretty easy. You just mount an engine hoist to the block and lift it out.

But you may not be fortunate enough to do that on your project, for one reason or another. If that's the case, you have other options to

tackle it correctly.

Engine Installation

The easiest way to reinstall the engine is to have a bare chassis. This way, you have 360-degree access to the mounting hardware, and you can see any potential obstructions to the frame without having to peer around sheet metal.

Rebuilding Basics

Once the engine is out of the truck, you can start the rebuilding process. Before you begin, make sure that you have clear access to all of your tools, the work area is clean, and you have lots of space for engine parts once they're off the block. An organized workspace is an efficient one, and you don't have to buy things twice because you lost something.

Disassembly and Machining

1 Put the engine on an engine stand. This is by far the easiest way to work on your engine because balancing the block in an old tire may get the job done, but with an engine stand you can apply the torque you need to the bolts without worrying about a 350 dropping on your foot. (Photo Courtesy Todd Ryden)

2 The first component off the block should be the starter. It's located on the passenger-side of the block, near the oil pan. Unbolting it is a straightforward process. If you see a shim or two between the starter and the block, keep them. You may need them again when putting everything back together. (Photo Courtesy Todd Ryden)

3 Remove the water pump next. This might be a tricky process because of the gaskets and sealants used to keep it leak-free. You may need to use some lubricating fluid on the bolts and a pry bar to pop it off the block. Just make sure that you don't apply leverage to the timing chain cover; that could cause some serious damage. (Photo Courtesy Todd Ryden)

4 After you've removed the rocker arms and pushrods using a ratchet and socket, unbolt the cylinder heads from the block with a 1/2-inch breaker bar and a 5/8-inch socket. If you're planning on reusing the original fasteners, keep them well organized and sorted so that you know which one goes where when putting things back together. (Photo Courtesy Todd Ryden)

5 *Keep everything organized, particularly your rockers and pushrods. They can wear specific to the cylinder, so you don't want to put them in the wrong position. (Photo Courtesy Todd Ryden)*

6 *Pull the lifters out of the block using a hooked probe. Make sure that you keep these organized and sorted by location as well; if you don't, you will destroy your original cam. If you're planning on replacing them anyway, sorting doesn't apply. (Photo Courtesy Todd Ryden)*

7 *Remove the 3/8-inch bolts from the crank pulley and put it aside. Then, using a three-bolt puller, remove the vibration dampener from the crankshaft, using a wooden handle between the crank and the block to keep it still. Once you've unbolted the timing chain cover bolts (they're 1/4-inch) and removed the timing chain cover, take the crank key out of the crankshaft with a non-tampering 5/16-inch drift punch. When about two-thirds of it is visible, pull it out with pliers. Remove the lower sprocket with a little pull or, if it's stuck, use a gear puller. Once the chain is off, use the cam sprocket as a handle to pull the cam out of the block. Be careful. You want to rotate and twist the cam on its way out so that it doesn't strike the bearings. (Photo Courtesy Todd Ryden)*

8 *Flip the engine over on the stand, making sure that everything is clear underneath so that any excess oil, fluids, or bolts aren't spilled and scattered across the room. Unbolt the oil pump and oil filter adapter with a ratchet. If you have one handy, use a crankshaft socket on a 1/2-inch ratchet to turn the crank as necessary. Number the rod and main caps using a set of steel number stamps. These components are not interchangeable and incorrect reassembly could cause your engine to fail. Rotate the crankshaft with the ratchet so that the piston to be removed is at bottom dead center (BDC), meaning that the piston is at the bottom end of its stroke. Loosen the connecting rod nuts with a breaker bar or long ratchet but don't take them off all the way. Protect the rod bolts using rubber hoses slid over the threads or special rod-bolt covers. Then remove the bolts. Using either a rod-removal tool or a 2-foot-long wooden dowel, tap the pistons out of the block, making sure that you keep the rod centered in the bore so that it doesn't damage the block. Once the piston is out, reinstall the rod caps and nuts so that you know which one goes where. Wash, rinse, and repeat until all of the cylinders are out of the block. (Photo Courtesy Todd Ryden)*

9 *Grasp the crankshaft by the ends and lift it straight up, occasionally twisting side to side. Take notice of the bearing shells: Some may stay attached to the crankshaft. Make sure that you don't let them drop or be pushed out of sequence. As with other engine components, you want to keep each bearing with its own cap; if they become separated you may have major issues later. (Photo Courtesy Todd Ryden)*

10 *Disassemble the heads with a valvespring compressor. (If you don't have one, get a shop to do the work.) Place the valvespring compressor over the valve you want to remove, and tighten it down to compress the spring. Take the locks off the valves using a magnetic tool or a probe, and then loosen the valvespring compressor to release tension on the assembly. Repeat for the remaining valves on each of the heads. (Photo Courtesy Todd Ryden)*

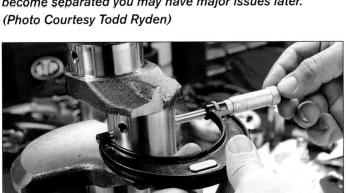

11 *With the engine completely disassembled, it's time to check the condition of each part. For the crankshaft, for example, you want to use a micrometer on the journal diameters to ensure that they're not more than .030 inch undersized. Also look for discoloration, make sure the keyways are perfect, and that the crank shaft surface is smooth. You will be doing similar processes with your cam, valves, and other components. (Photo Courtesy Todd Ryden)*

12 *Chances are you don't have the tooling available to perform align boring, so this is where a professional shop comes in handy. Align boring makes sure that the main bore alignment is perfect to give you a parallel crankshaft centerline, in case things were wonky on the block before. This is only one part of the machining process. (Photo Courtesy Todd Ryden)*

13 *Once all of the machine work is done and the cylinder heads are back on the block, check the fit of the intake manifold by loosely bolting it in place without the gaskets. Make sure that the manifold and heads fit perfectly and that the two edges are parallel; if they aren't, the machine shop may not have done the job correctly. Install the gasket and loosely place bolts in each corner. They should fit without any restrictions. Using a gapping tool, make sure there's between .060- and .120-inch clearance; if not, you may have to revisit the machine shop. (Photo Courtesy Todd Ryden)*

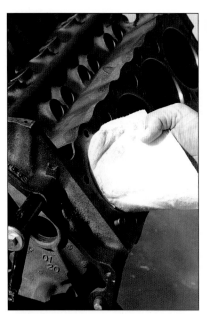

14 *Now that the machine work is done, you must thoroughly clean all components. To do this, put a light oil (ATF, WD-40, etc.) on a paper towel and scrub the cylinder bores aggressively. Switch out the towels with fresh ones on a regular basis, adding new oil as you go along. Continue cleaning each cylinder until the towels no longer show any dirt. Repeat on each cylinder. This process cleans out the cylinders and pushes lubricant into the cylinder walls. It helps with lubricating the rings when they are first installed and can reduce surface rust. (Photo Courtesy Todd Ryden)*

Engine Block Colors

From 1973–1976, Chevrolet used the same GM Orange on the V-8 engine blocks that was used in previous years. After that, GM Corporate Blue replaced the traditional orange. Now you'd think that would be that, but in 1982, General Motors went to a high-gloss black for its engines. So that's it, right?

Turns out, not so much. Some people claim that Chevrolet always used GM Corporate Blue on its 305 engines, making them easily discernible from the 350s. General Motors also used a red on some engines until 1979. So, there are quite a few options, as it turns out, for painting your engine block.

Point is, if you're looking to be absolutely period correct, be sure that your engine is the correct color. GM Orange (which is a very red/orange color) is a popular favorite, but you should stick with GM Corporate Blue if you own a 1977–1982. Anything later, go with high-gloss black, and anything earlier, use GM Orange.

Reassembly

1 *Before you finish putting everything together, check the critical clearances. You've likely just had a ton of (potentially expensive) machine work done, and there's no reason to waste that money by rushing through the final assembly. Take your time to make sure all of the clearances are where they need to be. (Photo Courtesy Todd Ryden)*

2 *As part of the final assembly process, check valve-guide clearance. To do this, you use hole gauges and micrometers to ensure that everything is done correctly. You also want to make sure that any parts that the machine shop worked on are labeled and organized thoroughly, so that you can put everything back together correctly. (Photo Courtesy Todd Ryden)*

3 Ensuring that the crankshaft is straight is crucial to several other steps, so you want to make sure that you get this part right. Once the front and rear main bearings are installed and lubricated, place the crankshaft into the block, being careful not to damage it. Place a dial indicator so that it reads off the center main. Spin the crank and watch the gauge on the dial indicator. It should indicate no more than .003-inch runout on a street engine. Use the dial indicator in the same fashion on the front sprocket and rear seal surfaces, where you're looking for no more than .002-inch runout. (Photo Courtesy Todd Ryden)

4 One method for checking the main bearing clearance is with Plastigauge. To begin, place the bearing shells in their respective locations, but do not put any lubricant on them or the crankshaft. Place the crankshaft onto the bearings, making sure not to spin it in any way. Put a strip of Plastigauge carefully on the center of a crankshaft journal. Bolt on and torque down the caps to their required specs. Then unbolt the caps and measure the Plastigauge strip as shown. The width shown on the chart corresponds to the clearance. This is an accurate way to get rod-bearing clearance readings. (Photo Courtesy Todd Ryden)

5 Checking the piston ring end gaps is a straightforward process. If the rings were previously machined by the machine shop, they should be labeled so that you know which ring goes in which cylinder. If you purchased rings from an aftermarket supplier, the ring gaps are built in. Regardless of your situation, you should always check the gaps to ensure they're correct before you install them on the pistons. To do that, put the ring into its cylinder and make sure that each ring is the same distance from the deck. Use a feeler gauge to check the gap, which should be within the manufacturer's specifications. If not, you need a replacement ring. (Photo Courtesy Todd Ryden)

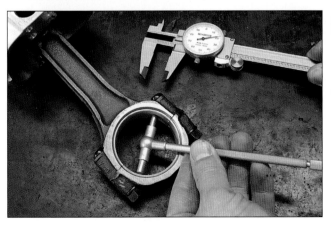

6 Another critical step in the process is measuring rod bearing clearance. To do this, you use either a micrometer or Plastigauge. Put the bearings in the rod dry, then tighten down the rod ends by placing them in a bench vise with soft jaws. Using an outside micrometer, determine the diameter of one rod journal. Then, measure the rod bearing diameter on another matching rod. To find out the bearing clearance, subtract the rod journal diameter from the rod bearing inner diameter. Do this on all of the rods in the engine. (Photo Courtesy Todd Ryden)

7 Locate top dead center (TDC) using a degree wheel and a piston-stop tool. Install the bearings for the No. 1 and No. 2 piston rods, making sure to use assembly lube on the bearings and front crank journal. Once you've lubed the piston skirts and cylinder bores using engine oil, put the protectors over the rod bolts (or use rubber tubing, as mentioned previously). Install both the No. 1 and No. 2 pistons without the piston rings. Once they're in place, and you have the caps torqued down, rotate the crank very carefully. Check the clearances with feeler gauges as well. (Photo Courtesy Todd Ryden)

8 Before assembling the cylinder head, lubricate the valve guides using assembly lube, making sure that all of the surfaces are thoroughly covered. Do this by moving the guides in and out of the head. (Photo Courtesy Todd Ryden)

9 To install the rear main cap, you should also use assembly lube on the bearing. Once you're sure that all surfaces are clean, place the cap on the block and, using a smoothed-face hammer, tap down the cap so that it sits correctly inside the block registers. Once you've lubricated the threads on the fasteners using thread assembly lube, make sure that everything is seated correctly, and then tighten the bolts by hand. Tap the back of the crankshaft two or three times using the same smoothed-face hammer to ensure that the thrust bearing is seated correctly on the block. (Photo Courtesy Todd Ryden)

10 With the rod in the piston, slide the piston into the bore. Remember those marks you wrote down during a previous step? Refer to them now to ensure that you have the correct piston installed in the right place and with the correct orientation. Using a piston ring compressor seated against the piston, tap the top of the piston using a wooden dowel, or the bottom of your hammer (assuming that it's also made of wood). Don't force it. (Photo Courtesy Todd Ryden)

11 Before installing the camshaft, apply assembly lube to all of the journals, making sure that every surface is lubricated. With the upper sprocket bolted to the camshaft, guide it into the block, making sure to keep it centered. Be sure to keep twisting it as you go, and don't try to force it in or you may damage something in the process. (Photo Courtesy Todd Ryden)

12 Installing the vibration dampener can be tricky, particularly if you don't have the right tool. Use a vibration dampener installation tool to insert it correctly. Make sure you use lubrication on the installation tool's threads, then work that lube through the crankshaft by threading it in place by hand. Apply assembly lube on the oil seal surface of the dampener. Place the vibration dampener on the end of the crankshaft, then carefully slide the roller bearing and thrust washer so that it sits against the dampener. Next, using a pair of wrenches, tighten the nut on the vibration dampener installation tool. Once the dampener is installed all the way, you're done. (Photo Courtesy Todd Ryden)

13 When you install the rocker arms, use assembly lube on the pushrod cup and valvetip contact points. Also, make sure that the valves, rocker arms, and pushrods are the same ones for the same cylinder as they were before. That way everything sits correctly. (Photo Courtesy Todd Ryden)

14 The fuel pump is located in the front passenger's side of the block, and installing it is quick and simple. Put some silicone sealant around the gasket on both sides, and then place the fuel pump onto the block. Tighten the two bolts in place using 30 ft-lbs of torque. That's it. (Photo Courtesy Todd Ryden)

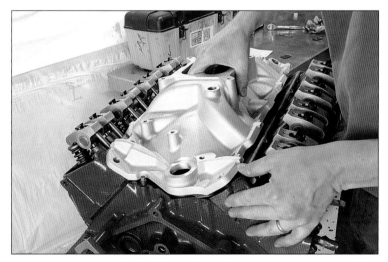

15 One of the final pieces of this puzzle is the intake manifold. The preferred method of installation is to put a 1/4-inch bead of silicone adhesive around the perimeter of the gasket rail. Also place a thin strip around the water passage holes (the ones located at the ends of the heads) and smooth it out so the remaining adhesive creates a thin skin. Place the head gasket in place, and then carefully lower the intake manifold onto the engine block, making sure that it is aligned correctly. Loosely place four bolts in the four corners of the manifold to ensure that a gasket doesn't slip out of place, and then install the bolts using the torque-sequence drawing that came with the intake manifold. (Photo Courtesy Todd Ryden)

TRANSMISSION

Rebuilding a transmission may not be for the beginner. It's a complex process that involves many moving parts, and it can be quite frustrating if you've never done it before. But don't let that stop you.

Yes, it's daunting, and yes, you could screw something up if it goes wrong. But you could do the same to an engine, right? And because you worked through that process with no problem, you will be able to do this.

If you have serious reservations, you can take the transmission to a qualified transmission rebuild shop in your area. If you go for it, get ready to have some fun.

Transmission Types

The 1973–1987 Chevrolet trucks had several transmission options. As a broad generalization, most V-6 trucks came with manual transmissions, and most small-block V-8s came with the TH350, also known as the Turbo 350. The TI1400 was more commonly found in big-block V-8s and 3/4- or 1-ton trucks.

There will always be debates about the best transmission for your application, and between the Turbo 350 and Turbo 400, it's pretty close. The 350 is a bit lighter and (according to some) has a stronger first gear, but the 400 is quite reliable and was built to sit behind a big-block engine. If you're building your truck according to factory specs, your choice is simple: Go with what the factory used. If not, it's all up to you.

Use a pressure washer for cleaning the transmission. It saves you a lot of time because you usually find loads of grease and gunk. This makes things go much more smoothly in the end. (Photo Courtesy Cliff Ruggles)

Available Transmissions: 1973–1987		
RPO Code	Years Available	Transmission Type
ZW4	1973–1980	3-speed Manual
M15	1981–1984	3-speed Manual
CH465	1973–1987	4-speed Manual
TH350	1973–1981	3-speed Automatic
TH400	1977–1987	3-speed Automatic
TH700R4	1982–1987	4-speed Automatic

Although you see a few specialty tools in this set, most are the same ones you use for the rest of your restoration. To the left of the flexible 1/2-inch ratchet and to the right of the large hose clamp is a funky-looking tool that looks like it was homemade. Well, it was. It functions as a spring compressor for the snap ring inside the case. If you don't have your own spring compressor, you can make something similar out of a 3/8-inch bolt and some flat steel stock. (Photo Courtesy Cliff Ruggles)

Turbo 350

Because these transmissions were used across the GM lineup, you might find them on everything from a GMC truck to a Buick. A Turbo 350 on a Pontiac is different from the rest, however. To figure out which is which, look at the top of the bellhousing. The traditional TH350 has a peak, like a mountain. One from a Pontiac dips and forms a valley. Otherwise, the two transmissions are identical.

Then there's the 700R4. It's a 4-speed automatic, so it kicks an extra gear into the mix, which can improve fuel economy. It was also standard in the later years and was quite popular across the GM lineup for years. If you like the 700R4 but can't find one under a truck, you can use one from an Astro van. The 4.3 V-6 also ran a 700R4 transmission, and they're common in some S10s and most Astro vans.

Of course, if you're looking for additional features, the 4L60E and 4L80E transmissions are also options.

They require more work to integrate into your system, but if you're doing an LS swap, this is the way to go.

Because the TH350 is one of the more common models around, particularly with this body style of truck, I'm going to cover rebuilding this transmission. Chances are good that it's already in your truck, and if it isn't, it might be what you want to install.

Be aware that this is an overview of the transmission rebuild process. There are other books dedicated to the rebuilding process (including

GM Turbo 350 Transmissions: How to Rebuild and Modify by Cliff Ruggles, who was immensely helpful with this chapter; I couldn't have done it without him). If you need more detail than is provided here, I suggest you also buy or borrow an entire book dedicated to that transmission.

Tools and Equipment

Taking apart a transmission is not easy, but again, it is doable. Fortunately, it doesn't take many specialized tools. If you don't have some of the ones I mention, your local auto parts store may rent them (both O'Reilly and Auto Zone have loaner tool programs). Also, many of them are affordable enough to buy. After all, you're saving a ton of money by doing the project yourself, so a few bucks spent on tools isn't the end of the world.

Workspaces

Let's start with the obvious: you need a clean place to work. An automatic transmission has many moving parts, and dirt and grime will trash them. Point is, you want to be sure that the place where you're working on the transmission is free of dirt and grime.

That work space should be fairly large and easy to clean up. You want to be able to lay out all of your equipment and parts in one area so they don't get lost in the process. A bench vice is handy, particularly if you have some of those soft-jaw attachments for the ends.

If you plan on doing multiple transmissions, or you just want to make the job go a bit easier, consider a dedicated transmission holding fixture. These fixtures have two parts: a sleeve that bolts to a workbench, and a scythe-like fixture with adjustable screws that slides into the sleeve. You can find them for around $140 by Trans-Tool online, and eBay also has a few options by Texas Auto Tools for around $125. If you want the job to go a bit easier, consider purchasing something like that.

Safety Gear

Working on a transmission means working with heavy parts all slicked up with ATF, and that can be an accident in the making. By using some additional, specific safety equipment, you should save yourself a (literal) headache in the end.

Eye protection is a must. At various stages in the process you will be using compressed air, and if you blast a piece of dirt or fluid in your direction, you will be glad that you are wearing safety glasses. Better yet, a face shield keeps you protected in those scenarios. As I like to joke whenever I put mine on, "I have to protect my moneymaker."

Hearing protection is also key. There will be a lot of loud noises, so make sure that you have either some disposable ear plugs or muffs handy.

A transmission is filled with ATF, and to clean it off you use solvents, so having gloves is critical. You need two kinds: chemical-resistant and Nitrile. The chemical-resistant ones are usually thicker and they extend past your wrist.

Cleaning Equipment and Products

If your transmission looks anything like mine did originally, you need some heavy-duty products to clean it. The basics are wire brushes of varying levels of hardness (you don't want to dig into the aluminum), plus a few scrapers. You don't have to buy a power washer, but if you already did for the rest of the job, it will be good to use here. You can use it initially to remove dirt attached to an engine once the case is empty. You don't want to blow dirt into crevices, only out.

You also want some solvents, such as brake cleaners and degreasers. Depending on how gnarly your transmission is, the cleaning process may be intense to get it back to new(ish) condition.

Hand Tools

For this part of the restoration, you need a full set of metric and standard sockets in varying sizes, plus ratchets and extensions. You need 1/4-, 3/8-, and 1/2-inch-drive versions of everything, and the matching torque wrenches as well.

Wrenches of varying sizes are also good to have on hand, particularly if they're ratcheting versions, as they help the job go quicker. You also need line, flare-nut, and tubing wrenches for specialty scenarios.

And then there's somewhat of an oddball that you might have in your collection already: a spin-handle wrench. There are lots of tight spaces to work within on a transmission, and having one of these on the job can speed things up. And because they're manual, it's much more difficult to strip out a thread when using them to tighten something.

Air Tools

One important item to have on hand is a long-tipped blow gun. You will be using one of these a lot during the build, so make sure you have one before you start turning wrenches. You want to have an air ratchet and an impact wrench on hand as well, but they are used for the removal process only. Remember, a lot of parts on the transmission are aluminum, and jamming them forward with an impact is a recipe for disaster. A 1/4-inch angle grinder with sanding discs helps to remove old gaskets and stubborn dirt. You want to use softer ones that don't bite into the aluminum; they are available from major manufacturers such as 3M.

Snap-Ring Pliers

If you're like me, you probably have one pair of snap-ring pliers that doesn't get a lot of use. That's going to change.

You need a wide variety of snap-ring pliers for this job, in both large and small sizes. There are lots of snap-rings in the case. Also, if you can get your hands on reversible snap-ring pliers, it will help with both installing and removing the various rings.

Screwdrivers and Picks

You want both flathead and Phillips-head screwdrivers, but probably not for the reasons you're thinking. The flatheads can be used on some of the larger snap rings found on the inside of the case. The Phillips-head style can help align the pump with the case when you're putting everything back together.

There are a lot of rubber seals that you are working with, so keep a pick and hook set around. Same with an awl, as it can be used as an alignment tool as well.

Calipers and Micrometers

During the process of putting together the transmission, you must measure the thickness of the steel and friction plates. For that, you need good calipers. Don't cheap out here; buy the good stuff. You also want a dial indicator, ball micrometer, and feeler gauge. There's a lot of measuring involved in rebuilding a transmission, so be sure to have these items on hand.

Spring Compressors

Now you might think that I'm talking about the kind of spring compressors that you use on the front suspension, but I'm not. No, I'm talking about the kind that you use to remove spring cages and rebuild clutch drums. If you don't have one, you could make one.

But unless you've done that before, I recommend that you buy one. Summit Racing and O'Reilly, for example, sell them. They're not all cheap, but they are worth it.

Bins and Trays

There are a lot of small parts involved in this process, and you need a place to put them all. That's why you want lots of tiny bins on hand, including baking trays.

No seriously, baking trays. The larger commercial ones are great for holding larger transmission parts while they're being removed.

Also, you want some 1-gallon plastic tubs. When you reassemble the transmission, you soak the frictions and bands in ATF for at least 15 minutes prior to installation. A small plastic tub holds everything well, and you can save it for later use, too.

Bushing Tools

An automatic transmission has a ton of bushings, and that means you need tools to take those bushings out and put them back in. That means you want bushing removers and bushing installers.

Bolt Extractors and Threaded Inserts

In my shop, I find that bolts have a tendency to break, particularly if they're old. And because of that, I have a lot of taps and dies around, as I never know when I'm going to need them. With taps come

bolt extractors, and, in the case of mixed-metal jobs, threaded inserts or Heli-Coils are needed, too.

Your transmission is most likely made of aluminum. Some of the components that bolt to it are made of steel, including the bolts that connect the two. When you work with dissimilar metals such as these, sometimes you can strip the threads out of the weaker one, leaving you with no way to fix it.

Now trust me when I say that most of the time you can't solve these problems with a tap. I've tried many, many times, and it just never works quite right. Instead, I suggest installing a Heli-Coil and using other threaded inserts. You should be able to solve any stripped bolt problem you come across.

But what if the problem is that the bolt broke on the way out? In that case, you need bolt extractors. Having a pair on hand is good no matter where on the truck you're working, but they are especially useful here. The bolts on your transmission may be old, rusted, or just worn out from overuse, and so when they're called upon to break free, they may call it quits. When they do, you're usually left with the stub of a bolt and nothing to grab onto. Bolt extractors thread into the center of the bolt, grabbing on and pulling them out. I recommend having these in your toolbox even if you weren't working on a truck. They're just that handy.

Files and Other Small Tools

A good set of small files is great to have, particularly jeweler's files. They fit into small spots, and they can work out small imperfections found along the way. Punches and chisels fall into the same category, so pick up a wide variety of sizes, from small to large.

Tools for Lip Seals

The pistons and servos in the transmission use seals to keep the fluid and pressure in its place. Reinstalling those seals isn't always fun, as there are multiple versions. For that, you need some specialty equipment.

Removing seals, on the other hand, is pretty straightforward. Get yourself a good razor blade, preferably one with a long handle for safety, and cut the seals off. No big deal.

Oil Pump Band

The oil pump in your transmission comes apart in two pieces. You pull those pieces apart to access and rebuild the components inside, but putting them back together requires clamping them together. For that, you need a pipe clamp. A large one, or multiple small ones, work well, so keep a few around during the transmission build.

Miscellaneous and Special Tools

There's a bunch of other stuff that you should have on hand just in case. A slide hammer is one, and you might have it nearby because of the bodywork. You need two of them to take the oil pump out of the transmission case. Pick up a spare if you don't have one already.

You will be lining up multiple pieces with 5/16-inch alignment studs, so pick up some of them, too. Alternatively, you can cut the heads off some 5/16-inch bolts and use those.

Know what else comes in handy for disassembly? A magnet or one of those magnet-tipped extension tools for grabbing metallic objects from a distance.

Specialty tools can be expensive. Fortunately, you can use some homemade options instead.

For example, you can use large channel locks for removing valve

If you want to avoid a mess in your shop, drain the transmission pan first. Place a drain pan under the transmission to catch any fluids. Check the transmission pan to see if it has a drain plug. If it does, unbolt it and let the fluid drain out. If it doesn't, unbolt the entire pan and let it tip backward to pour into the drain pan. (Photo Courtesy Cliff Ruggles)

body accumulators, and then use needle-nose pliers to take out the retaining clips. If you don't have channel locks, a C-clamp can work; you just might have to modify it slightly to work best.

Removing the Transmission

Because you're doing a full restoration, I'm going to proceed on a few assumptions. First, that your engine and transmission are either out of the truck, or are easily accessible. At this point in the rebuild, you should have either the cab off or the engine out, which means that

the transmission has likely come out with it.

What that also means is that you're not starting the rebuild before any of that happens. You aren't pulling the transmission out solo, it's coming with its friends. If that's not the case, be aware that taking out the transmission by itself means supporting the engine so that it doesn't tilt backward on its way out.

Start with the Driveshaft

With the truck secured on jack stands and unable to roll, one of the first things to do is to remove the driveshaft.

If you have a standard-cab truck, taking the driveshaft out the rest of the way is easy. Place a pan under the back half of the transmission to catch any fluids, and pull the driveshaft straight out.

If you have a crew cab, you have one additional step: Unbolt the carrier bearing from the crossmember, and then pull the assembly toward and under the rear end.

Separate the Engine from the Transmission

With the engine and transmission out of the truck and on the ground, you need to separate the two so that you can proceed.

Remove the inspection cover from the transmission if one is present. It's located at the front of the transmission (the rear of the engine) and is usually bolted in place. Depending on the type of truck, it may not have an inspection cover. In fact, my latest project didn't have one, and neither did the one before it. If that's the case, congrats, you just saved yourself a step.

Separating the torque converter from the flywheel is fairly straightforward. Use a wrench to unbolt the two. Next, you have to rotate the engine to gain access to the next bolt. You can do that either by using a pry bar to turn the flywheel or having a helper turn the crank with a ratchet and socket. Dealer's choice. (Photo Courtesy Cliff Ruggles)

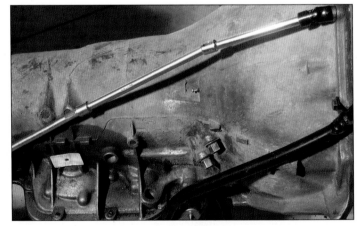

If the transmission came out of the truck with the engine, you don't need many extensions to separate the two. If they are still together, it may be difficult to access the upper bolts. Either way, unbolting them is the next step. The transmission is then free from the engine and you can proceed. (Photo Courtesy Cliff Ruggles)

Disassembling the Transmission

Now it's time to take this thing apart. Again, if you're concerned because you've never done this before, don't be. Your nicely restored truck will be shifting smoothly in no time. And don't stress out if your transmission isn't sparkling clean. Right now, during the disassembly process, that's not a big deal. You can handle that later.

The first step is to remove all of the transmission fluid from the case. If you already removed the pan, you're ahead of the game, but there may be some fluid trapped in various passages. If you have one of those holding fixtures that I mentioned earlier in the chapter, attach it to the transmission and set it vertically. With a pan under the tailshaft, let the fluid drain out. As you continue, keep that pan there; sometimes removing one part allows more fluid to escape.

Another thing to talk about here is cleanliness. I like to spread out some shop rags on my workbench for any hardware I find. This is only a short-term thing, but it helps remind me to clean those parts with the rags before I put them in bags for sorting. Nothing's worse than removing oily parts from plastic bags.

Remember, oil makes parts stick to one another, so once you pull out a component, make sure that there aren't any washers or bearings tagging along for the ride. Once a part is removed, check all sides for extra pieces, then place them on the rags.

Valve Body and Servo Assembly Removal

1 Disconnect the kick-down cable from the case, then remove the retaining clip that holds it in place and take it off the valve body entirely. Remove the S-link (at pencil point), and set it to the side. (Photo Courtesy Cliff Ruggles)

2 The servo assembly is under the valve body on the case. Grip it by the pin and pull it out firmly. (Photo Courtesy Cliff Ruggles)

Separator Plate, Check Balls, and More Removal

1 Gently pry out the fluid filters, and be careful not to nick or scratch the throttle body. Not every transmission rebuilder uses them. You might need to use a tiny flathead screwdriver (or similar) to remove them. (Photo Courtesy Cliff Ruggles)

Manual Shaft, Accumulator, and Vacuum Modulator Removal

1 The parking pawl guide is located at the opposite end, and is held in place with Grade-8 bolts. Remove them and the parking pawl guide, and make sure to keep those bolts separate from the rest, as most are only Grade 5. Pull the manual shaft out from the case. (Photo Courtesy Cliff Ruggles)

2 Locate the small hole on the outside of the case right next to the accumulator. Insert a tiny flathead screwdriver or an awl in the hole, then strike the back of it with a hammer. This pops the snap ring out; you can then pry it off with another flathead screwdriver or a pry bar. Remove the cover of the accumulator with a flathead screwdriver. Then remove the spring (usually, on a truck that's been used a lot, it's broken) and accumulator from the case and set them to the side. (Photo Courtesy Cliff Ruggles)

3 The vacuum modulator is on the back of the case on the passenger's side. Unbolt the bracket that holds it to the case using a 5/16-inch socket (some newer models use a 1/2-inch bolt) and ratchet, and then remove it and the vacuum modulator. You can toss the O-ring on the modulator as you install a new one. Then, pull the modulator valve out of the case using a magnet or something similar. (Photo Courtesy Cliff Ruggles)

Oil Pump Disassembly and Clutch Removal

1 Attach a dial indicator to the case and properly align it with the end of the input shaft. Take an endplay reading before you start so you have a baseline. Optimal endplay is between .044 and .010 inch. As you disassemble the pump, you might find washers that are used to adjust the endplay. Make sure to keep them handy for reassembly. (Photo Courtesy Cliff Ruggles)

2 Unbolt the multiple 5/16-18 bolts around the perimeter, and then use slide hammers with 3/8-16 threads to pop the oil pump free from the casing. Lift out the assembly in one unit and set it to the side. Peel off the pump gasket by hand. Take out the wavy spacer first, and then pull out the clutch packs using a pick tool (or something with a hooked end) at a 90-degree angle. Take out the backing plate next, and then pull the notched end of the band out. Remove the entire band and set it to the side. Alternatively, there is a slot in the corner where you can see the end of the band. If you stick a flathead screwdriver in and push the band so it releases pressure, the entire assembly pops loose. (Photo Courtesy Cliff Ruggles)

3 Take out the forward and direct clutch packs next. The easiest way to do this is to grab the input shaft and lift, pulling them straight out of the case. There are a few things to take note of here, including the two washers, one between the drums and one under the forward drum. Most of the time the last washer comes out in the process by adhering to the bottom of the drum. If it doesn't, make sure to pull it out by hand. (Photo Courtesy Cliff Ruggles)

Governor and Speedometer Gear Drive Removal

1 The first part of the planetary gear assembly lifts right out, as does the metal washer behind it. At this point, stop and do not proceed until you've removed the speedometer gear drive. If you don't, you will damage other components, and that can be pricey. (Photo Courtesy Cliff Ruggles)

2 On the driver's side of the case a large domed cap houses the governor. Holding it in place is a large retainer clip (if you don't see one, the dome is press fit in place). Remove the retainer clip with a pry bar, and then use a screwdriver and a mallet around the perimeter of the dome to tap it off the transmission. Make sure not to angle the screwdriver too far inward, as there's a seal inside, and you don't want to slip and damage it. Now you can slide the governor gear out of the case. If you want to verify that it still works, hold it vertically so the large portion is at the bottom, and look between the top lobe and the one below it. Open and close the bottom switches and notice if the valve between the lobes opens and closes, too. If it does, you're good to proceed. (Photo Courtesy Cliff Ruggles)

Planetary Gear Set and Low Reverse Removal

1 To remove the planetary gear set inside the case, use snap-ring pliers to pop off the snap ring (and don't lose it, as replacements don't often come in rebuild kits) and wiggle it out. (Photo Courtesy Cliff Ruggles)

2 The sun shell should lift straight out. Underneath it is a thrust washer; you want to be sure to have that on hand later. (Photo Courtesy Cliff Ruggles)

3 *The low reverse and center support area comes out next. It's held in place by a large snap ring. A long flathead screwdriver with a wide end pops it off nicely. Then you can hold on to the shaft and pull out the entire assembly. If the case is worn out, this part may be difficult because the clearances are much tighter from heat damage. Consider buying a new case at that point. (Photo Courtesy Cliff Ruggles)*

Low/Reverse Apply Piston Removal

1 *This is where things can be tricky. Start by looking for the opening in the snap ring at the bottom center of the low/reverse apply piston. Position your spring compressor so that it doesn't block access to the snap-ring gap; it still needs to function. Tighten the spring compressor. Now you can remove the snap ring with your snap-ring pliers. Loosen the spring compressor, take it out of the way, and lift out the spring cage by hand. (Photo Courtesy Cliff Ruggles)*

2 *You can either reposition the case so that it's angled slightly upward, or with the bellhousing downward, angle it toward the back of your bench. Aim a blow gun into the oil-feed hole on the bottom of the case. This pops off the low/reverse piston. Be sure to remove the parking pawl before you proceed. (Photo Courtesy Cliff Ruggles)*

Rebuilding Basics

Feels good to have the transmission apart, right? Fortunately for you, you just have to put it all back together in the reverse order in which you disassembled it. Easy as pie. Mostly.

Admittedly, there's a lot to do here, which is why many people throw in the towel and either buy a remanufactured transmission or simply have theirs rebuilt by a professional. If you're not that person, you will be shifting smoothly (or firmly, depending on your preference) soon.

Many truck owners want a bit more performance out of their transmission, so they install a shift kit. It's nothing radical, but it provides enough added gains so that it's worth the modifications.

Of course, you need to make sure that you have a clean workspace for

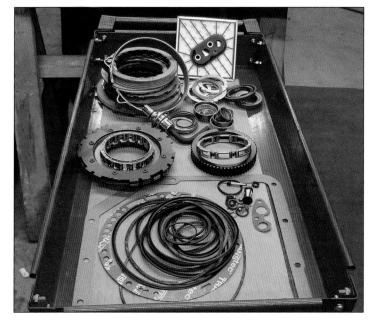

Having parts laid out on a clean surface and in an orderly system makes the entire process go much more smoothly. Before you start the assembly process, pressure wash the transmission and use compressed air and your blow gun to remove water from all channels and passages. From start to finish, an experienced transmission tech can complete the disassembly process in less than an hour. It may take you longer. (Photo Courtesy Cliff Ruggles)

this process. It was important when you took things apart; now it is absolutely critical. After all, you don't want to throw in a gear set with chunks of dirt. If you did, what was the point of a rebuild? Make sure that everything is clean beforehand, then keep it that way by protecting parts and pieces as you go.

That also means that you should clean all of the parts that you will be reusing. Using a pressure washer is a good start, but you can also put them into a solvent tank if necessary. You know, "cleanliness is next to godliness," and all that.

Having an organized workspace is especially important here. You will be dealing with a lot of small parts and other things that are easy to misplace. By now you likely have already laid out your parts carefully and sorted them accordingly, so keep things flowing that direction.

Again, keep it clean. I can't stress that enough.

Depending on the age and use of the transmission, it might be damaged. Now is the time to repair any damage from disassembly. That includes threads. Look for stress marks and chips in all components. Dig around the transmission case and look for signs of wear or damage.

Now you can begin the rebuild.

Case Bushing Removal and Installation

With the case either in the fixture or securely mounted elsewhere, use a bushing driver and a mallet on the end of the case to drive out the bushing. Once it's out, inspect the area for signs of damage. Take a moment to test fit the new bushing as well, just to be sure it works. You can't install the new bushing with the case in the same position because the governor pin is in the way. Instead, flip the case and drive the bushing in from the bellhousing side. This requires a long driver handle; a metal rod works as well. Apply some red Loctite on the end of every bushing before it's installed. It must be driven in just slightly below flush so that the output shaft's bearing functions correctly. (Photo Courtesy Cliff Ruggles)

Begin Reassembly

Using trans gel or clean ATF, apply the replacement seals to the low/reverse piston. The square block on the bottom is a key that correlates to a square hole in the base of the transmission case. After the case and the low/reverse piston are lubed with clean ATF or trans gel, place the low/reverse piston into the case and push it down firmly, either by hand or with a wooden dowel, to lock it in place. Alternatively, you can mark the case and the piston with a felt-tip pen to help line things up. The low/reverse clutch springs are next. Use the same process that you did when you removed them. Tighten the spring compressor, then use the snap-ring pliers to lock the snap ring into place. (Photo Courtesy Cliff Ruggles)

Output Shaft Bushing Removal and Assembly Installation

2 Using an appropriate bushing driver, install the new bushing with a fresh application of Loctite. The bushing should sit just below flush to function properly. (Photo Courtesy Cliff Ruggles)

3 Soak all Torrington bearings in ATF prior to installation. Then lube the output shaft and all mating surfaces with clean ATF and slide it into the casing. (Photo Courtesy Cliff Ruggles)

1 At the end of the output shaft is a tiny bushing that should be swapped out. To do that, use a tap that fits into the bushing to draw the bushing out of the shaft. If you see any remaining metal shavings or other debris, clean them out. (Photo Courtesy Cliff Ruggles)

Low Planetary Bushing Replacement and Assembly Installation

1 *Remove the old planetary bushing, then install a replacement with the appropriate bushing driver by sliding it onto the output shaft to make sure it spins freely. Take a moment to inspect the planetary gears. Check for looseness or endplay on the gears, as any excessive play requires replacing the entire assembly. (Photo Courtesy Cliff Ruggles)*

2 *Dip the gears of the planetary assembly into clean ATF to ensure that they're properly lubricated. Then install the entire assembly into the casing. (Photo Courtesy Cliff Ruggles)*

Low/Reverse Clutch Pack and Center Support Installation

1 *You have four or five steels and frictions for this assembly. The first thing to do is soak the frictions in clean ATF for at least a few minutes. Then place them into the case starting with a steel, then a friction, and repeat until you have a friction on the top. (Photo Courtesy Cliff Ruggles)*

2 *Install the center support retaining spring into the case. Then slide the center support into the case, and install the retaining ring to keep the assembly solid and fixed. (Photo Courtesy Cliff Ruggles)*

Center Support Assembly Installation

Installing a bolt-in center support beefs up the transmission substantially and is affordable. Do this by sliding the assembly past the case lugs and pushing it firmly into place. Then apply some red Loctite on the bolts, and tighten them with a ratchet and long extension. (Photo Courtesy Cliff Ruggles)

Sun Gear Refurbish and Installation

To remove the bushings from the sun gear, use a punch to drive out the upper and then the lower bushings. Reinstall them in the opposite sequence (lower then upper) using a bushing-driver kit. Lube the sun gear with plenty of ATF and lower it into the case. Rotate the gear as you lower it, and make sure it engages with the planetary gears. (Photo Courtesy Cliff Ruggles)

Front Planetary Gear Installation

Dip the front planetary gear in clean ATF; be sure to coat all of the surfaces. Then place it into the sun gear, making sure that it slides onto the output shaft correctly. Push down on the planetary gear with a long flathead screwdriver, and install the snap ring to lock it in place. Clean up the front Torrington bearing, then dip it in ATF and install it on the output shaft. (Photo Courtesy Cliff Ruggles)

Front Planetary Reaction Carrier Bearings and Assembly Removal and Installation

Remove the original bearing using a sharp punch and a hammer, then install the new bearing (coated with Loctite) into the front planetary carrier with a bushing driver. Next, set the reaction carrier onto the front planetary gear. To do that, slide it over the output shaft, then turn it until it locks into place on the planetary gear. Install the final thrust washer with some trans gel. (Photo Courtesy Cliff Ruggles)

Forward Clutch Rebuild

1 *Install the seals on the forward clutch apply piston with a pick or similar tool, and make sure that the drum spins. Install the spring cage using a spring compressor, then lock it in place with a snap ring. If you look closely, you see two raised marks on the retainer. You want the ends of the snap rings to line up with those marks to ensure that everything works properly. (Photo Courtesy Cliff Ruggles)*

2 *Now it's time to install the steels and frictions, starting with a wavy steel. Then you want to install the rest in the following sequence: flat steel, friction, repeat. The last one is a friction and goes under the backing plate. Put the snap ring back in place, double-check the clearances (it should be between .020 and .040 inch), and you're good to go. (Photo Courtesy Cliff Ruggles)*

3 *Slide the assembled forward clutch into the case, and then spin it to make sure it is connected properly. Place the ATF-soaked Torrington bearing over the shaft, and make sure it's seated securely. (Photo Courtesy Cliff Ruggles)*

Pre-soaking Steels and Frictions

If you've purchased steels and frictions that were pre-soaked, it's still a good idea to soak them before installation. This is one of those times when it's best to overdo it, rather than underperform.

Intermediate Clutch Reassembly

Install the seals on the direct drum, then install the apply piston and seals while using a liberal amount of trans gel. Spin the drum during the installation process, being careful with the seal. Install the spring cage onto the apply piston, then lock it in place using a spring compressor and snap ring. Install the ATF-soaked steels and frictions next with a flat steel first, then a friction, and alternating from there. A friction goes last, and once the backing plate is installed, you can lock that down with the snap ring. The bushing is the last thing to be installed. The intermediate roller clutch assembly goes right onto the direct drum with the rollers and the notches on the drum lined up. The intermediate clutch outer race goes around this, then the roller clutch retainer, and finally, the snap ring. Lower the assembly into the case, making sure it's latched and bottomed out. (Photo Courtesy Cliff Ruggles)

Pump Installation

Install the band; it should align with the notches in the case. A large flathead screwdriver helps you lock it in correctly. Install the intermediate frictions next, with the backing plate in the case first. A friction plate (soaked in ATF) goes in next, then steel, friction, etc., until the wavy top spacer is installed last. Put some assembly lube on the case, then put the replacement pump gasket onto the assembly. (Photo Courtesy Cliff Ruggles)

Speedometer Gear and Tail Shaft Installation

1 *The speedometer gear clip installs onto the output shaft the same way it came off. Slide the speedometer gear over the clip so that it locks into place. Be sure that the end of the clip curls up against the end of the gear; that keeps it in place. (Photo Courtesy Cliff Ruggles)*

2 *You must remove and install a new bushing before you install the tailshaft housing. Use a bushing driver to handle the job. (Photo Courtesy Cliff Ruggles)*

3 *Once you've installed the O-ring onto the tailshaft housing, bolt it in place. Tighten the bolts to 35 ft-lbs with a torque wrench. (Photo Courtesy Cliff Ruggles)*

4 *Install new seals onto the speedometer housing, then lubricate the end and slide it into the tailshaft. Bolt down the retainer clamp, and the install is complete. (Photo Courtesy Cliff Ruggles)*

5 Slide the governor into the tailshaft, turning it as you go to ensure that it engages with the output shaft. Place a replacement seal on the governor cap, then tap it into place with a mallet. If your transmission had the retaining clip in place over the cap, reinstall it with a flathead screwdriver. (Photo Courtesy Cliff Ruggles)

Accumulators and Valve Body Installation

1 After you replace the seals on the 1-2 accumulator, lubricate it with some clean ATF, then slide it into the case. Follow that with the 1-2 accumulator spring, and finally, the cover, complete with a new seal. Lock everything with the stock retainer clip. (Photo Courtesy Cliff Ruggles)

2 Reinstall the manual shaft hardware using an open-end wrench. Install the parking brake pawl, which bolts in place with the original hardware. (Photo Courtesy Cliff Ruggles)

3 Start installing the modulator valve by first cleaning it with ATF, then sliding it into the case. After installing a seal on the modulator, slide that into the case, and bolt it down with the retaining clamp. (Photo Courtesy Cliff Ruggles)

4 Earlier, you marked the check ball locations in the case. Now place the replacement balls in those positions. (Photo Courtesy Cliff Ruggles)

5 *Place the lower valve body gasket in place. Apply trans gel to the separator plate, then put the separator plate and upper gasket in place. Place two pan bolts into two of the gasket holes and thread them in loosely so that you can keep the gaskets aligned with the case. Install the support plate bolts and tighten them to 10 ft-lbs of torque. (Photo Courtesy Cliff Ruggles)*

6 *Place the spring and the accumulator in the valve body. Then install it completely using the retainer clip. If necessary, use some channel locks to compress the spring. (Photo Courtesy Cliff Ruggles)*

7 *Slide the manual valve into the valve body, and connect it to the case and linkage with the S-clip (as you did during disassembly). Install the valve body to the case with the hardware, just tightening everything by hand. Torque the bolts to 10 ft-lbs. Under no circumstances should you use air tools; that may damage the components. (Photo Courtesy Cliff Ruggles)*

8 *Place a filter in the proper location in the valve body and a new gasket on top of it. Then bolt it in place using a flathead screwdriver. (Photo Courtesy Cliff Ruggles)*

9 *Install the transmission pan gasket and then the transmission pan with the factory hardware. The final step? Fill the transmission with fluid. (Photo Courtesy Cliff Ruggles)*

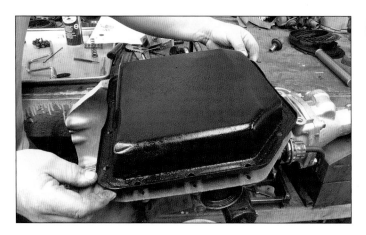

DRIVETRAIN

In the grand scheme of a restoration, rebuilding the rear axle is often overlooked because it is often in usable shape, and other than a bit of paint and cleanup work, you should be good to go. But after countless miles and years under severe use, rear axles can be in dire need of a rebuild. Even it's not on the verge of failure, a rebuild makes sure that it doesn't cause you problems in the future. After all, if the backlash isn't set correctly or your mesh is off, you can go from having a noisy rear end to one that completely detonates, leaving the truck dead and you on the side of the road.

Of course, there are other considerations. Can the rear end handle the horsepower your engine is putting out? Will the truck get good gas mileage with your current gearing setup? Will it be able to tow if it needs to? Because of all that and a whole lot more, I need to discuss gearing. There's a whole lot to be done in that category.

Axle Identification

For the most part, you find one of two axle types underneath these trucks: 10-bolt and 12-bolt. You can determine which one you have based on the number of bolts that hold the differential cover in place. The types and styles varied from year to year, but typically the 12-bolt was used until 1981, and the 10-bolt has been used since the 1982 model year.

In general, 12-bolt axles are considered to be stronger. Although you can easily build a 10-bolt version to handle some decent horsepower, the 12-bolt can take more abuse, making it the preferred model among enthusiasts. Of course, if your truck is a 1981 or newer, chances are pretty good that you have the 12-bolt, anyway. Now you just have to figure out what's inside.

The first step is to look for identifying marks on the axle itself. On some models a stamp on the passenger-side tube indicates what's inside; on others, a cast alphanumeric code on the driver's side of the pumkin gives you all the details.

You will need to do some digging to figure out what those codes mean. The problem, however, is that

Whether your truck is equipped with a Chevy 10- or 12-bolt differential, you need to support it safely with jack stands before you perform a rebuild. After more than 20 years and hundreds of thousands of miles, many rear differentials need a complete rebuild and that includes a new ring and pinion gears.

This 12-bolt axle has a stamping on the side of the pumpkin that reads "ON2." Unfortunately, I couldn't find that number referenced anywhere, and neither could my local GM dealer, so I still don't know what it is.

On the passenger's side of the axle tube is another number. The closest I could find from a GM dealer was that this KAA code matched the axle code on a 1977 C10 with a 3.07 gear ratio.

After I removed the differential cover, I counted 43 teeth on the ring gear, and the pinion had 14. Dividing 43 by 14 is 3.0714285714, so this axle has a 3.07:1 gear ratio.

General Motors doesn't have records stored electronically for models that old. Instead, you either have to find someone at a dealership who knows those codes or do some online sleuthing. Even then, you might not find everything you're looking for.

If you can't find any information, you can determine the gear ratio by doing some math and counting. Crack open the case, and count the number of teeth on the ring gear. Then, with a flashlight, count the number of teeth on the pinion. Divide the ring gear by the pinion, and you have the gear ratio.

Gearing

Because you're rebuilding the rear differential, you can make a gearing change so the axle ratio is suited to your application and driving preferences. Common ratios are 3.08, 3.42, 3.73, and 4.10:1. You need to decide what you want versus what you need.

Well, entire books are dedicated to the subject, such as *Chevy Differentials: How to Rebuild the 10- and 12-Bolt* by Jefferson Bryant. Any one of them delves into the subject more deeply than I do here. There's a lot to factor in: transmission gearing, tire size, engine, etc., and the combination of them gives you the results you want.

Gear ratios are often referred to as "short" or "tall." Short gears are 3.73 or 4.10, which are high numbers, but low gear ratios. Tall gears, therefore, are lower numbers, such as a 3.08. Many factors are at play here: A shorter gear is better for acceleration; a taller gear is better for the freeway.

Think of it like this: The ratio basically tells you how many times the driveshaft is going to turn for every rotation of your tire. So if you have a 4.10 ratio, the driveshaft rotates a little more than four times for each tire turn. You give up a bit of top-end speed with shorter gears, but you get there more quickly.

Long story short, you have identical trucks with identical transmissions and engines, the only difference is the gearing. The one with the shorter gear ratio will win off the line. The one with the taller gear set gets better mileage and hits a higher top speed over the long haul.

Rebuilding an Axle

At first, this seems like a straightforward job, and essentially, it is. But you need a few tools to do the job correctly. A hydraulic press is the first thing that comes to mind, as you will be pressing bearings into place during the course of the install, and it's critical that you either use a hydraulic press or have access to one. Without it, you will be unable to do the job yourself. Harbor Freight, for example, sells them starting at $175. You also need a bearing and seal driver kit, which is made up of various-size pieces for installing the bearings and seals in the axle shafts and pumpkin. You can pick up an affordable kit at

Eastwood for $26, and O'Reilly has them as low as $10. Then there's the bearing separator tool. National Tool Warehouse and Harbor Freight sell them for just over $50.

An extremely important tool to have is a torque wrench, specifically an inch/pound model. It is critical because you need to set the drag on the pinion to the correct amount so you don't burn out the bearings. Make sure to purchase one that measures less than 20 in/lbs. Otherwise, you're just wasting your money. Precision Instruments sells one at Sears for $165.

You also need a magnetic-base flex-arm caliper. Fowler sells a kit on Amazon for $60.

Most of the other tools that you need are standard fare. The exception is a long piece of 1½-inch tubing, which you use to remove the axle bearings.

Axle Disassembly

1 One of the first things to do is stamp the bearing caps and axle housing with an "E." On one side the E is straight; on the other, it is tilted to the right, so the parts go where they should upon reassembly.

2 The bearings on the axle are machined specifically for that housing, so you can't swap them left to right. This is so you know which side is which when you reassemble the axle.

3 A pin on the center of the carrier holds in the spider gears, as well as the axles. You unbolt it and slide it out to access the axles.

4 Each axle shaft is held in place with a C-clip. Just push in the axle, then use a magnet to pull the clip out of the axle. The axle slides right out of the body, and you reinstall the pin to keep the spider gears in place during disassembly.

5 Once the bearing caps are unbolted, use a pry bar and a little persuasion to take out the pinion ring and carrier assembly in one piece.

6 The pinion comes out next. Use an impact wrench to remove the nut that retains the U-joint to the tailshaft. A number of seals and bearings also come out at the same time. Clean the housing thoroughly. Be sure that you have these seals and bearings in the rebuild kit.

7 These shafts are worn, as you can tell by the pitting and marring at the end. If yours look like this, they need to be replaced.

8 Press all of the original bearings off the stock pinion. You need a bearing puller and separator set as well as an arbor press for this procedure. Place the pinion gear into a clamp with two pieces of metal stock on the end. Use an old steel shaft to press on the pinion shaft and drive off the pinion bearing. You need a press for this; it can't be done easily otherwise.

Test Fit Ring and Pinion

1 To test fit everything, you can use a bearing that was slightly reamed out on the inside so it can slide over the shaft of the pinion easily. This way, it doesn't have to be pressed and unpressed constantly, and you can determine the right amount for the shims.

2 If you swap a 3.07 gearset to a 3.73 to better match up with the rest of the drivetrain, the height difference between the ring gears is visible. That means you need a new carrier. Attach the ring gear to the carrier, use red Loctite on the nuts, and torque to the correct specification.

3 *Align the spider gears in the housing and then slide the retaining pin through the housing and gears. If necessary, use a soft plastic mallet to tap the pin through the housing and gears, but do not force it. You install the retainer pin and spider gears in the new carrier so that the assembly can be placed in the axle as one unit.*

4 *After applying red Loctite on all of the bolts, put together the new ring gear assembly and then torque the bolts to the proper specification.*

5 *Press the bearings onto the assembly with a bearing press. Use a block of aluminum to space out the distance between the press and the housing, as well as to disperse the pressure to the entire bearing. This way, it doesn't tilt one direction or the other. When you're done, it sits flush against the housing.*

6 *Prior to test fitting the ring gear assembly, knock the axle bearings out with a deadblow hammer and a long piece of steel tubing. The idea is to seat the steel tubing on the inside of the bearing, inside of the axle tube. By striking the tubing with the hammer, you can remove the bearing from the inside out. The rebuild kit should include brand-new axle shaft bearings.*

7 Install the pinion with a temporary bearing and no crush sleeve. This way, you can determine what the pinion depth needs to be without damaging good bearings and crush sleeves in the process.

Backlash Measurement and Pinion Depth Determination

1 With everything reassembled and tightened, check the backlash of the ring gear. To do this, you put the magnetic base of the gauge onto a flat surface, and then position the end of the dial indicator onto the gear teeth, making sure it's about midway depressed compared to its full range of travel. Adjust the dial to zero, so that by rocking the pinion gear back and forth, you can see how much the gear moves forward or backward. For this particular model, the movement needs to be between .006 and .100 inch. This is extremely important, and needs to be done within specs or you will have problems with the rear end.

2 Painting the ring gear with gear marking compound is critical. By doing this, you can see the mesh pattern between the pinion and the ring gear; this helps you determine if you should add or remove shims between the gear and the bearing. By adding shims, you move the pinion gear farther into the case, and vice versa.

3 After rotating the ring gear a few times, you can see the marks where the two gears meet. You want a nice, smooth pattern that's mostly centered on both sides of the ring gear, although it can go to opposite sides and be just fine. Ultimately, the idea is that the pattern is smooth and oval, not a half-moon with harsh edges. In addition, the pattern should be roughly equal on both the coast and drive sides. Otherwise, the gear wears out sooner, and you have excessive noise. Here, I wanted more pinion depth, so I added a shim.

4 Adding or removing shims means disassembling everything, putting in (or taking out) the new shims, and then putting it all back together again. Use the old bearing to test the pinion depth and shim spacing. You don't want to ruin your new bearing by pressing it in and out of the tail section multiple times. When you're satisfied with the fit, you can press the new bearing in place and use the appropriate shims.

Reassembly

1 Give all of the seals (pinion, axle shafts, and differential cover) a thin coat of silicone sealant around the border. This helps keep the gear oil from leaking. It also adds an extra layer of protection.

2 Set the preload on the pinion to ensure that it turns properly. The idea is to use an inch/pound torque wrench to rotate the pinion bolt until you have between 12 and 15 in/lbs. This example is right at 15, so it's good. If it were more, you'd have to disassemble the pinion, install a new crush sleeve and bearings, and then do it again. Most mechanics have a ft-lb torque wrench but not an in-lb wrench.

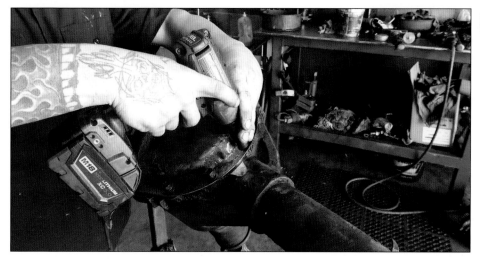

3 With everything reinstalled and torqued to specs, place a gasket on the differential cover. Torque bolts in a star pattern to 20 ft-lbs. Fill the differential with 80W-90 gear oil up to the fill hole.

BRAKES

The brakes on your truck are a vital safety and control device, and therefore brake system refurbishment is an important part of the restoration process. After all, your brakes need to be in working order because your life depends on them. Fortunately, you picked the right truck. The previous generation (1967–1972) carried drum brakes all the way around in the early years, and most of them had six-lug axles. Starting in 1973, Chevy and GMC trucks were equipped with modern disc brakes and five-lug wheels, making them both easy to purchase wheels for and reliable in stopping situations. They didn't have ABS or any fancy computerized options, but

they were as modern, and yet retro, as you can get.

Remove or Replace

So here's the next big decision: Do you replace or repair your brake components? You can go in several directions, and they all come from what your plan is for your truck. If your decision is to restore the truck to be as factory accurate as possible, and you only want original parts and components on the vehicle, you either have to find used parts at a wrecking yard or look into what your options are on online auction sites. If you either can't find the parts you

need or want to keep as many original components as possible, you may have to repair what you have.

You could also buy a parts truck, but there may be some quality issues with it. Bushings and ball joints need repair or replacement eventually, for example, and because these trucks are at least 25 years old, the components may not be ideal replacements.

Another option is to upgrade your brakes with an aftermarket kit. Prices vary, but Wilwood, Baer, and others offer brake kits. These are typically four-piston calipers with 12-inch or larger cross-drilled and slotted rotors. When you compare the results versus the cost, it's clear that the benefits far outweigh the potential consequences. You can step up to a larger rotor and calipers, switch from drum brakes to disc brakes in the rear, and improve the booster, if you like. And that's before you get into the crazy stuff that this book doesn't cover.

Finally, you can upgrade to high-performance aftermarket brakes, which includes 14-inch big-brake kits with steel alloy rotors and even carbon fiber. Dozens of brake upgrade kits are available for these trucks, which include larger discs and calipers that provide bet-

It seems obvious, but let me just put it out there: Brakes are important. Your restoration isn't complete if your truck can't stop on a dime, and making sure that happens is what this chapter is all about.

ter stopping power. Many brake kits include cross-drilled slotted rotors, six-piston calipers, and lighter aluminum parts. They also usually have a hefty price tag, often upward of $2,000. This is the ultimate stopping upgrade to do to your truck, but it's not factory. And this means that (not to beat a dead horse here) it depends on the type of restoration that you want to do.

Brake Lines

Depending on the year and condition of your truck, you have options to consider regarding brake lines. If the truck is drivable and the brakes work well, chances are pretty good that you can get away with a quick inspection to make sure the master cylinder, brake lines, calipers, pads, rotors, and all related parts are in proper working order.

Safely raise the truck on a lift or jack stands. With a creeper and flashlight, inspect the entire length of the brake lines, which are located inside the frame. Look for rusty spots, splits, or damage in the line, which are usually wet from brake fluid seeping out. Then, search further for problems with connections in the lines, and finish by looking at the rubber lines up front that connect to the drums or calipers. If any of these components look perished, are weeping fluid, or generally seem in need of repair, it's time to replace them.

If you're going for original appearance for your Squarebody, install factory brake equipment. In the interest of safety, go with new parts. You can upgrade to Baer, Wilwood, or another aftermarket brake system, but that is outside the scope of this book. Many companies manufacture aftermarket brake kits to suit your needs; they

offer brake line setups as well. You can continue using rubber hoses where needed if you like, or upgrade to stainless steel if you want a little more longevity and improved pedal feel.

Classic Tube sells stainless-steel brake lines for this body style, so for around $120 you can swap out the current rubber lines (that are probably damaged by now) for better ones. Dorman Products also carries these rubber lines for the entire truck, and Eckler's Chevy Truck has a ton of brake line options.

If you're having trouble finding aftermarket steel brake lines, you can always bend some yourself. This is not a task to be taken lightly. The tools required for the job are specialty versions, and if you kink your brake lines, you risk forming a crack or crease that could erupt at any time. That's not to say that it's impossible to do, far from it. But just know that it's not an easy job, particularly if you're a novice.

Removal and Installation

The sequence for all brake jobs, whether disc or drum, starts the same. Park the truck on a level surface, then set the emergency brake if it has one. Lift the truck using a floor jack (or use a hydraulic or pneumatic lift). Position jack stands underneath the frame and/or axle, and then lower the floor jack to put the weight of the truck onto the stands. The wheels that you're working on should be off the ground, and all four wheels should be if you're working on the entire system.

Unbolt the wheels using either an impact wrench or a lug wrench and tire iron, then remove the wheels and tires. Place them somewhere safe so they do not roll away. Now you have access to work on the brakes.

Front Disc Brakes

The front brakes on a 1973–1987 Chevrolet or GMC trucks are disc brakes, which is a step up from the previous body style. Because disc brakes are now standard on most vehicles, you've likely worked on them before, so you probably understand the basic process. If you haven't, don't worry, it's a straightforward process.

Front Disc Brake Installation

The process starts with a bare spindle with no brake rotor at all. Although you could have the original rotors turned, the argument could be made that's it's cheaper on multiple levels to buy and install new rotors. No matter which way you go, you're going to need new wheel bearings (see the next section).

1 *Before you install any braking components, spray the area with brake cleaner, and dry it with a paper towel or lint-free rag. If any grease is on the rotor, it could cause problems with braking. In addition, many rotors come with an oily surface to protect them from rust, and the brake fluid removes it.*

2 To help keep the brakes from squeaking, apply some disc brake quiet to the moving components. The slides mount inside the caliper, and using the disc brake quiet minimizes any friction that could cause excess wear and make noise.

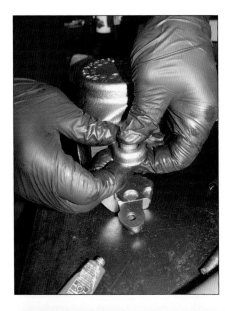

3 Push the slides into the calipers once you have applied disc brake quiet around the entire perimeter.

4 When the original brakes wear, the caliper applies continuous pressure to the brake pads. It sticks out farther than needed after you install new (and thicker) pads. To fix that, use an old brake pad and a C-clamp to push the piston as far into the caliper as possible.

5 Replacement brake pads have clips and pads that match the contour of the brake. Install them by clipping them in place.

6 Install new pads into the caliper, making sure that the grooves on the sides face the same direction. This is where the caliper bolts slide into place, so you don't want anything blocking their movement.

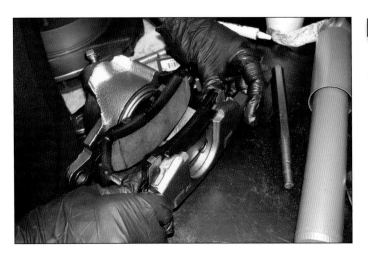

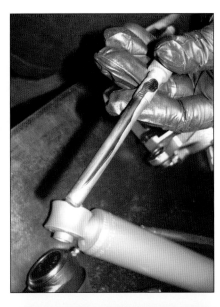

7 *Also place some disc brake quiet onto the caliper bolts. This ensures that there is no metal-to-metal contact.*

8 *The caliper is now ready to be installed onto the rotor. Slide it on carefully.*

9 *Install the caliper bolts using a 3/8-inch ratchet and an Allen socket. Check the manufacturer's installation instructions and torque to the correct space, which is often between 40 and 50 ft-lbs.*

10 *Install new brake lines as well. Two copper washers go onto the replacement brake line's connection to the caliper. When both washers are installed, they flank the brake line's end (shown).*

11 *Install the brake line into the backside of the caliper using an open-end wrench.*

Wheel Bearings

On modern Chevrolet and GMC trucks, the wheel bearings come in sealed units. When they need to be replaced, the entire assembly unbolts from the steering knuckle, and a new one is bolted on.

With 1973–1987 Chevrolet and GMC trucks, however, the wheel bearings should be replaced anytime you remove the rotors. This means that (ideally) anytime the brakes are replaced, so are the wheel bearings. This can make a brake job an expensive proposition.

Fortunately, replacing the wheel bearings on these trucks is not difficult, particularly if you start from scratch, as you do with a restoration. After all, you're likely not going to install worn-out brakes and rotors onto a truck with a ton of money and time spent on the rest of it, right? Changing the bearings requires new bearings, seals, and, at a minimum, turned rotors (although replacements are the usual choice).

Wheel Bearing Installation

1 Start with all of your parts laid out on a workbench, where you have lots of room to work. You're going to want bearing grease handy as well; you will be using a lot of it.

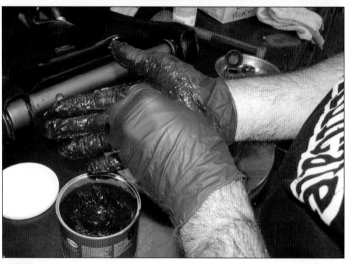

2 To pack the bearings, start by scooping up a dab of the bearing grease and putting it in the palm of your hand.

3 Hold the bearing in your left hand. Push the bearing into the grease on the palm of your right hand, working the bearing grease through the assembly, so that it oozes out the other side. Rotate the bearing as you do this, to ensure that all sides are covered by grease. You don't want to install dry bearings on your truck; that's an accident waiting to happen.

4 Once the bearing has been lubricated properly, place another dollop of bearing grease on your index finger, and work it around the inside of the brake rotor (the part that faces the engine). Make sure it too has plenty of grease.

5 Insert the inner wheel bearing into the brake rotor, then add more grease to the backside of the bearing.

6 Lightly tap the bearing seal into place with a hammer. You just want to begin the seating process; don't pound it into place all the way.

7 Using a socket to provide equal pressure, tap the bearing seal until it sits flat against the inside of the rotor.

8 The completed bearing and bearing seal should look like this.

9 Do the same process for the outer bearings, except that you don't have a seal to install.

10 *With the front suspension assembled, apply bearing grease to the spindle on the steering knuckle.*

11 *Slide the rotor onto the spindle, making sure to keep everything centered on the bearings. Be careful not to contact a bearing with the spindle.*

12 *Install the two washers. The first is round, and the second is round with a slot in it that keys to the flat spot on the spindle.*

13 *Install the spindle castle nut onto the spindle using a wrench or socket. The goal is to tighten it firmly, then back the nut off about 1/4 to 1/2 rotation. The rotor should spin freely, but not so much that it feels as if it has some play.*

14 *Slide the cotter pin for the spindle through the castle nut, then pull apart the two ends so that they hold the pin in place. Use a screwdriver and mallet for some extra assistance. Install the dust cap, which you can do with a mallet or a mallet and a drift.*

Rear Drum Brakes

If you've never replaced a set before, drum brakes can be intimidating. That's because they have many springs and moving parts, and each one needs to be set correctly. You should consider changing the rear brake lines on the axle as well. Sometimes they can corrode over time, and because they're so close to the ground, they can take on salt and road grime.

Always change both rear brakes at the same time. If you don't, you risk having serious braking issues.

Rear Drum Brake Installation

1 Usually, sliding off the brake drums is straightforward. Occasionally, you may need to loosen the shoes a bit to release their grip on the drum. To do that, look for the access hole on the lower portion of the brake drum, and push in the sprocket using a flathead screwdriver.

2 Taking off the rear drums can be a bit tricky, but one way to simplify the process is to remove them as one unit. To do that, remove the clips holding the shoes to the brackets using a flathead screwdriver. Once the springs have been removed, the drum assembly can come off most of the way. All that's left is removing the hold-down pins and retainers at the bottom.

3 Almost every brake drum kit comes with all of the replacement springs you need, so just take lots of pictures and notes as you go so everything is replaced correctly.

4 Clips hold the rear shoes to the brackets; they come out with a pair of needle-nose pliers. Once they're free, the brake shoes come free of the brackets. These brackets usually look a bit rough after decades of braking. By disassembling everything, you can take your time to clean them.

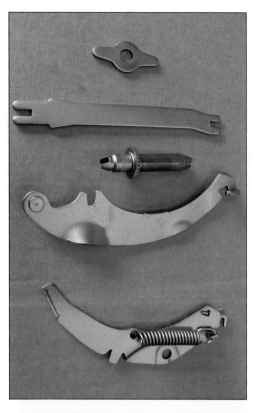

6 You can paint the brackets with a factory-looking matte silver from a local auto parts store. They look as good as new.

5 Depending on the condition of your parts, it should be quick and easy to remove any scale from the brake brackets. A wire wheel does a good job.

7 Because you're already replacing the brakes, you should replace the wheel cylinder, too, which is as simple as unbolting the old one, removing the brake line connection, and bolting in the replacement. When you install the pistons, make sure to use some grease because they may resist fitting. Slide the pins into notches on the brackets, and make sure you line them up correctly.

8 On the backing pad of the brakes, raised portions are shaped like rectangles with rounded corners. By lubricating them with grease, you ensure that the brakes move smoothly.

9 *The first bracket to mount is the one for the emergency brake cable. Hook it around the end so it stays in place.*

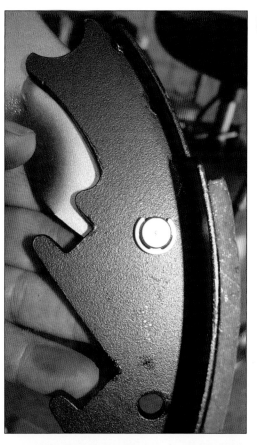

10 *To connect the brake shoe to the bracket, you can usually push the clip in place using your hands. Needle-nose pliers work, too.*

11 *The actuator lever needs to be attached to the brake shoe bracket, and the actuator spring also needs to be set in place. To hold down the lever, use a hold-down pin coupled with a hold-down spring and retainer.*

12 *The parking brake strut sits behind the axle shaft and connects to the mounted shoe. The strut spring goes on the forward end of the parking brake strut, and it sits against the forward shoe once everything is complete.*

13 *Mount the forward shoe using a hold-down pin, spring, and retainer.*

14 *The pivot nut and adjusting screw assembly sit at the bottom of the brakes, and are held in by the adjuster screw spring. One half sits on the adjusting screw, and the other half sits on the forward-mounted shoe. You also mount an actuator lever return spring on the actuator lever.*

15 *After the shoe guide slides to the top of the brakes, install the actuator link with the return springs.*

16 *With all of the brakes complete, slide the rear drum into place.*

17 *If you adjust the shoes out too far, roll the adjuster screw back until it fits, and there's a light amount of drag on the drum.*

18 *You can purchase complete rear brake line kits online. The rear soft line attaches to the frame with a clip, and you connect the brake lines using a brake line wrench.*

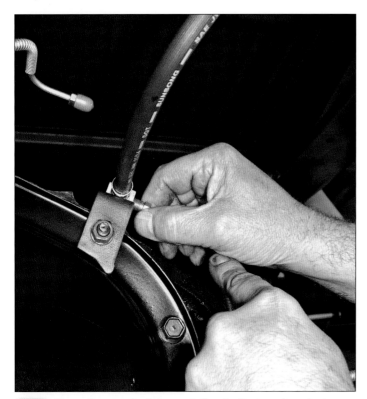

19 *The other end of the soft line bolts to a bracket on the axle. Loosely fit into place the hard brake lines that run to the drums. This allows you to flex the hard line as necessary to fit into the drums.*

20 *Run each brake line to its designated location, then tighten it in place on both ends. Once that's complete, use a flathead screwdriver to push in the tabs on the axle that hold the line.*

Whether you use a vacuum pump or the manual method, you start by opening the hood and taking the cover off the master cylinder.

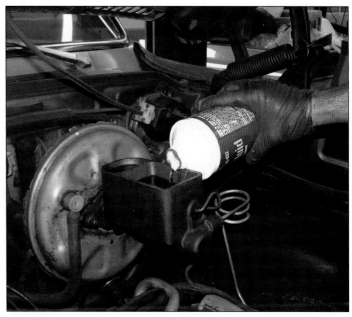

Next, fill the master cylinder with brake fluid, making sure to fill both chambers.

Bleeding the Brakes

If your truck has been apart for any period of time, the brakes must be bled before you put it back on the road. By removing components such as the calipers, rotors, and wheel cylinders, you introduce air bubbles into the system. Hydraulic fluid, such as the kind in your brake system, doesn't compress, but air does. This means that if you have air in your braking system, the brake pedal feels soft and mushy. If you have too much air, you might not "feel" the pedal at all.

To fix that, bleed the brakes. You have two primary ways to do it. The first is to use a vacuum pump, which sucks the air out of the lines directly. The second is done manually, with a wrench, clear tubing, and an assistant to pump the brakes. Both are effective, but using a vacuum pump is a one-person job.

If you use the manual method, buy some clear plastic tubing of approximately 1/8-inch diameter, and about a foot long. Connect the tubing to the bleeder valve on the bleeder screw, starting at the right rear wheel. Loosen the bleeder screw with a wrench. Have an assistant pump the brakes. When the brake fluid coming through the line is free of air, tighten the bleeder screw and move on to the next wheel, the left rear. From there proceed to the passenger-side front wheel, and finally, the driver-side front wheel.

Start with the passenger-side rear wheel, and work your way to the driver-side rear, then the passenger-side front, and finally the driver-side front. Place the clear tubing from the vacuum pump onto the bleeder screw located on the caliper or the back of the drum. Loosen the bleeder screw slightly, then pull the trigger on the vacuum pump until no more air comes through the line. Tighten the bleeder screw, top off the master cylinder with more brake fluid if it's low or close to low, and then move on to the next wheel.

CHAPTER 9

SUSPENSION

Squarebody trucks have a tried-and-true conventional suspension setup. Up front, they are equipped with a double wishbone with stamped upper and lower control arms, coil-over springs, shocks, sway bar, and related parts. The rear suspension is a common live axle with leaf springs. The restoration process is straightforward mechanical work that most at-home restorers can tackle. For me, it's one of the more enjoyable components to work on. If you are just freshening the suspension, you usually can see (and feel) the results immediately, and that's awesome.

This is also one of the more accessible parts of a truck to work on; even more so if the truck is torn apart down to the chassis. The only downsides are that some parts require specialized tools for installation, and the components are very heavy.

DIY Versus Paying a Professional

The suspension on 1973–1987 Chevy and GMC trucks is extremely common. Its basic principles have been used on both cars and trucks for decades. They're quite easy to work on, and with the exception of a few frustrating moments when it's time to separate a ball joint from a spindle, these trucks come apart easily. I recommend that you do this part of the restoration yourself.

The only other mitigating factors come down to the time and tools required. Most of the tools you need for this job you likely already have in your toolbox. However, specialty tools, such as a coil spring compressor, are required, but those are either cheap or easy to rent at a local parts store. When it comes to time, it is almost always faster for you to work on the suspension yourself, unless you need a specialty tool that you don't have.

There are a few exceptions of course. For example, if you decide that refurbishing your stock suspension is what you want to do (which means that you need new ball joints and bushings), you may want to

You need to make sure to use the proper tools and safely disassemble the front suspension so you can replace damaged control arms, sacked out springs, failed shocks, old ball joints, and other parts. A moderately skilled person can perform all of the suspension restoration at a home workshop.

consider taking those parts to a shop. The bushings in these trucks are pressed into place, and removing them can be quite the chore if you don't have the right tools. However, rather than taking the entire truck to a shop, you could take just the control arms, which leaves you to do the rest of the work yourself. If the factory ball joints are in place, you have to drill out a series of rivets. That's time consuming, but you can do it in your garage.

Another exception comes with the alignment. Although you can ballpark your truck's alignment with a few tools, the fact is that today's alignment shops use lasers and other precision tools to do the job quickly and efficiently. A proper alignment is crucial to the handling of your truck, so when the time comes to get it dialed in, you should take it to a shop.

In the end, the suspension can be one of the fun projects that you tackle yourself. It's relatively easy to do and shouldn't be intimidating.

Removal and Installation

The process of taking apart the suspension starts with securing the truck on jack stands. Because you're taking apart the entire suspension, it makes sense to do this at a place where the truck can sit for a minimum of a few hours. Make sure that the frame is supported by at least four jack stands, and place another two underneath the axle as well. There's no harm in having additional stands in place if it makes you feel safer, too.

You can look at the process in two ways. If you remove the entire front suspension and replace it with new parts from the aftermarket (including brakes), the process becomes fairly

---

Working with Coil Springs

The coil springs on the front suspension are under a tremendous amount of tension. Professionals who remove springs have years of experience, so the way they approach the problem is arguably different than the way you do.

I recommend using coil spring compressors. You can rent them at AutoZone for around $40. Simply slide a pair through the lower control arm and into the coil spring. Hook one end around a top wrap of the coil and another on the bottom. Repeat for the other coil spring compressor, on the opposite side of the coil.

Tighten the compressors with either an impact wrench or a socket/ratchet combo, and alternate sides so that the spring doesn't bulge out one way or the other. Once the coil wraps are touching and you can freely move the coil with your hands, you can take out the lower control arms and springs.

The coil springs on these trucks typically aren't under the kinds of pressure found on a lot of cars, but that's no reason to neglect safety. (Plus, who knows what previous owners did to the front suspension, including taller-than-factory springs.) Take your time, use some coil spring compressors, and be safe.

---

simple and straightforward. You could have the entire front end and rear end removed in an hour or so.

If you remove the upper and lower control arms together, you can slide everything off the truck in one unit, brakes included. The only problem is the spring, which is under tension, meaning that you don't want to just unbolt something and hope you'll be fine. You won't.

Instead, place a jack underneath the lower control arm and lift it enough so that it's not lifting the entire frame off the stands, but it stops the arm from slamming down. Then unbolt the sway bar and tie-rod ends from the suspension, and remove the brake line leading from the frame to the suspension on either side. Unbolt and remove the shock as well. Then, use a pair of spring compressors to remove the tension from the coil spring. You won't be able to compress it all the way, but go as tight as you can.

Coil Spring Removal

1 One of the first quick and easy things you can do is remove the tie-rod end. Pull out the cotter pin first with pliers, then remove the tie-rod bolt from the spindle with a 1/2-inch ratchet and socket.

2 *Remove the brake caliper. It uses a hex-head bolt to hold it to the stock spindle. Then you can pull the brake line over the upper control arm and out of the way.*

3 *Remove all of the cotter pins. One connects the upper control arm to the spindle, and one connects the lower. Pliers make quick work of this.*

4 *The sway bar is bolted to the lower control arms. Use a wrench on one end and a 1/2-inch ratchet and socket on the other end to remove it. Loosen them on both sides before proceeding.*

5 *Once the sway bar is unbolted from the frame, pull it away and set it to the side.*

6 *After placing a jack under the lower control arm, use a sledgehammer against the spindle to knock the ball joints free. Then you can pull the spindle and disc brake assembly out of the way.*

7 By pushing the lower control arm down and using a pry bar, you should be able to pull out the stock spring. If you can't, or if you don't feel comfortable doing it, you may want to use a spring compressor for a more manageable size.

8 This particular project truck was a 1973 GMC with 40,000 original miles, and the original shocks and shock mounts were in place. You have to access these from the inside of the frame, just to the side of the oil pan, so it's tricky to access. Most replacement shock kits come with new mounts, so it isn't a big deal.

Unbolt the lower control arm U-bolts from the frame, making sure that the jack is still in place. Unbolt the upper control arms from the frame next, making sure to take note of the shims between the upper control arm cross-shaft and the frame. This will help you with alignment later (take a picture for reference). Lower the jack so that the suspension rests on the end, and slide it away from the frame. Now one side of the front suspension is free, and you simply do the same thing on the other side.

If you want to take everything apart to recondition them yourself, the process is a bit different. You start in the same fashion with the jack, lower control arm, and coil spring. Once the spring compressors have done their job, remove either the drums or the discs (see Chapter 9). Disconnect the upper and lower ball joints from the steering knuckle.

Once the ball joint is unbolted from the knuckle, you can use a pickle fork between the ball joint and the knuckle to knock them free. This will likely destroy the ball joint boot in the process but if they need replacement anyway, no big deal. Then repeat for the remaining ball joint and the tie-rod end. With those complete, you can lift the knuckle away from the suspension.

Control Arm Refurbishment

1 Looking at the condition of the ball joints on this truck, I decided that it was a good idea to replace them with new ones. Removing these is not fun; usually the easiest method is to cut an X into the rivet heads using an angle grinder, then use an impact hammer with a cutting attachment to cut off the heads. A quick jolt or two with the air hammer should knock the rivets out of their spot. Replacement ball joints always come with new bolts so they can be bolted in place. The lower control arm ball joints must be pressed out completely, which requires special tools.

2 *The bushings on the control arms also require pressing, and they're tricky to do, because you have the cross shafts in there as well. To do it properly, press out one side with a hydraulic press, then press out the other side; it can be frustrating. Again, this is something that you probably want to take to a shop, unless you have experience with it.*

3 *Before removing the upper control arms, make sure to unbolt the brake lines from the arms using a 3/8-inch ratchet.*

4 *The upper control arm bolts can be tricky to remove, but you can do so with either a breaker bar on a 1/2-inch drive ratchet or an impact wrench (shown).*

Next, remove the arms. Unbolt the shocks and sway bar from the lower control arms, then unbolt the U-bolts that hold the lower control arm in place and lower it. The spring should fall out. Unbolt the upper control arm cross-shaft from the frame, noting how many alignment shims are on each bolt, and remove the upper control arm from the frame.

After you repeat the process for the other side, you've removed the bulk of the suspension. All that's left is the sway bar, which is held in place by four bolts (two on each side) on the underside of the frame.

Disassemble Brake/Spindle

1 *It's easier to pull the discs apart on the bench. Start by popping off the dust cover on the brake rotor using a flathead screwdriver.*

2 *After removing the cotter pin, use an impact wrench to remove the center bolt on the spindle.*

3 *With the disc out of the way, it's easy to remove the dust shield. Just three bolts, and it's off.*

Rear Suspension

Before you start on the rear suspension, it's critical that you support the frame and the axle with jack stands. If you're using a lift, you still need some kind of support on the axle; otherwise, you risk a serious catastrophe.

Rear Suspension Removal

1 *U-bolts hold the leaf spring to the top of the axle. These are best removed with an impact wrench, because they're usually locked on solidly.*

2 *The shocks mount to the frame and to the axle via through-bolts. These come off with an open-end wrench and a ratchet, although an impact works just as well.*

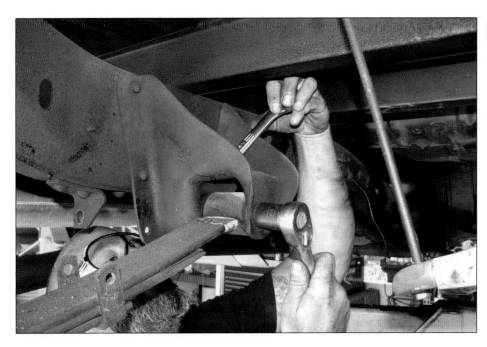

3 Disconnect the leaf springs from the front hangers, which are just forward of the axle. You need a ratchet and an open-end wrench for this, and possibly some penetrating fluid. It's a relatively simple task.

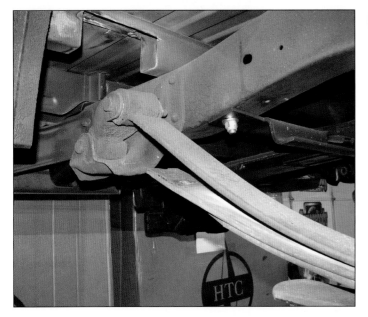

4 The aft portion of the leaf spring consists of the hanger (mounted on the frame) and the shackle (the pivoting bracket). It's usually easier to remove the shackle from the hanger with a 1/2-inch ratchet and open-end wrench, but you will eventually take off the leaf springs from the shackle, so you could do it either way. Have a friend support one end of the leaf while you remove the bolts, then lift the leaf spring out of the rear suspension.

Steering Linkage

You can remove the steering linkage in a few different ways; it depends on your intentions with the project. Removing the entire linkage as a single unit is a pretty smart way to go for a number of reasons. First, reassembling the linkage can be confusing, particularly when some of the parts are similar and yet are still side specific. Second, even if you reassemble the truck with new parts, having the originals as an assembled reference is a good idea. Finally, it all comes out fairly easily as one unit.

If you don't want to use that method, you can remove the pieces one at a time, making sure to note where each one goes and in what orientation. This is important because some year trucks have slight variations compared to others (the 1976 trucks, for example, have a tie-rod end that orients differently on the steering knuckle).

No matter which method you choose, make sure to keep all of the original components. You will want to reference them later when giving your truck a rough alignment. When the time comes to reassemble the steering linkage, make sure to take your time so that none of the components are switched.

New Pitman Arm and Tie Rod Installation

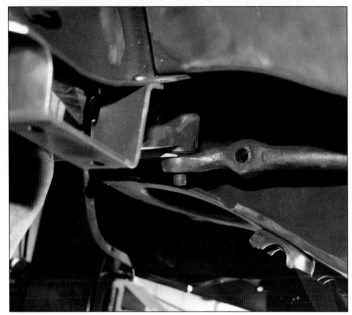

1 With the truck on jack stands or a lift, start separating the steering components. If you plan on replacing most of the parts, use a ball joint separator (also called a pickle fork) and a hammer. Just know that the pickle fork will destroy the rubber ball joint bushings, and you will need to replace the component entirely.

2 If all-new components are installed, use a pickle fork to separate the idler arm from the drag link.

3 Remove the idler arm frame mount using a 1/2-inch wrench and socket so that you can paint the chassis as well as the mount.

4 When it comes time to remove the pitman arm from the steering box, use a pitman arm puller. Although it's a specialty tool, it's fairly easy to find at your local parts store.

5 When reassembling the steering, keep everything loose to start. It's a bit of a puzzle under there, and it takes patience to sort it all out.

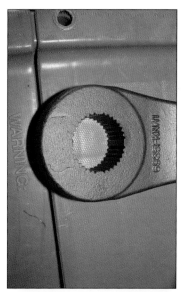

6 The pitman arm mounts on the steering box in the same orientation as the original, but take note of those four flat spots located at the 12-, 3-, 6-, and 9-o'clock positions. There are corresponding marks on your steering box, and it's designed this way so that if the steering is off, it is off by 90 degrees.

7 If you keep the steering wheel locked straight forward, reinstalling the pitman arm in the correct position isn't difficult.

9 Use copper anti-seize on all of the alignment bolt threads to ensure that it will be easy to adjust the linkage in the future.

8 The clearance between the drag link and the front crossmember is tight, and it may cause some issues when reinstalling the linkage. If you keep everything loose, it goes together fairly smoothly. Keeping the original tie-rod assemblies is critical if you want the alignment to be within the ballpark once it has been reassembled. Before you install the adjustment sleeve, lay out all of the components to inspect everything.

10 Thread the new tie-rod ends into the sleeves to match the old ones. Once the correct spacing has been achieved, cinch down the tie-rod sleeves before installing them on the pitman arm. You may want to keep a bit of play in the sleeves to be able to adjust the alignment once everything is completely reassembled.

11 Installing the tie rod ends on the spindle is fairly straightforward; the ends were connected to the drag link and spindle with the new castle nuts and a 1/2-inch ratchet and socket, then the cotter pins were installed to keep everything locked in place.

Rebuilding Basics

Once your chassis is ready for reassembly, it's time to put the suspension back into place. This is easiest with just a bare chassis because you're not working around any sheet metal. However, it can be done either way and it's not particularly difficult.

Front Suspension Installation

1 Before you bolt in the upper control arms, make sure you have the shims in place. Alignment shims come in various sizes, and they're necessary to keep the truck's front end aligned properly.

2 Replacement ball joints aren't too pricey and can be found at most major auto parts stores such as AutoZone and O'Reilly. They bolt into place on the control arms and include zerk fittings for easy serviceability.

Wheel and Tire Conversion

Most factory C10s of this era ran a 15-inch wheel, although some were equipped with 16-inch wheels. Increasing the diameter of the wheel while decreasing the profile of the tire (thus keeping the overall aspect ratio of the tire size accurate, which means you also don't have to adjust the gearing in the rear end) is very popular. The question then becomes, why would you want to do this?

When Chevrolet introduced its "new body style" trucks in 1999, it switched to a six-lug bolt pattern on the two-wheel-drive models. This was a pretty big shift because even though there were six-lug trucks in years prior, the five-lug from 1973 to 1998 was incredibly common. So common that you could buy wheels for everything from your truck to your trailer in that bolt pattern.

Because Chevrolet has continued with the six-lug system, it's become more difficult to find five-lug wheels. If you decide that you want to install a rear axle from a 1999-up truck for the rear disc brakes and so on (a common modification), you have to switch to a six-lug wheel. And that means going to a 16-inch wheel because you can't run a 15 with brakes that large.

Today, it's easier to find six-lug wheels, and most of them are at least 16-inchers, if not 17. Therefore, if you have a rare two-wheel-drive six-lug 1973–1987, or you want to convert for more wheel options, you may need to change the tire size to match.

To find out what size wheel and tire combination works for your particular truck, you can search online to find interactive calculators that give you a visual idea of what various options will look like. If you prefer to do the math, the following is a quick primer.

A tire size is written like this: 265/55R15. The first number (265 in this example) is the width of the tire in millimeters. The second number (55) is the percentage of the width that is the height of the sidewall. The last number (15) is the diameter of the inside of the tire, which also equals the diameter of the wheel in inches. To figure out what the overall diameter is of the wheel and tire combination, you have to do some math.

To convert the metric numbers into standard inches, you divide by 25.4. For example, 265 mm ÷ 25.4 = 10.43 inches. That is the width of the tire.

To find the height, you multiply the second number (55), which is a percentage, by the first number (265).

$$265 \times 0.55 = 145.75 \text{ mm}$$
$$10.43 \times 0.55 = 5.74 \text{ inches}$$

If you want to calculate the overall diameter of the combination, you multiply the height of the tire by 2 (there are two sidewalls that go around the wheel, with one being the top portion and the other part being the bottom). You then add that number to the diameter provided on the tire (15).

If you want to convert the diameter of the tire to metric, you multiply it by 25.4 to get 381.

$$(145.75 \times 2) + 381 = 672.5 \text{ mm}$$
$$(5.74 \times 2) + 15 = 26.48 \text{ inches}$$

There is one other thing to consider in this whole process: The width of the tire dictates the width of the wheel that it can be mounted on, and that's usually determined by the manufacturer. For every half inch that you vary outside that range, the overall size changes .2 inch. If you choose wider wheels, the size increases .2 inch. If they are narrower, it decreases .2 inch. ∎

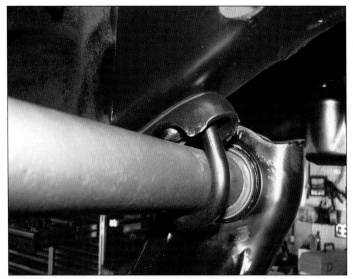

3 The lower control arms are more difficult to install than the upper arms. A round alignment dowel is located above the lower control arm cross shaft inside of the frame. To align the lower control arms properly, the hole in the cross-shaft must fit over that alignment dowel.

4 It's handy to have an assistant for this step. Lift the lower control arm into the frame and line up the round alignment dowel with the holes in the cross-shaft. Loosely install the U-bolts that hold the cross-shaft to the frame. Once you're sure everything is still aligned, tighten everything with a 1/2-inch ratchet.

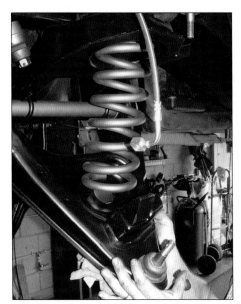

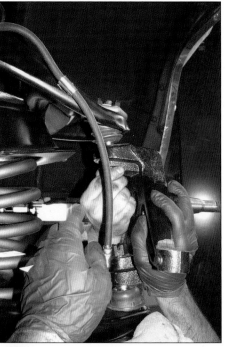

5 Before you install the spindles, install the springs using one of two common methods. You can use a transmission jack placed on the lower control arm and a hydraulic lift to lower the truck, compressing the coil in the process. Another method is to use spring compressors on the springs, and then remove them once the spindles are installed.

6 Place the spindle on top of the lower control arm ball joint, and loosely thread it in place.

7 As the spring is compressed, be ready to align the upper control arm ball joint with the spindle, and then put on the nut, but don't tighten it 100 percent. Release pressure on the spring carefully, and then tighten things up.

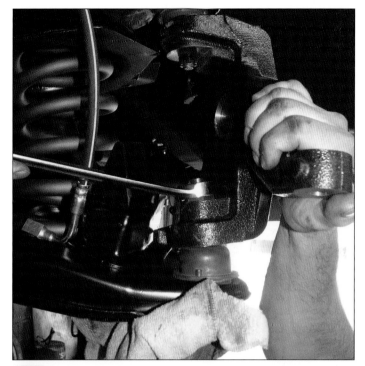

8 *As you tighten the castle nuts for the spindles (approximately 12 ft-lbs), be mindful of the cotter pin location. If necessary, back off the nut a touch to allow you to place a cotter pin through the nut and ball joint.*

9 *Because the caliper's brake lines run under the spindle, it's important to keep the cotter pin as tight as possible against the castle nut. After placing one through the ball joint and spreading it out using pliers, use a chisel and hammer to sit it flush against the nut and spindle. Use a similar process on the lower control arm.*

10 *The front shocks use a through-bolt from the backside of the frame; it sits aft of the front suspension. Bolt it in place using a ratchet. Apply some grease on the upper shock bolt to ensure that nothing squeaks while going down the road. Slide the new shocks over the bolt and tighten in place.*

11 *On the bottom of the shock, a single bolt holds it in place to the lower control arm.*

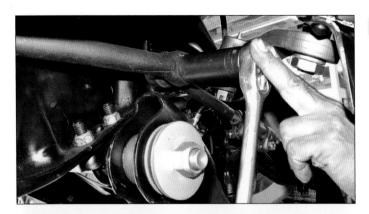

12 *Mount the tie-rods to the steering linkage and the spindle.*

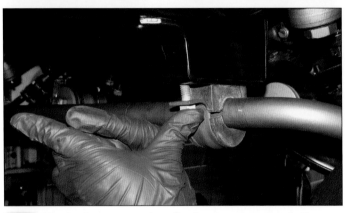

13 *The last component on the front suspension is the sway bar, which is optional on some years and models. It bolts to the frame and the lower control arms using factory hardware. It's good to keep these bolts loose during the process, because not only is it a bit easier to install then, but it also allows the suspension to cycle to its resting point once the wheels and tires are on the ground. Once they are in position, tighten the bolts using a 3/8-inch ratchet.*

14 *Once everything is complete, grease all of the zerk fittings using a grease gun. In the case of the ball joints, make sure that the grease leaks out a bit from the boot seal.*

Rear Suspension Installation

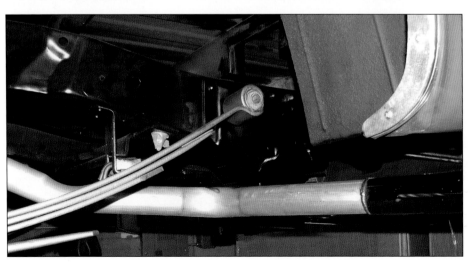

Put the rear leafs back together in the reverse order of disassembly. Once the U-bolts are connected to the axle, connect the front of the leaf spring to the hanger. Mounting the rear of the leaf spring to the shackle and rear hanger is also straightforward.

ELECTRICS

If there's one task during the restoration process that both excites and terrifies many at-home restorers, it's electrical work. I love the idea that you can control so many devices using wiring, but diagnosing and fixing a problem may seem to be a mysterious art. It's not, and with the right tools and process, you can identify and fix problems.

You could always rewire your complete truck yourself, crimping and soldering your way to running

Your truck's safety and function depend upon a sound electrical system. Over time, wires, terminals, and junction boxes degrade and often fail. A new fuse panel, such as this one, will help restore the function and reliability of the electrical system.

and driving it. But I don't recommend that unless you're extremely comfortable and experienced working with automotive electrics. There's a lot of potential for making a serious mistake, and if you're looking for a period-correct restoration, worrying about tucking or hiding wires just doesn't make a lot of sense. Instead, consider a pre-built harness with a period-correct wiring loom.

Many companies make quality wiring harnesses for your vehicle. And you can purchase either a full-chassis harness or one for specific areas. If you can follow directions and use a crimping tool, chances are pretty good that you can wire up your Squarebody just fine.

Where do you find these harnesses and what kind of options do you have? If you want the whole kit and caboodle, Painless Perfor-

mance and American Autowire have full-chassis kits that do everything from the headlights to the taillights. Both run around $800 and include everything you need, minus the wire loom. If you want to go the piecemeal route (either because you only want to replace parts of your harness or otherwise), you can get individual sections from many of the usual suspects. Brothers Trucks, Classic Parts, Jegs, USA1 Industries, LMC Truck, and Eckler's Chevy Truck have various smaller harnesses available, for anywhere from $100 to $500.

In my personal hunt for a harness, I had a hard time finding smaller pieces in stock. I attempted to order a headlight harness from both Brothers and Classic Parts, and both were backordered for three to four weeks. I tell you this so that you can plan early. Place your orders with enough lead time so you're not left waiting for the UPS driver.

Tools and Equipment

Although many of the tools that you need fall into the "general" category, some pieces are specialized. Even if you buy a full harness, at a minimum you will most likely have to crimp on your own terminals, and maybe fit your own plugs as well. So be sure to have some quality tools on hand to do the job right.

A cable-tie gun can come in handy. It looks like a small gun, and you slide the end of a zip tie into the end. When you pull the trigger, the grips at the end grab the zip tie and pull it tighter until it reaches the tension point that you pre-set. It stops pulling and cuts the end of the tie, giving you a nice, clean end. Today, you can find these for around $30 from online sources, or as little as $15 on Amazon.

Quality wire strippers are absolutely critical. A pre-built harness is often not pre-terminated, which makes a lot of sense. After all, if you're running your own wires, you don't want to have to bundle up excess material because you have to make that plug work; or the opposite, extend a harness for the same reason. Instead, you want to put on some connectors and do your own plugs, and for that, you need quality wire strippers. Make sure they don't remove any excess copper. I use a Mac Tools wire stripper that I purchased at the same time as a cable-tie gun, and it's been a lifesaver. Ideal Industries has one that sells for around $40. You can also source one from Irwin Industrial for about $20.

A 10-amp battery charger is another solid purchase. You don't want to just put the key in the ignition and crank it over, hoping that everything works perfectly. Painless Performance recommends a small 10-amp charger, which is what I've used. Thing is, they're difficult to find. Walmart sells them for around $125.

Another essential tool is a multimeter. I use a Mac Tools model (I spent a lot at that tool truck), but if I were to buy a new one today, I'd buy a Fluke. They start around $110, and it's what my father, a former electrician, also recommends.

Some people prefer the tried-and-true option of soldering and heat shrinking their connections. For that, you need a solder gun, solder, a heat-shrink torch, and heat-shrink tubing. The soldering gun must be portable and easy to work with. I found a Weller kit at Grainger for $80 that comes with solder. A heat-shrink torch may seem like overkill, but Grainger sells one for $30.

Finally, arguably the most important thing on the list is a quality crimping tool. An overcrimped connection isn't as solid and could fail over time. Assuming you're not soldering your connections, an auto-matic crimping tool is your best bet. It ensures that everything is crimped just enough, and never too much. I found some on American Autowire's website, ranging from $80 to $170.

Full-Chassis Harness

As mentioned previously, you have a lot of options when it comes to wiring your truck, but the simplest and most straightforward of all of them is installing a new full-chassis harness. It covers everything from the headlights to the taillights, and if you buy a decent kit, it has all of the instructions and components that you need to do a proper job.

Again, this can be a daunting task. When you first open the box of wiring, it's easy to become overwhelmed. But if you follow the

Begin by removing the entire truck interior. That includes the carpet, seat, and console if so equipped. This is my 1981 Silverado in the middle of that process. I ended up removing the dashboard, too.

instructions and take it one section at a time, it's an enjoyable process.

That's because wiring is one of those things that's necessary for your truck, but also can show exactly how much detail you're willing to put into your ride. You should run the wiring down the factory paths, use zip ties every 1½ inches, and use a wiring loom that's period correct.

If your project truck is anything like mine, the factory wiring probably is a total mess. Over the course of 30 or more years, these trucks have typically been exposed to harsh conditions, and the wiring harness ages and deterio-rates and therefore needs replacement. I found multiple home electrical wire nuts during the removal process, and what looked like the remains of an old car alarm that was likely causing the starting issue.

Here's my Painless Performance chas-sis harness kit plus a ground-strap kit. When I spoke to Painless about the project, they told me that most of the problems that peo-ple have with their installs come from the grounds. This kit includes ground straps for the engine and chassis, so I should be covered.

My most recent project truck came with a few issues. It was miss-ing a radiator, the transmission had "problems," and there was some kind of electrical gremlin that had taken over the vehicle. I knew that I would have to replace the wiring harness at some point, but to learn if the original 305 had any value, plus get a head start on some of the proj-ect, I figured I'd install a new Pain-less Performance kit. Yes, a lot of it would have to be removed later on, but it was a solid way to determine what worked and what would need replacement along the way.

You can tackle a project like this in many ways, but it really comes down to organization. By laying out the harness and making sure you know what goes where, you save yourself a lot of hassle. Hold every-thing in place using factory hard-ware, including the clips under the dash and the plastic in the engine bay, or use zip ties that are kept very loose. And don't cut any wires before you know for sure that you're good to go. Once you are in a rhythm, everything is pretty much the same: run wiring, terminate as necessary, cover with loom (if required), wash, rinse, repeat.

Disconnecting the Speedometer Cable

If you're anything like me, you may become frustrated the first time you try to disconnect the speedometer cable from the back of the gauge cluster. The trick is to remove the out-side A/C vent to the left of the steer-ing column. Then you reach your hand behind the cluster, and push down on the tab to release the cable from the panel. Just like that, you're done.

Wiring Harness Installation

1 *Removing the factory harness starts with taking out the engine plug. It's located on the driver's side of the firewall, to the outside of the brake booster. You remove it with a 5/16-inch socket and 1/4-inch ratchet.*

2 *On the passenger's side of the firewall sits the fuse block. It also comes out with a 5/16-inch socket, and once the two bolts are free, it slides away from the firewall, supported only by the remaining wiring.*

3 *You have to pull all of the remaining wiring out from behind the dashboard and throughout the truck. You will probably run into a bunch of these metal strips along the way. They're like twist ties installed by the factory that hold up the harness. They're even rubber coated so they don't chafe anything. Remember that, because you will likely use them during the reinstallation.*

4 *The Painless Performance fuse block mounts in the factory location. The only difference is that the stock block mounts with screws, and the new one uses 1/4-inch bolts. Drill out the stock holes and thread in the new fasteners to mount the block.*

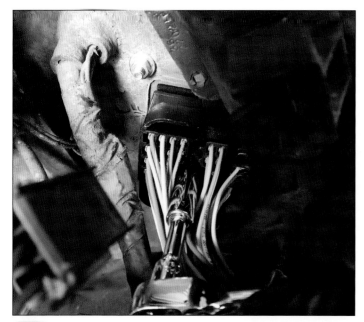

5 On the engine side of the firewall, the new engine harness bolts in using the same method as the original. You just press in the plug, then tighten it with the bolt.

6 Now it's time to run all of the new wiring. This is a test fit, so nothing is going in permanently, but you want to have an idea of your best path and what obstacles you might hit along the way.

7 Because nothing is going in permanently yet, it's best to leave yourself some options. You can use blue painter's tape to hold the wiring for the dome light to the floor. That way you can make sure it works. Because I typically use sound deadener on all of my projects, I use small strips of tape to hold the wiring once I'm done.

8 After dropping the steering column, you have access to the ignition harness, column wiring, and neutral safety switch. This particular plug is special because it comes in two sizes: $4\frac{1}{8}$ inches long, and $3\frac{7}{8}$ inches long. The kit has two of each plug, so you want to be sure that you've measured correctly before you start plugging in the wiring.

9 Each of the wires for this section of the harness are pre-terminated, so by following the guide in the manual for your particular year and model, you can plug everything in correctly. Make sure you orient the terminals so that the flat side slides into the notch on the plug, and that you're putting the correct color in the labeled slot.

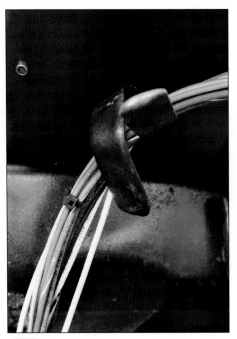

10 While you figure out where the wiring should go, you can use the factory wire ties to keep things out of the way. Not only does it save on zip ties, but this makes it easy to reorganize when necessary.

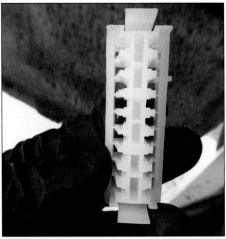

11 The harness for the back of the gauge panel is a little tricky. There are two horizontal slots at the top and the bottom of the plug; the wider one corresponds with the slot toward the top of the gauge panel. Because you're plugging in the wires yourself, it's important to keep all the wires organized. You might want to label the top of the plug with a "T." It will make things easier.

12 Plugging in the gauge-panel wiring is done using the same method as for the column. This time, however, there are multiple variations based on the year of your truck, so make sure to pay attention to that as you push in the terminals.

13 The nice thing about a quality harness is that everything is labeled clearly and pre-grouped for easy sorting.

14 Under the hood, you want to install some wire loom (here, Painless Performance's Classic Braid) around the wiring for the taillights and fuel pump. Because it must be run under the truck, installing the loom beforehand is helpful. It also helps to have the installation tool for this product. It makes the process much faster.

15 The wiring for the taillights and fuel pump runs along the outside of the driver's side of the frame and is held in place with brackets. Fortunately, I have a bare chassis to work with as well, which is why you can see things so clearly.

16 The rear harness snakes to the inside of the frame right after the rear cab mount.

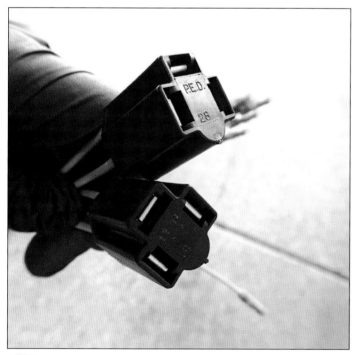

17 The kit comes with four headlight pigtails and sockets. If you have a truck with four headlights (as does my 1981 model), you use all of them; if it doesn't, you use just two. You then group the green wires with the tan wires, and connect them to the harness either by soldering or with the provided butt terminals.

18 Installing ground straps is another key part of the equation. Make sure the engine is grounded solidly to the frame, as well as the cab. By doing both, you ensure that the truck doesn't have any grounding problems.

INTERIOR

The interior of your truck is your living room, and therefore you want a clean, comfortable, and functional interior. As with the suspension, interior work is a job that even amateurs can accomplish because restored, NOS, and aftermarket parts are available for everything on the inside of these trucks.

For upholstery projects, you have two options. If you're handy with a sewing machine (or know someone who is), you may be able to do that part on your own. The only upholstery in the truck is on the seat; anything else requires glue. If you don't have any sewing skills, taking your seat to an upholstery shop is a good choice.

The only other issue to consider is sound deadening and carpet. The factory sound-deadening material is little more than cloth fiber packed densely together or Hushmat and Dynamat that stick to the metal directly. You can buy a carpet kit that drops into place, or you can have an upholstery shop install a carpet kit for you. Keep in mind that the factory used drop-in carpets, so if you decide to glue it, that's on you.

The entire job (minus any outsourced work) can be done in a weekend, sooner if you have everything prepared in advance. It's not complicated, nor is it difficult; it just takes time to do correctly.

DIY Versus Paying a Professional

And that brings us to that all-important question: DIY or shop it out?

Disassembly of the interior is not complex. There are very few hidden bolts, almost everything is a Phillips-head screw, and with the exception of the seat (or seats, depending on what the previous owner did), you can lift everything yourself. So the disassembly of the interior is fairly straightforward.

It seems logical that reassembly wouldn't be that difficult, and for the most part, that's correct. However, it's the part in between removing

The interiors of many trucks have suffered through years of severe use and harsh weather conditions. As such, many trucks need seats reupholstered, carpet replaced, and new dashes installed.

and reinstalling that's much more complicated.

You have two options when it comes to redoing your interior. You can buy NOS and/or reproduction parts to replace what you currently have, or you can dye and/or recondition the existing parts.

One problem with these trucks is that almost everything on the inside is made of plastic. It's not the type of plastic that we have today because it dries out and cracks easily. If your truck has an interior that's in good shape, it's a rarity for sure. Years of poorly applied Armor All treatments and neglect usually mean that your interior is just toast, and you're going to either spend the next few months scouring junkyards to find what you need, or purchase new stuff. If your interior plastics are in good condition, you can dye them to the original color. Simply clean them up with

NOS upholstery material may be difficult to find, but you can if you do some digging. This particular roll is designated for restoring a 1973 Chevrolet Super Cheyenne, and it complements the green paint nicely.

soapy water and a green Scotch-Brite pad, then spray them with the vinyl dye and clear coat that you can find at any upholstery store. It's a pretty straightforward process.

The most expensive purchase will likely be having your seat(s) reupholstered. Although the factory vinyl was good enough for Chevrolet, you may want a higher quality product than even the aftermarket can provide.

A good portion of the interior is metal, and it came painted body color from the factory. This means that you have to strip out all of the interior before you paint the cab (which you want to do for a quality job anyway). It also means prep time for the interior.

This situation then puts you at a crossroads. For a higher quality job, you may want to seek the help of a professional, which costs more money. If you're fine with leveraging the aftermarket for parts, you can do everything yourself with some careful planning. I've found that I can handle most of the interior jobs myself. I've also wrapped interior panels myself (I discuss that later), which is not an incredibly complex process. But the two things I don't do on my own are the seats and carpet.

On my last project, the carpet needed to conform to some modifications to the floorboards. I decided to hire an interior specialist. He did a phenomenal job laying down the carpet, which looked stunning when it was done. How? Lots of cutting, steaming, and gluing so it contoured around everything nicely. It looked like a factory drop-in by the time it was done. It's amazing what a high-end carpet does for any project, enough so that you should consider it for your truck.

Sometimes I want to do something custom with the seats, but I find that many (not all) of the kits on the aftermarket are just not up to my standards. Having a skilled tradesperson do the stitching cleans up the job substantially and gives me the results I desire.

Trim Removal

The 1973–1987 GMC and Chevrolet trucks are simple in many respects, particularly when it comes to the interior. Although you have a wide variety of trim levels for the Squarebody, almost everything on the inside of the truck can be removed with a Phillips-head screw driver or a ratchet.

Pillars? Phillips-head screwdriver. Sill plates? Phillips-head screwdriver. Dashboard? Phillips-head screwdriver, ratchet, and sockets, if you count the gauge cluster.

You need only a limited tool set to take apart the interior of your truck, and you will be thankful for that in the end.

Interior Disassembly

Stripping down the inside of these trucks can be both a chore and super easy, depending on how far you want to go and the trim level of the truck. Base models rarely had carpet or headliners, and then there are the crew cabs, which sometimes had both.

Seat Removal

There are many places that you can start on the interior, but generally beginning with the seat gives you more accessibility to other components. Also, it's an easy place to start because it's such a straightforward process.

Bench Seat Removal

1 Four bolts hold the seat to the floor of the cab. Two are located just below the front of the seat toward the outside edges but parallel to the dash. The remaining two are behind the backrest.

2 Start with the front bolts because they're the most accessible. Just take them out with a ratchet. If rust is a problem, consider spraying some WD-40 or similar rust penetrating fluid on the bolts to help them move.

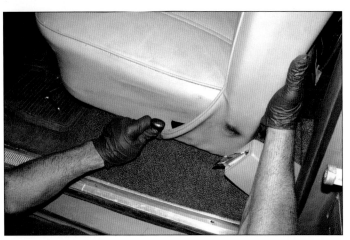

3 Many truck owners don't adjust their seat more than once, and rarely are items stored behind the seat. This particular truck was a one-owner vehicle owned by a GM stockholder, and even though it was in immaculate condition, sliding the seat forward to access the rear seat bolts wasn't easy. The solution was to put someone in both the driver's and passenger's seats, and have them slide the seat forward while the adjustment arm was held in place. It took a bit of work, but it eventually moved.

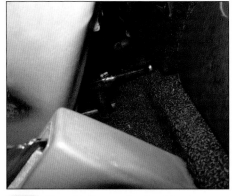

4 Two bolts are tucked just behind the seat near the outside edges (I added the ratchet for better visibility). Once those two bolts are out, the seat is almost ready to remove.

5 Taking the seat out is a two-person job. While one pulls it out of the cab through one side, the other has to crawl through the cab from the other side. It also helps to have someone hold one of the doors open so you don't damage the truck in the process.

Door Panel Removal

The door panels on these trucks varied in size through the years, but the basic process for removing and reinstalling them is basically the same, with more or fewer Phillips-head screws along the way. Unlike modern door panels, there are few Christmas tree clips or pins guiding your way; they're mostly screws.

Dash Bezel Removal

Depending on the year and trim level of your truck, it has either a wood- or aluminum-trimmed bezel (assuming it was not replaced by a previous owner). Although some aluminum bezels have fared well over the years, wood ones tended to take more of a beating because it was more of a sticker on top of plastic than anything else.

In addition, almost everything on the dash that needs to be replaced requires that the dash bezel comes off first. Fortunately, it's a straightforward process and shouldn't take you more than a few minutes.

Dash Pad Removal

One area that's sure to take some abuse is the dash pad. Tinted windows weren't a thing when most of these trucks were new, and so the plastic and vinyl finish of the original pad is likely cracked and damaged. The aftermarket makes plenty of replacement options, which is a good thing, because most dash pads end up being beyond repair.

Removing the dash pad means that you first have to remove the bezel.

Steering Wheel Removal

If your project truck is unrestored, it's likely that the steering wheel is in some state of disrepair. Maybe the plastic is chipping or the trim is peeling off. Or, the wheel could be in rough shape overall, and you want to swap it out for a new one.

Even if your steering wheel is fine, the parts behind it may not be. If the turn-signal column is broken off, pull the wheel. The same goes for the ignition cylinder.

Steering Column Refurbishment

1 *After disconnecting the positive and negative terminals of the battery, the next step is to remove the horn button. This is as easy as using a flathead screwdriver to pry it up and away from the wheel.*

2 *Make sure that the front wheels are straight, and lock the steering wheel in position so that it's as straight and centered as possible. (You will thank me for this later.) Unscrew the cup from the wheel using a Phillips-head screwdriver. There's another washer behind it. You can use the screwdriver to wedge it out (shown), or you can use a magnet on an inspection tool.*

3 With a ratchet and socket (and likely an extension, depending on the socket's depth), loosen the steering wheel bolt. Don't remove the bolt completely. If you do, when you pull the wheel off the column it could come back toward you with a decent amount of force. At best, it would be a bit shocking; at worst, a potential injury. Keeping the bolt in place with just a few threads allows you to free the wheel off the splines, but not remove it completely.

4 You need a steering wheel puller for this step, and you can rent one at many automotive parts stores or buy one for around $30. There are threaded holes in the steering wheel on either side of the center of the shaft. Place the puller so that the large center bolt is centered on the column, then thread the included bolts and washers through the puller and into the steering wheel (shown). Adjust everything by hand until you have some tension and the bolts and washers have a solid tooth on the wheel. Using a ratchet and socket, tighten the center bolt on the steering wheel puller until the steering wheel pops off the column (you'll know it when it happens). Finally, remove the steering wheel puller from the steering wheel.

5 Use both hands to grip the steering wheel and pull it toward you to remove it from the column. Pull off the metal washer, which slides off easily.

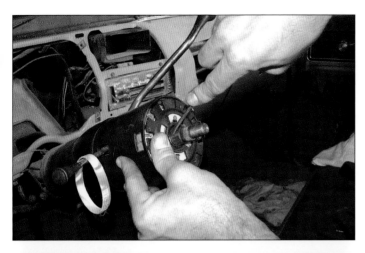

6 *If you look at the center of the steering column shaft, close to where it meets the black metal washer around it, you see a metal retaining clip. This metal washer (which has slots in it to lock the steering wheel in place) holds pressure via a spring between the metal washer and the ignition cylinder assembly behind it. You can buy a specialty tool just for the purpose of removing tension on the column spring. Or, you can push forward on the metal washer and use a variety of tools to remove the retaining clip from the column.*

7 *Remove the metal washer from the column, as well as the column spring and the plastic horn-button connections. Here, the broken white plastic on the inside of the column is where this particular truck's turn-signal switch used to be. If yours is still in place, remove it using a Phillips-head screwdriver.*

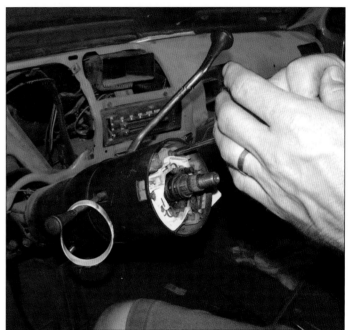

8 *Three screws hold the turn-signal switch in place. The first is easily accessible and is located on the left side of the column. It comes out with a Phillips-head screwdriver. The remaining two screws are on the right side of the column shaft: one above it and one below it. Depending on what position the turn-signal switch is in, one or both of those screws may be inaccessible. To access them, push the turn-signal switch with your hand to provide clearance. Then remove the screws with a Phillips-head screwdriver.*

9 *Use a Phillips-head screwdriver to take the hazard switch out from the bottom right-hand corner of the steering column.*

10 On the bottom of the steering column near the steering wheel sits a long, horizontal plug with several wires. Separate the harness using your hands, then trace the wires back up the column. You will notice a plastic shield around the wires. You must place the harness and plug through that plastic piece, and up through the end of the column with the turn-signal switch. And yes, it is possible.

11 To access the plastic shield, you have to drop the column using a ratchet and socket. With the column brackets out of the way, you can manipulate the plastic shield a bit more easily, and that helps you remove the harness and wiring from the column. (Photo Courtesy Ronnie Wetch)

12 Although it may seem impossible, removing the turn-signal switch is doable. Installing the replacement is the reverse of removal. I suggest wrapping some home wire around the replacement harness using electrical tape so that you can pull on the wire to move the assembly through the plastic channel. Then you just remove the tape and the home wire.

Turn-Signal Switch Assembly Removal

If your turn-signal switch isn't working and/or missing entirely, you're going to have to remove and replace it. This is not a fun process, so prepare yourself before you dive in, and if you can find an obvious way to fix the problem, consider that option as well.

Ignition Cylinder Swap

If the key doesn't start your truck, something to try is to swap out the ignition cylinder. It's cheap to replace, and it's a good place

The plastic piece sits at the end of the original ignition cylinder. That's all that holds the cylinder in place on the column, so it's an easy fix.

With the turn-signal switch out of the way, look for the vertical slot in the column located at about the one o'clock position. Inside is a thin, dark gray piece of plastic. Press it toward the firewall using a flathead screwdriver as you pull on the ignition switch. Once the plastic piece is free of the column, the ignition switch pops out of the dash.

to start your work on the ignition. It's also handy to do if you don't have the original keys, or if the switch is dinged and dented from years of use.

Interior Reassembly and Refurbishment

The materials you use on your truck will set the tone for the rest of the build. They should pair nicely with the outside but be comfortable for your everyday (or occasional) use. And, of course, they should be period-correct for your restoration. No pressure.

Seat Upholstery

There are several methods to reupholster seats. One involves a lot of time and the other involves a lot of money.

You can purchase pre-done seat kits for your truck from a wide variety of sources. These include new foam, pads, upholstery, and hog rings; all you need is some hand tools. Brothers Trucks sells a bench seat kit in vinyl, for example, for $230. You can buy the rare bucket seat vinyl kit for the same price. These are relatively easy to install, but they take time. And to get it right, you want to be sure to pull the fabric tight, so there are no wrinkles or other issues. In my experience, this is a totally doable process, but it can be frustrating, so know your limits.

Unless you're handy with a sewing machine (or know someone who is), automotive upholstery can be expensive and is something that you should leave to the professionals. All of these trucks came with a bench seat standard, although in some years bucket seats and a center console were options. (One popular conversion in these trucks is to install the 1995–1998 Chevrolet Silverado buckets and console because they bolt in easily and include seat belts). However, you're most likely going to recover a bench.

As with engine work, I'm not going to delve into every detail of the seat upholstery process. Instead, the following is an overview of how a professional upholsterer does the job; these are the results you should look for.

Bench Seat Reupholstery

1 The stock bench was first placed on a table, where a rough outline of the pattern was sketched in chalk. The owner of this truck used an old Chevrolet brochure as a reference. In fact, there were two of them, as the owner of this truck was building a second vehicle simultaneously.

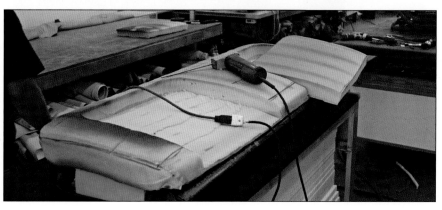

2 Here, the upholsterer has already disassembled the base of the first seat and cut out a portion around the middle. These seats are often a combination of springs and foam, but they provide very little support. One thing that this shop crew does is cut out the center portion of the seat around where your butt sits and replace it with memory foam. This results in a super comfortable seat that still looks stock but performs admirably.

3 *Using the original portion of the seat as a guide, a tech traces the pattern onto the memory foam using a permanent marker.*

4 *Using an upholstery foam-cutting tool, the tech cuts out the pattern so that it's ready to place in the seat.*

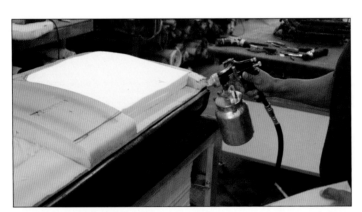

5 *When working on upholstery, Weldwood Contact Adhesive's Spray Grade is a good product. When I used to do interiors, I bought an older suction-feed spray gun designed for primer and used it to spray. The tech sprays both the surface to be covered and the backside of the cover material because the glue bonds to itself. After spraying glue into the void on the seat and installing the memory foam, the tech next sprays the back part of the base of the seat so that he can install one last piece of foam. This part sits where the top and bottom of the seat meet, and also provides some extra support for the lower back.*

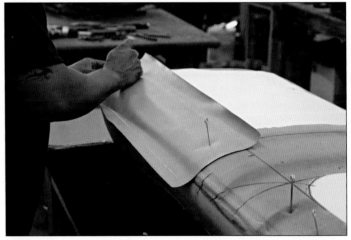

6 *Using a photo on his phone as reference, the tech then lays out the basic structure of the upholstery on the seat using a straightedge and permanent marker. The seats have NOS vinyl inserts where the memory foam sits. Leather will replace the original vinyl for the rest of the seat. It also has welt cords through multiple sections, which increases the complexity of the install.*

7 *To make the seat cover, the tech starts by cutting out sections of a scrap material and pinning them in place on the foam. The goal is to create patterns of each component of the cover and then use those patterns to create the actual pieces in the leather. By doing it with scrap materials, he ensures that he's not wasting the expensive stuff.*

8 *With all of the patterns cut, the tech lays out the green leather (it matches the original vinyl nicely) and marks the patterns using chalk that he occasionally sharpens with a scissors. It's tricky to do this on leather because there are often brands on the material to work around, and the material is never quite flat.*

10 *After the tech flips the two pieces, he lays down another stitch on each side of the seam, mimicking the pattern done by General Motors on the factory upholstery. He repeats this process for the entire seat.*

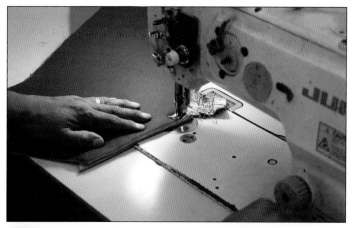

9 *Before stitching the patterns together, the tech stitches some thin, low-density foam to the leather. Both leather and vinyl are thinner materials, and without the foam, they would show any ridges or imperfections in the hard foam underneath. This keeps everything looking clean. Once all of the foam is added to the leather, he adds a line of stitching to the inside of the two pieces. Basically, he lines them up so the leather is face-to-face with the adjacent piece. Then he runs the pieces through the sewing machine. This not only hides the stitch, but also provides extra strength to the pieces when combined with the rest.*

11 *An interesting thing about the upholstery is the factory welt cording throughout the design. To replicate it, the tech stitched some 1/8-inch plastic cording into some scrap fabric. This way, he had something to attach to the leather.*

12 *With a chalk line indicating the placement of the welt cording as a guide, the tech stitches the cording into place. In this case, it goes right across the other seams, which is quite challenging.*

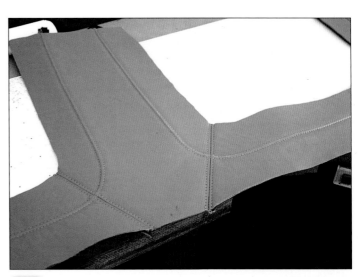

13 One of the ways that the tech made the process go more smoothly was by cutting relief slots in the welt cording cloth using scissors. That allowed the piece to fit around the corners easier.

14 Here are all of the leather pieces assembled for the first time. The factory vinyl is installed in the seating area.

15 As with leather, the tech used a light foam as a backer for the factory vinyl. This was held together using contact cement. After careful measurements, he starts laying down stitching to pleat the factory vinyl. This is tricky because he wanted to complement the pattern; the overall width shrinks with all of the extra stitches, and he had to match the original layout.

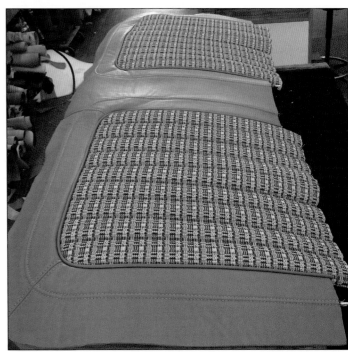

16 The completed seating area has rounded corners and a line of stitching around the border to seal things up. The tech stitches the vinyl seat inserts into the leather then adds a line of welt cording to the border.

17 From the start to this point of the process, the shop put in about 10 hours of work, and there's still a lot to go.

Door Panel Refurbish

You have several options for the door panels. You can find a pair of NOS models that are in good shape, replace them with new aftermarket models, or refurbish them.

Because they're made of plastic, repainting them is also an option. Companies such as SEM sell vinyl dye, which comes in a can and is applied just like typical rattle-can jobs. The difference is in the prep and breakdown, both of which are more detailed.

Door Panel Replacement

1 *You start by pulling off the chrome trim that bolts onto the front by unbolting it from the backside. There's typically a strip around the interior door handle and the insert. A felt strip at the top of the door panel is pretty simple to remove. Just pull back the metal tabs that hold it to the plastic using a flathead screwdriver. It slides right out.*

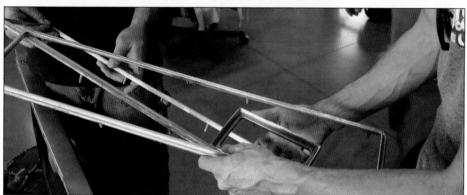

2 *With all of the chrome removed and the pieces disassembled, you can begin the cleaning process.*

3 *Thoroughly wash each door panel using degreaser, a green Scotch-Brite pad, and water. The point is to ensure that it's completely free of grease and any residual oils from the plastic. The panel on the left has been dyed, and the difference between the two is clearly visible. One thing that's really nice about vinyl dye is that you can use it to change the interior color or to make a replacement panel match the rest of the interior.*

5 *You can use spray chrome, which can look pretty good. It gives the door panel a matte chrome effect. If you want to go with something more authentic, plastic chroming is your best bet. Reinstalling the door panels is the opposite of removal.*

4 *Reinstall the chrome with the factory hardware, and it's good to go.*

6 *These modern Christmas tree clips fit into holes around the perimeter of the door panel. You want to use these because the factory clips are likely dry rotted. You can buy them at most auto parts stores. To install the clips, just slide the old ones out of the hole, and put the new ones in.*

7 *To install the panel, you lay the felt strip into the window ledge, and push it down. Then, once the window crank is aligned, push it forward so the clips can lock into place.*

8 *A Teflon piece goes between the door panel and the window crank. It simply presses into place, and sits there without locking.*

9 *The window crank retainer clips resemble a horseshoe or the omega symbol. They slide into a slot on the handle.*

10 Push the window crank onto the gear, and it locks into place.

11 These door panels have ashtrays. They slide and lock into place easily.

12 The armrest on these panels screw into place with a Phillips-head screwdriver. You screw the bottom half of the panels in place with a Phillips-head screwdriver as well.

13 The front door panels have an upholstered pocket that install with a Phillips-head screwdriver.

Dash Bezel Refurbishment

The black trim piece around the gauges can be something of an eyesore. It has chrome accents, but when it wears, it sometimes exposes more chrome and looks shabby. In addition, some models have wood trim options, and that can be even trickier.

Complicating things further, it's not easy to buy a replacement. The bezels vary depending on the model year, and whether or not the truck has air-conditioning. If you decided to go hunting at a junkyard for one that's in better shape than the one you have, take your original one with

After scrubbing the dash bezel with a green Scotch-Brite pad and degreaser, rinse it thoroughly and paint it with plastic dye.

Reinstalling the dash bezel is the reverse of installation, but all it takes is a Phillips-head screwdriver and a little time.

The completed panel looks a ton better than before, and it's much cleaner.

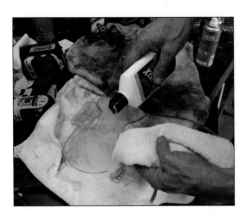

The plastic panel on the front of the gauge cluster unbolts easily. The first step in refurbishing it is to clean off the gunk and dirt that's built up over the decades. If your panel has fine scratches on it, use a plastic polish and a microfiber towel to work them out. Replacement pieces are available, but the quality varies wildly, so keep that in mind before you pull the trigger on a new model.

you. Otherwise, you risk having one that doesn't work in your vehicle.

Gauge Cluster Refurbishment

It's hard not to notice the gauge cluster; it's one of the things you look at every time you enter the truck.

With age, many of these clusters are worn, faded, scratched, or have other damage. You have a few options for restoring them.

If the cluster has non-functioning gauges, bad electrics, and is in generally poor condition, sourcing a replacement

is probably your best option. Contacting a professional speedometer repair shop is also a viable option, as they can usually sort things out for you.

However, if your cluster is just a bit faded and sun worn, you may want to consider taking on the job yourself. With paint, polish, and cleaning, you can knock it out in a few hours and have substantially better results.

Carpet Installation

Lots of these trucks came without carpet, but you can install it in all of them. Plus, there are many companies that make carpet kits, and there are tons of variations so you have options.

To brighten the gauges, use a cotton swab to apply neon orange paint to the needles. If you don't have steady hands (or you're just nervous about hitting the gauge faces with the paint), you can mask off the area with light-tack masking tape from a home supply store.

With the gauge cluster reassembled, everything looks better. You still have some cleanup work to do on the surrounding area, but it's definitely an improvement.

Interior Carpet Installation

1 *The carpet in a kit comes balled up like this, and that's an issue. If you were to unfold it as-is, you'd have wrinkles all over the place and it wouldn't match the humps and curves in the floor. (Photo Courtesy Jefferson Bryant)*

2 *When you first test fit the carpet, it may still have some wrinkles. That's okay because you have more options to remove them. First, make sure that the carpet is laid side to side correctly, and that there's a roughly equal amount of carpet on each side.*

3 *Depending on your truck's options, you might have to add some relief cuts on the carpet. Here, the factory A/C was causing some issues. Fortunately, this section of carpet isn't visible, so won't be a problem.*

4 *Once the carpet is in place, use a screwdriver to locate the mounting holes for the seat. Do this in each of the four bolt holes, making sure the carpet is as flat as possible. All you have to do before you bolt in the seat is cut out the holes for the bolts with a razor blade.*

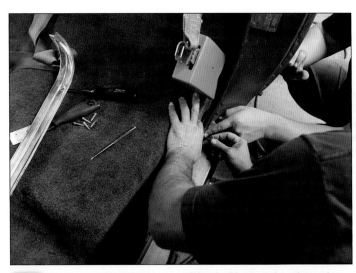

5 *To help remove carpet wrinkles, use an upholstery steamer. Most big box stores carry them. It helps the carpet conform to the floor, which is handy around the transmission hump.*

6 *Use a razor blade or utility knife to trim the edges of the carpet. Make make relief cuts only where absolutely necessary; otherwise, you risk ruining the entire piece.*

7 *Finish off the sides by installing the factory trim panels along the rockers. Use a screwdriver to tighten the screws that secure the plastic or stainless steel trim panels to the floor and over the carpet. In this case, they were brand new from a reproduction company.*

Dashboard Reinstallation

The dashboard of your truck goes back together just like it came apart, except now you want to be extra careful so that you don't damage anything.

Weather Stripping Removal and Installation

As these trucks age, the rubber is one of the first things to go. You may find that your project truck has tons of cracked and broken pieces that do very little to keep water out, which can lead to rust. That's why you need new weather stripping.

Removing the old stuff can be a bit of a trial by fire, depending on the age and condition of the truck. In the end it's a relatively simple job, and you should be able to do it in a few hours.

MISCELLANEOUS MECHANICALS

Restoring your truck is going to take some time, and somewhere along the way you're going to realize that there are a ton of little things that make up the whole picture. Fuel systems, gas tanks, badges, and more should be inspected and double-checked to make sure that they are safe and up to specs.

Fuel System

If you have a running and drivable truck, your fuel system is at least in fair shape. You still want to give everything a once over, but you know that the plumbing has worked so far and could last longer.

If the vehicle has been sitting for a long period, the fuel could have gone foul, causing it to no longer start the truck. Or worse, it could have gummed up the lines, making it necessary to redo the entire system. Inspect the truck thoroughly to see what you need to either clean or replace, and go from there. Put the truck on jack stands or a lift. Give yourself enough room so that you can inspect the fuel lines with a flashlight. You're looking for cracks in the rubber, flexed lines that have cracks or look as if they might crack, and weeping or oozing.

Gas Tank(s) Removal and Replacement

Even if the fuel in your truck is fine, and everything runs and drives great, you should probably consider taking a look at your gas tank. Because the tank is located outboard of the frame, there's the chance that it's been damaged in a side-impact collision. If the surrounding sheet metal had been repaired or replaced, checking the state of the tank is the

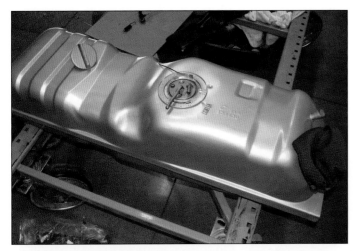

Of the many odd jobs that make up a restoration, replacing or refurbishing the gas tank should be high on the list. A tank that is gunked up can wreak havoc on your engine, and that won't be any fun to fix.

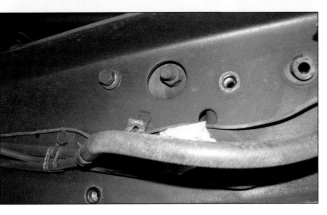

The fuel lines run on the passenger's side of the truck, alongside the inner frame rails. (If your truck has dual tanks, they cross over around the back of the cab.) Make sure all of the lines are in good condition; if not, replace them.

only way you can know about the damage.

Another reason to do a good inspection is that the tank could be starting to rot, and thin sheet metal could form a leak in the near future. Or, possibly, the fuel sending unit seal could be close to failing, causing the truck to smell like gasoline. You can handle the inspection process in multiple ways and multiple steps, depending on what stage of the restoration you're in.

Although it may sound daunting, removing the bed is one of the easier ways to access the tank. Grab a few buddies, remove the six to eight bolts holding the bed in place (depending on if it's a short- or long-bed), disconnect the wiring to the taillights, unscrew the gas filler neck from the bed side(s), and lift the bed straight up and away from the truck. This exposes the tank(s) on the outside of the frame, giving you access to both the connections on the top and the sending unit.

This method is likely the easiest way to fix things if your tank is in good condition and the truck has been driven on a regular basis. If it has spent any period of time off the road, or you suspect that the tank has stored fouled fuel, you should pull it from the truck and either repair it or replace it.

The first step in any gas tank restoration is to have the tank thoroughly cleaned and steamed. Although you could attempt this at home, you should seriously consider sending it to a professional shop. They have experience working with a hazardous material such as gasoline, and they know how to clean the tank correctly. In addition, the same shop should be able to pressure test the tank. This step is crucial in ensuring that the tank lasts, because if it fails, it won't be able to contain the pressure that it needs to function, and it will likely have one or more leaks. Finally, if this shop also repairs gas tanks, and you decide

that it's important to keep the stock tank rather than replacing it, you definitely want a shop to perform that task.

As you likely know, gasoline fumes are flammable. A gas tank holds gas, and no matter how much you think you've removed yourself, there's always the possibility that there are still fumes present or even some gas. By introducing heat and sparks via a welder, you risk serious injury. Tank restoration really is better left to the professionals.

Another option, which some folks opt for no matter how good the stock tank(s) look, is replacement. The aftermarket has dozens of replacement options available, and they're typically designed to fit in the factory location(s). By purchasing a replacement tank, you can eliminate variables that might be present in your stock tank.

You also could purchase an NOS tank that's been restored completely, but those can be more expensive.

Fuel Tank Replacement

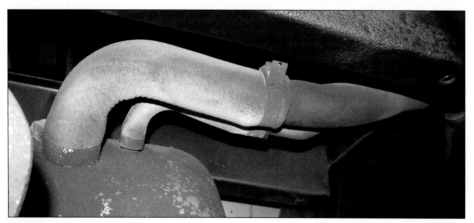

1 *The stock position of the main fuel tank in a 1973–1980 Chevrolet/GMC truck is on the passenger's side; it switched to the driver's side in 1981. To access the tank, put the truck on a lift and remove the passenger-side rear tire for clearance. This could also be done with the truck on jack stands positioned on the frame. If the truck runs, make sure to use up as much fuel as possible before you start; lifting all that heavy gas in the tank is not fun.*

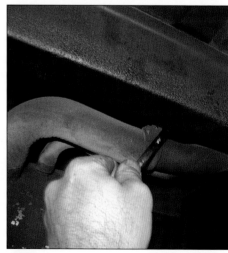

2 *Disconnect the filler neck from the tank. A good place to start is to loosen the hose clamp on the connection, which is secured with a bolt.*

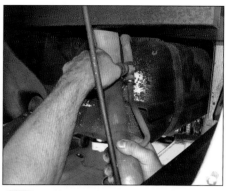

3 The second hose on the filler neck is held in place with a spring clamp, and pliers makes removing it easier. Just clamp down on the two tabs, then slide the clamp farther down the rubber or steel line so that it's no longer over the connection point.

4 On the older trucks, the gas filler neck is exposed on the bed side. Use a Phillips-head screwdriver to separate the filler from the bed side. Also unscrew the cap. Newer trucks have a gas door, which you have to open first.

5 Pull the fuel filler neck to the inside of the bed side, then pull it apart from the rubber hoses. You may want to use a flathead screwdriver to separate the two lines. If they're stuck, you can cut them off because you will likely replace them anyway.

6 At the inside of the frame, disconnect the fuel lines from the tank using pliers to release the spring clamps. These lines run both over and through the frame, so make sure to take note where they go for reinstallation. If you truck still has fuel, make sure to clamp the lines with a fuel line clamp before disconnecting them.

7 Here's a better look at the lines as they run through the frame. An electrical connection runs to the top of the tank. It's extremely difficult to reach (and impossible to photograph without removing the bed), but it's easy to feel. Just pinch the connection on the single wire and it pops off.

8 The tank is held to the frame by two brackets that wrap around the outside of the tank. These are then held in place with four bolts that are visible on the inside of the frame. Remove these bolts with an impact wrench or a ratchet and socket. Also, be sure to have some kind of support underneath the tank before you remove the bolts. If you don't have a lift, you can use a jack stand.

9 Removing the tank using a two-post lift may be more difficult than using jack stands because the tank hits the arms of the lift on the way down. With a little maneuvering, you can lift it out. Make sure to move the tank away from any heat or ignition sources so that you don't cause a fire.

10 When placed side by side, it's clear that the replacement gas tank (left) is in better condition than the stock unit. Use all new parts to install the new tank, while reusing the plastic skid plate and brackets fitted to the tank.

11 The straps loop around the gas tank and then secure to the bracket. To remove the straps and bracket assembly, remove the top bolt that holds the top of the strap to the bracket. You can then remove the strap from the bracket, and pull both out as one unit.

12 Before you can remove the forward-facing bracket, remove the skid plate from the front of the tank. Unbolt the skid plate from the bracket with a ratchet and then slide the plate off the front of the tank.

13 Using the combination of a wire wheel on a grinder and a sandblasting box, clean the gas tank brackets. Then paint them the same color as the chassis.

14 Replacement tanks come with felt pads that sit between the gas tank straps and the gas tank to reduce friction between the two metal pieces. Wrapping them around the tank is a straightforward process.

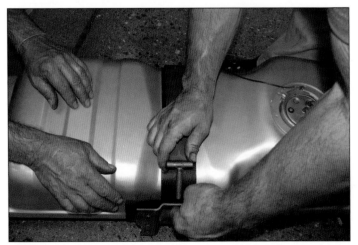

15 Wrap the straps around the tank and through the brackets, so that they can be bolted together.

16 With both straps bolted in place and the skid plate reinstalled, the tank is ready to go. Here's a tip: The strap nuts are located in holes in the frame. If, for some reason, you wanted to leave the brackets on the frame and just unbolt the straps, you could. Just be sure that the access holes are lined up properly. Otherwise, fitting the tank on the frame becomes difficult.

17 Because access is limited under the truck, you want to attach all of the replacement fuel lines beforehand. Keep them long to avoid issues with fitment. Camp them in place with hose clamps. Here, you can see the grounding stud on the top of the fuel-sending unit.

18 Install the hoses to the fuel filler neck with the same type of clamps that were used by the factory.

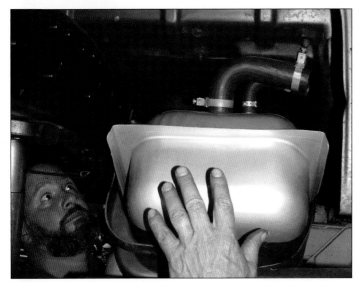

19 Putting the tank into place while the truck is on the lift is difficult, but by angling it, you can fit it correctly. In hindsight, removing the bed and using jack stands instead of a lift would have made this process easier.

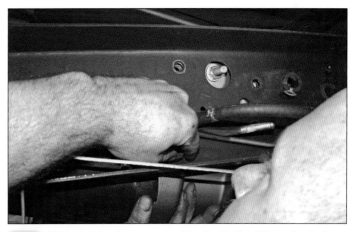

20 With the tank supported by both the lift and a helper, install the bracket mounting bolts place loosely. Note the hole at the top of the frame where you can see the strap bolt protruding through. By ensuring that this fits and that you can still position a socket in place, you can be sure that the brackets are mounted properly. Secure the electrical connection on top of the tank at this time.

21 *If your brackets are just a touch off, you can adjust them by loosening the mounting straps through the access holes in the frame. Then, tighten the bracket bolts using an impact wrench.*

22 *Reinstall the filler neck onto the bed side using the factory Phillips-head screws and a screwdriver.*

23 *Finally, reconnect the hoses to their appropriate lines using hose clamps.*

Badge and Emblems

Often, on these trucks, the logos located on the B-pillars start to fade over time. You can purchase reproduction parts that come close to matching the color, but the yellow in the emblem often looks a bit off. Fortunately, I have a fix.

The colors are Fl. Yellow (PN 1169-RM11691_0611) and Fl. Brown (PN 1166-RM11661_0611); both have a matte finish. If you mix them in a 1:1 ratio, you have the correct color for the B-pillar emblems.

Kimball Midwest carries this color, New Equipment Yellow (PN 80-832), which is perfect for the yellow emblem on the center of the factory hubcaps. Mask off the area, prep it for paint, and spray it on.

The Chevy bowtie is pretty iconic, and most of them were either a sticker or painted on. As the result of age, they're usually pretty faded. Restoring them does take time, but not much else.

Long-Bed to Short-Bed Conversion

The 1973–1987 Chevrolet pickup has the largest production numbers of any previous model Chevy truck, but you may not find the short-bed truck you want, or you may find an excellent deal on a long-bed. It's a dilemma.

The short-bed (the 6-foot model) is considered to be more desirable, particularly for standard-cab trucks. With crew cabs, some prefer long-beds and others prefer shorts. Chevrolet never made an extended cab, nor did it make a short-bed truck with a crew cab.

Wrecking yards, swap meets, and online sales have beds all over the place, usually for reasonable prices. If, for some reason, you can't find the bed you want, you can cut up a long bed to make it shorter.

Here, I discuss the most difficult part of the conversion: shortening the frame and driveshaft. For this procedure, you need to possess moderate plasma cutting and welding skills for the necessary modifications. In addition, make sure that the frame is square and properly aligned.

Converting a long-bed truck to a short-bed is not technically difficult. If you've done work on frames before, you should be comfortable doing this modification because it is literally one cut in the frame (per side) and one spot (per side) to weld. If this is new to you, it may be a bit more daunting, and you may want to consider getting some help.

Long- to Short-Bed Conversion

1 Once the front end is lifted onto jack stands and the rear section of the frame is level, you tack weld some pipes to the frame. They act as stands for the back half of the frame and allow you to cut the front from the back while keeping things aligned. In this process, you remove a few other parts, including the driveline, gas tank, and rear brake lines. Place the tank far away from the work area to avoid a fire. Pull any electrical connections toward the center of the frame, away from the welded area. (Photo Courtesy Todd Burton and Lowboy Motorsports)

2 A total of 14 inches must be removed from the front of the frame, just behind the farthest-forward bed mounts next to the cab. By removing this section, you ensure that all of the factory mounts on the bed line up perfectly. Mark where the cuts are to be made at an angle. Why? Because this gives you more surface area for welding, which makes the joint stronger. This section of the frame is also perfectly straight, which makes the alignment process simpler. (Photo Courtesy Todd Burton and Lowboy Motorsports)

3 Using a straightedge as a guide, use a plasma cutter to cut the frame. (Photo Courtesy Todd Burton and Lowboy Motorsports)

4 Here, you can see how big the cut is and its position relative to the bed mounts. (Photo Courtesy Todd Burton and Lowboy Motorsports)

5 Even though the front receives the majority of the work, the rear needs a little help as well. Cut it off with the plasma cutter about 3 inches from the farthest portion of the frame. Clean up the slag from the plasma using a sanding disc. (Photo Courtesy Todd Burton and Lowboy Motorsports)

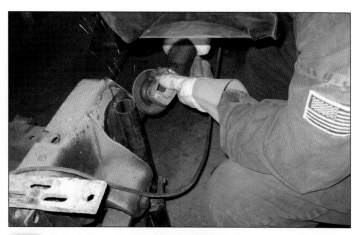

6 Grind the edges of each half to a slight angle with a die grinder and grinding disc. This beveled edge gives the weld better penetration, and it also ensures that no paint is left on the surface to be welded, which would cause problems with the weld. (Photo Courtesy Todd Burton and Lowboy Motorsports)

7 After you pull the rear of the frame forward to meet the front, measure diagonally from bed mount to bed mount to make sure that the frame is still square. Use a clamp to hold a piece of square tubing behind the frame to keep it straight and solid while you weld. (Photo Courtesy Todd Burton and Lowboy Motorsports)

8 Weld the frame together using a MIG welder. Weld the entire outside edge completely, including the top and bottom, on both sides. (Photo Courtesy Todd Burton and Lowboy Motorsports)

9 Cut an oval-shaped piece of 1/4-inch steel out of some scrap tubing and then weld it to the inside of the frame. Plug weld through the factory holes on the frame to this new oval piece. This keeps the cut-out section of the frame strong, even stronger than the original. Remove the temporary supports from the frame. (Photo Courtesy Todd Burton and Lowboy Motorsports)

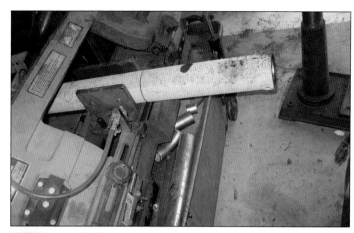

10 *The driveline needs to be shortened 14 inches as well. Use a band saw to remove the yoke on one end. (Photo Courtesy Todd Burton and Lowboy Motorsports)*

11 *Cut off the 14-inch section using a band saw. After you clean up the edges of the tubing, weld them in place with the MIG welder. The driveline needs to be balanced to avoid vibrations, but by doing the shortening yourself, you save money and time. (Photo Courtesy Todd Burton and Lowboy Motorsports)*

12 *Reinstall the driveline and bolt the tank into the factory location. If you want to run new brake lines throughout the truck, the original lines can be maneuvered to fit without being shortened. Otherwise, you cut and re-flare the brake lines to fit properly. Bleed the brake lines now. You can either bundle and keep the factory wiring as is, or, particularly if you're rewiring the truck, you can run new wiring to the taillights. (Photo Courtesy Todd Burton and Lowboy Motorsports)*

13 *Finally, you bolt the bed to the truck, and it is ready to cruise down the road with its newly shortened bed. (Photo Courtesy Todd Burton and Lowboy Motorsports)*

73-87ChevyTrucks.com
1145 Arlington Dr.
Birmingham, AL 35224
73-87chevytrucks.com

aFe Power
232 Granite St.
Corona, CA 92879
888-901-7693
afepower.com

American Classic Truck Parts LLC
3301 NW Tullison Rd.
Kansas City, MO 64150
816-741-5255
americanclassic.com

Brothers Trucks
801 E. Parkridge Ave.
Corona, CA 92879
800-977-2767
brotherstrucks.com

Carolina Classic Trucks
336-298-4168
carolinaclassictrucks.com

Carolina Kustoms
Portland, OR 97218
503-954-1369
carolinakustoms.com

Chevrolet Performance
chevroletperformance.com

Cheyenne Pickup Parts
PO Box 959
Noble, OK 73068
405-872-3399
cheyennepickup.com

Classic Industries
18460 Gothard St.
Huntington Beach, CA 92648-1229
714-847-6887
classicindustries.com

Classic Muscle
Division of Modern Chevrolet
5415 Kelley-Moore Dr.
Winston-Salem, NC 27105
888-302-7699
classicmuscle.com

Classic Parts of America
1 Chevy Duty Dr.
Riverside, MO 64150
800-741-1678
www.classicparts.com

Classic Performance Products (CPP)
378 E Orangethorpe Ave.
Placentia, CA 92870
800-522-5004
classicperform.com/contact.html

CMW Trucks
1351 S. Cleve-Mass Rd.
Unit W-8
Copley, OH 44321
330-212-5030
cmwtrucks.com

Competition Cams
3406 Democrat Rd.
Memphis, TN 38118
800-999-0853
compcams.com

Dino's Chevy Only
dinoschevyonly.com

Ecklers Classic Trucks
6150 Donner Rd.
Lockport, NY 14094
800-853-6360
ecklerstrucks.com

Edelbrock
2700 California St.
Torrance, CA 90503
310-781-2222
edelbrock.com

FAST
3400 Democrat Rd.
Memphis, TN 38118
877-334-8355
fuelairspark.com

Frontier Shop Supplies
4551 E. Ivy St., #101
Mesa, AZ 85205
480-981-1126
frontiershopsupplies.com

General Motors
gm.com

Goodyear Tire & Rubber
200 Innovation Way
Akron, OH 44316
800-321-2136
goodyear.com

Holley Performance Products
1801 Russellville Rd.
Bowling Green, KY 42102
270-782-2900
holley.com

Hubcaps Hotrod and Custom
1700 E. Robin Ln.
Phoenix, AZ 85024
602-410-1211
hubcapsrodandcustom.com

Hughes Performance
2244 W. McDowell Rd.
Phoenix, AZ 85009
602-257-9591
www.hughesperformance.com

JC Whitney
866-529-5530
jcwhitney.com

Little Shop
150 Mahr Ave.
Lawrenceburg, TN 38464
littleshopmfg.com

LMC Truck
15450 W. 108th St.
Lenexa, KS 66219
800-562-8782
lmctruck.com

Manes Truck Parts
Odessa, MO 64076
816-230-5949
manestruckparts.com

MCB Parts
156 W. Linda Mesa Ave.
Danville, CA 94526
925-828-5555
mattsclassicbowties.com

MSD Performance
888-258-3835
msdperformance.com

Painless Performance
2501 Ludelle St.
Fort Worth, TX 76105
817-244-6212
painlessperformance.com

Powermaster
1833 Downs Dr.
West Chicago, IL 60185
630-957-4019
powermastermotorsports.com

Precision Replacement Parts
4611 Camp Phillips Rd.
Weston, WI 54476
800-367-8241
prp.com

Pro Performance
218 W. Hampton Ave., Ste. 3
Mesa, AZ 85210
azproperformance.com

Rock Auto
rockauto.com

Rockland Standard Gear
150 Rte. 17
Sloatsburg, NY 10974
877-774-4327
rsgear.com

Ron Francis Wiring
200 Keystone Rd., Ste. #1
Chester, PA 19013
800-292-1940
ronfrancis.com

Southern Trucks
784 N. Van Dyke Rd.
Imlay City, MI 48444
810-724-3590
southern-truck.com

Squarebody Syndicate
squarebodysyndicate.com

Switch Suspension
6005 S. 40th St., Ste. #4
Phoenix, AZ 85042
800-928-1984
switchsuspension.com

Summit Racing
800-230-3030
summitracing.com

TCI Automotive
151 Industrial Dr.
Ashland, MS 38603
888-776-9824
tciauto.com

Tilden Motorsports
565 Rossi Ct.
Gilroy, CA 95020
408-600-0122
tildenmotorsports.com

Toyo Tire & Rubber Company
toyotires.com

Tuckers Classic Auto Parts
800-544-1955
tuckersparts.com

USA1 Industries
1676 Anthony Rd.
Burlington, NC 27215
336-792-2011
usa1industries.com